UNDERSTANDING HUMAN RIGHTS PRINCIPLES

Edited by

JEFFREY JOWELL QC

AND

JONATHAN COOPER

·HART·
PUBLISHING

OXFORD AND PORTLAND, OREGON
2001

Hart Publishing
Oxford and Portland, Oregon

Published in North America (US and Canada) by
Hart Publishing
c/o International Specialized Book Services
5804 NE Hassalo Street
Portland, Oregon
97213-3644
USA

Distributed in Netherlands, Belgium and Luxembourg by
Intersentia, Churchillaan 108
B2900 Schoten
Antwerpen
Belgium

Hart Publishing is a specialist legal publisher
based in Oxford, England.
To order further copies of this book or to request a list of
other publications please write to:

Hart Publishing,
Salters Boatyard, Folly Bridge,
Abingdon Rd, Oxford, OX1 4LB
Telephone: +44 (0)1865 245533
Fax: +44 (0) 1865 794882
email: mail@hartpub.co.uk

British Library Cataloguing in Publication Data
Data Available

ISBN 1-84113-169-5

Typeset by
John Saunders Design and Production, Reading
Printed and bound in Great Britain
by Biddles Ltd. www.biddles.co.uk

UNDERSTANDING
HUMAN RIGHTS
PRINCIPLES

Contents

Foreword

I had the privilege of chairing the series of JUSTICE/UCL seminars that was the genesis of this book. It was a resounding success. The sheer number of conferences, seminars and talks on human rights can sometimes seem excessive, if not oppressive. No doubt they all have a value, given how much there is to learn in this unfamiliar field. The JUSTICE/UCL seminars, however, stood out for the contribution they made to an understanding of the subject and of some of the difficulties that we all face in developing our domestic law on human rights.

The main reason for their success was the quality of the principal speakers, all experts on the subject. But seminars also depend on the quality of the other participants. In this case the invitees, who included leading practitioners and academics, members of the government legal service and representatives of organisations in the public law field, provided an excellent mix for fuelling the debate. The format may also have helped; a main paper, followed by a response by a commentator, which served as a catalyst for discussion.

The papers now published, although based on the main papers at each of the seminars, have benefited considerably from revision in the light of the commentators' responses and the ensuing discussion. As a result they are even better than the original versions. In some ways it would have been valuable to include the responses themselves, many of which were masterly pieces deserving of publication in their own right. As it is, the commentators must content themselves with the knowledge that their contributions were greatly appreciated and have helped to mould the final papers published.

The topics covered embrace many of the central principles with which all those concerned in our domestic law on human rights will have to wrestle. In some cases they also take the debate onto a higher plane, examining the relationship between human rights and principles of democracy and thereby assisting in an understanding of some of the broader policy questions on which decisions will have to be taken.

I am pleased to give this book my wholehearted commendation and would like to take this opportunity to thank UCL and JUSTICE for organising the seminars and to thank Clifford Chance for sponsoring them.

The Hon. Mr Justice Richards

Contributors

Jonathan Cooper is Assistant Director at JUSTICE. He is editor of the *European Human Rights Law Review* (Sweet & Maxwell), and co-editor of *Legislating for Human Rights* (Hart Publishing).

Thomas de la Mare is a barrister at Blackstone Chambers who specialises in public, EC and ECHR law. He has contributed to numerous books and journals, including *Human Rights Law and Practice* (Butterworths) and *The Evolution of EU Law* (Oxford University Press).

Michael Fordham is a barrister at Blackstone Chambers. He specialises in public law. He is the author of the *Judicial Review Handbook* (Wiley Chancery Law Publishing), editor of the quarterly journal Judicial Review, and College Lecturer in Administrative Law at Hertford College Oxford.

Javan Herberg is a barrister at Blackstone Chambers, principally in the fields of judicial review and human rights, commercial law and financial services. He is the Assistant Editor of the *Judicial Review of Administrative Action* (Supplement, 1998), and is a contributing author of *Human Rights Law and Practice* (Butterworths).

Murray Hunt is a barrister at Matrix Chambers and specialises in the law of human rights and judicial review. He is the author of *Using Human Rights Law in English Courts* (Hart Publishing) and co-editor of *A Practitioner's Guide to the Impact of the Human Rights Act 1988* (forthcoming). He has published articles in *Public Law*, the *European Human Rights Law Review*, the *Journal of Law & Society*, and the *Judicial Studies Board Journal* and contributes an annual survey of the case law of the European Court of Human Rights to the *Yearbook of European Law*.

Jeffrey Jowell QC is Professor of Public Law and Dean of the Faculty of Laws at University College London and a practising barrister at Blackstone Chambers. He is author of a number of articles and books on administrative law and human rights and was a member of the Bowman Committee on the Crown Office List. He is the UK member on the Council of Europe's Commission for Democracy through Law (the Venice Commission).

Andrew Le Sueur is Barber Professor of Jurisprudence at the University of Birmingham. He was formerly Reader in Laws at University College London.

Jane Mulcahy is a barrister at Blackstone Chambers. She specialises in public law and human rights.

Rabinder Singh is a barrister at Matrix Chambers, who specialises in public law, employment law, European law and human rights. He is a Visiting Fellow at Queen Mary and Westfield College, London and is the author of *The Future of Human Rights in the United Kingdom* (Hart Publishing).

Helen Mountfield is a barrister at Matrix Chambers, where she specialises in human rights, discrimination, employment and public law. She is co-author of the *Blackstone Guide to the Human Rights Act*, and has trained judges, practising lawyers, diplomats and NGO's on human rights issues, in the UK and abroad.

Keir Starmer is a barrister at Doughty Street Chambers specialising in human rights law. He has extensive experience of criminal and civil cases in the UK and abroad. He is also a senior research fellow at the Department of Law at King's College, London University, where he is actively engaged in work for the Human Rights Act Research Unit.

C L I F F O R D

C H A N C E

JUSTICE and UCL are grateful to **Clifford Chance** for their sponsorship of the seminar series upon which this book is based.

Introduction:
Defining Human Rights Principles

Jeffrey Jowell QC and Jonathan Cooper

The Human Rights Act was passed in 1998. Because of the complex changes it will bring to our law and to the practice of public administration, the full implementation of the Act was delayed until 2 October 2000. During that interval a large number of conferences and seminars explaining the provisions of the Act took place. Unusually, even our most senior judges were required to attend training sessions at which they would sit at the feet of human rights experts. Public authorities of all kinds held human rights workshops and audits. In large part the various conferences dealt with the substantive provisions of the European Convention on Human Rights, which the Act seeks to make directly enforceable in our law. Issues such as the scope of freedom of expression under Article 10 of the Convention, and the extent to which it could be tempered by the Convention's right to privacy under Article 8, occupied the attention of audiences up and down the country for many months.

Hidden in the interstices of the substance of the Convention rights, however, are key concepts, techniques and values which the various conferences often tended to ignore. Your editors – on behalf of JUSTICE (the all party legal human rights organisation) and University College London Faculty of Laws – therefore arranged a series of seminars between November 1999 and February 2000 for the purpose of examining those interstitial issues from the point of view of the practising lawyer. Some of those issues are fundamental to an understanding of the techniques by which to judge the scope of Convention rights – proportionality, for example, or the notion of interference that may be "prescribed by law". The notion of "civil rights and obligations" needs careful consideration and, underlying all of the Convention rights, the need to delineate what is required or forbidden in a "democratic society". In addition, we looked at the potential horizontal effect of the Human Rights Act and the question of the positive obligations that it will induce – both in decision-makers and the courts.

The invited audience at the seminars were leading practitioners in the field of human rights and public law. They included judges, practising barristers, solicitors, government lawyers and academics. At each seminar a paper was presented by a practitioner experienced in the application of human rights principles. Seminar papers were circulated to participants in advance. The paper was then responded to by an expert academic lawyer or practitioner. That response highlighted the key issues and concerns raised by the paper. Following the response there was lively discussion of both the paper and the response to it, skilfully controlled and supervised by the series chair, Mr Justice Richards. This was no straightforward task: discussion was wide-ranging and informed. The process leading from seminar paper to completed chapter for this book was rigorous. Following the seminar, each presenter was given the opportunity to revise the paper to take account of the response and the general discussion.

The seminars were as follows: *The Concept of Lawful Interference with Convention Rights* presented by Helen Mountfield (Matrix Chambers) and responded to by James Goudie QC (11 Kings' Bench Walk); *Identifying the Principles of Proportionality* presented by Michael Fordham and Tom de la Mare (Blackstone Chambers) and responded to by Professor Jeffrey Jowell (UCL and Blackstone Chambers); *Determining Civil Rights and Obligations* presented by Javan Herberg and Jane Mulcahy (Blackstone Chambers) and Andrew Le Sueur (UCL) and responded to by Richard Gordon (Brick Court Chambers); *Positive Obligations Under the Convention* presented by Keir Starmer (Doughty Street Chambers) and responded to by Professor Christopher McCrudden (Lincoln College, Oxford); *The Horizontal Effect of the Human Rights Act* presented by Murray Hunt (Matrix Chambers) and responded to by Professor Conor Gearty (King's College, London and Matrix Chambers); and *The Place of Human Rights in a Democratic Society* presented by Rabinder Singh (Matrix Chambers) and responded to by Professor Stephen Guest (UCL).

During the course of the seminars two features of the Human Rights Act became apparent. First, although on its face it is just another statute – it is not entrenched or conferred any higher-order status – in practice the Act has profound constitutional significance. This is not only because, for the first time, legislation will be able to be placed under the scrutiny of the judiciary. It is also because the Act imports into our law a notion that government, in a democratic society properly so called, is limited in its scope by the requirement to observe fundamental rights that are themselves necessary for democracy. This model of limited government differs from the model of majority rule by insisting that certain fundamental rights must be protected even if Parliament, representing the majority of the electorate, decrees otherwise. Of course, the Act does not go so far as to permit the courts to strike down legislation that offends Convention rights. A subtle compromise has been reached with the notion of Parliamentary sovereignty, so that the courts may only issue a declaration of incompatibility with the Convention rights. Legislation which is declared incompatible still stands. However, such a declaration will no doubt carry great moral weight, and the relevant Minister is given power to amend the offending legislation by way of remedial order, which can have retrospective effect. And, on the face of all government legislation, Ministers must certify whether they believe the Bill complies with Convention standards.

Secondly, it was apparent that the principal effect of the Human Rights Act will not be (as is so often alleged) to increase the power of the judiciary over the other branches of government. The duty to implement and protect human rights rests with each branch of government and with all decision-makers who could be said to be exercising "public functions". Each has clear duties and responsibilities and these cannot be ignored. Courts will have the ultimate say when it is alleged that legislation or official action offends Convention rights, but it is intended that much of the Act should be self-implementing, as individuals and public authorities come to appreciate their rights and duties under the Act.

The effect of these two features of the Human Rights Act is that all law must now be looked at through the prism of human rights standards and that those standards must be defined by methods of interpretation which acknowledge the constitutional context of the Act. A purposive process of reasoning is required; one that imports the notions and techniques discussed in this book, and which will permit all UK law to be "rinsed with a human rights dye".[1]

We do not think it necessary in this introduction to summarise the chapters below; we are confident that they are sufficiently clear to merit

---

[1] Sir Stephen Sedley, *Freedom, Law and Justice* (Sweet and Maxwell, 1999).

the reader's full scrutiny. We should like to thank the authors for their efforts, as well as the responders to the discussion, mentioned above. The papers presented by the responders were not prepared for publication and therefore do not appear in this text. Their wise and thoughtful involvement was essential to ensuring the success of the seminar series and the quality of this publication as a whole. We thank also Mr Justice Richards for chairing the series; the distinguished audience who attended so assiduously at the Moot Court Room at UCL's Bentham House; Ruth Allen (JUSTICE) and Lisa Penfold (UCL) for their excellent organisation of the seminars; and Clifford Chance for their generous support.

The Concept of a Lawful Interference with Fundamental Rights

Helen Mountfield[1]

OVERVIEW

The concept of the rule of law infuses the European Convention on Human Rights. It is described in the preamble to the Convention as part of the "common heritage" which the signatories share, and is one of the "fundamental principles of a democratic society".[2]

Rights and freedoms can compete, and states may limit citizens' rights or curtail their freedoms for certain specified and legitimate purposes. But in Convention jurisprudence, a legitimate aim and a proportionate response alone are insufficient to justify derogation from a right. A derogation must also have an ascertainable legal basis, that is, be "prescribed by law" or "in accordance with the law".[3]

---

[1] I am grateful to Lord Lester of Herne Hill QC and to my colleague Murray Hunt for their comments on an earlier draft.

[2] *Iatridis* v. *Greece* (judgment 25 March 1999, para 62).

[3] In this chapter, I have, unless the context otherwise required, referred to an interference with a Convention right being "prescribed by law". The Convention uses a number of variants on this phrase: the death penalty can be used only as "provided by law" (Article 2); arrest and detention are permitted only if in accordance with a procedure "prescribed by law" and if "lawful" (Article 5); tribunals must be "established by law" (Article 6); punishment may only be for "a criminal offence under national or international law at the time when it was committed" or where "criminal according to the general principles of law recognised by civilised nations" (Article 7); interference with respect for private and family life, home and correspondence must be "in accordance with the law" (Article 8); limitations to freedom to manifest beliefs, of expression and of association must be "prescribed by law" (Articles 9, 10, 11), and deprivation of possessions must be subject to the "conditions provided for by law and by the general principles of international law (Article 1 Protocol 1). The European Court of Human Rights has specifically stated that the phrases "prescribed by law" and "in accordance with the law" must be given an identical interpretation in order to ensure that Articles 8 and 10 (privacy/freedom of expression) can be read as a coherent whole. See *Silver* v. *UK* (1983) 5 EHRR 347, para 85.

These phrases mean more than a simple search for a national legal rule which permits the derogation. To be "prescribed by law" for Convention purposes, the starting point is that there must be a basis for what is done in national law. But this is no more than a starting point. The idea of a lawful action is also "imbued with a Convention idea of the essential qualities of law".[4] This idea connotes concepts of accessibility, foreseeability and certainty, whose meanings vary from context to context. They may not always be fully met by provisions of our own legal system.

A national rule will not constitute a law for Convention purposes unless it has appropriate qualities to make it compatible with the rule of law[5]. In summary:

> A State may interfere with citizens' rights or regulate their freedom to act for specified legitimate aims but if it does so, it must do so by law, and a norm cannot be classified as a law unless it is accessible and also foreseeable to a reasonable degree in its application and consequences.[6]

It is the essence of a democracy that people can know the laws which define their rights and responsibilities. Blackstone's *Commentaries on the Laws of England*[7] said that a "law" must be "prescribed", because,

> a bare resolution, continued in the breast of the legislator, without manifesting itself by some external sign, can never be properly a law. It is requisite that this resolution be notified to the people who are to obey it [though] the manner in which this notification is to be made, is a matter of very great indifference.[8]

---

[4] D.J. Harris, M. O'Boyle and C. Warbrick, *Law of the European Convention on Human Rights* (Butterworths, 1995). Cf. W.H. Auden "Law, says the judge as he looks down his nose/Speaking clearly and most severely/Law is as you know I suppose/Law is but let me explain it once more/Law is The Law" (from "Law Like Love" in *Collected Shorter Poems* (Faber)).

[5] See *Kopp* v. *Switzerland* (1999) 27 EHRR 91, paras 55 and 64.

[6] Karen Reid, *A Practitioner's Guide to the European Convention of Human Rights* (Sweet & Maxwell, 1998) p. 35.

[7] (1765) Volume 1 pp. 45-6.

[8] See also *Blackpool Corporation* v. *Locker* [1948] 1 KB 349 CA at 361 in which Lord Justice Scott said:

> The maxim that ignorance of the law does not excuse any subject represents the working hypothesis on which the rule of law rests in British democracy. That maxim applies in legal theory just as much to written or to unwritten law, i.e. to statute law

The requirements that a law be accessible, certain and foreseeable are servants to the overriding concepts of legal certainty and accountability. In legal systems founded on the common law this is expressed as the principle of the rule of law, and, in civil law systems, as the principle of legality.

This chapter is in two parts. The first is an overview of Convention case-law (and some from other jurisdictions) on what it means to say that there is a lawful basis for a derogation from a Convention right. The second is a preview of the potential impact of this case-law on English jurisprudence, if the duties under section 2 of the Human Rights Act 1998 to have regard to Convention principles are taken sufficiently seriously. I argue that the Convention concept of legality is capable of having a substantial effect on the development of English law. It can be used as a powerful democratic tool for accountability: to ensure that the executive legislates accessibly, creating a positive and foreseeable legal basis for its actions, and to strengthen the powers of the courts to restrain interference with fundamental rights.

THE CONVENTION MEANING OF "PRESCRIBED BY LAW"

An identifiable and established legal basis

The Convention seeks a positive basis for an interference with rights. The Convention concept of legality requires first that there must be an identifiable and established legal basis in domestic law for restrictions on Convention rights. In the absence of such a basis, no derogation from rights can be justified, no matter how worthy its objects.[9] Statute law, secondary legislation, applicable rules of European Community law,[10] ascertainable rules of the common law,[11] and even the rules of professional bodies may be sufficient.[12] The European Court of Human Rights (ECtHR) is unlikely to contradict the findings of a domestic

---

as much as to common law or equity. *But the very justification for that basic maxim is that the whole of our law, written or unwritten, is accessible to the public* – in the sense, of course, that at any rate, its legal advisers have access to it, at any moment, as of right. (my emphasis).

[9] *Iatridis* v. *Greece* (supra).

[10] *Groppera Radio AG* v. *Switzerland* (1990) 12 EHRR 321.

[11] *Sunday Times* v. *UK* (1979-80) 2 EHRR 245 at paras 46-53.

[12] *Barthold* v. *Germany* (1985) 7 EHRR 383, para 46.

court as to interpretation and application of the domestic law.[13] The existence of a domestic legal basis for an action, however, is a necessary but insufficient condition to render lawful, in Convention terms, an infringement of a right.

Accessibility: availability and foreseeability

To constitute a "lawful" fetter on a Convention freedom, the applicable law or rule must be accessible, in two senses. First, it must be available to people likely to be affected by it, at least with the help of a lawyer.[14] Internal guidelines from government departments or other public authorities will probably not fulfil the accessibility requirement unless they are published or at least unless their content is sufficiently made known.[15] Second, the citizen must be reasonably able to foresee how the legal rules are likely to be applied to the circumstances of a given case.[16]

Norms are unlikely to be sufficiently "accessible" in this second sense to constitute law if the criteria for interpreting them are themselves secret and unpublished:

> a norm cannot be regarded as "law" unless it is formulated with suffi-
> cient precision to enable the citizen to regulate his conduct: he must be
> able – if need be with appropriate advice – to foresee, to a degree that is
> reasonable in the circumstances, the consequences which a given action
> may entail.[17]

If an ostensible "rule of domestic law" does not fulfil these criteria,

---

[13] *Barthold*, para 48; *Casada Coca* v. *Spain* (1994) 18 EHRR 1, para 43; and *McLeod* v. *UK* (1999) EHRR, 493 para 44, though it may sometimes do so (see the recent Commission decision in *Lukanov* v. *Bulgaria* (1998) 26 EHRR CD 21. The Court also has a power to review whether national law has been complied with: see *Tsirlis & Kouloumpas* v. *Greece* (1998) 25 EHRR 198, para 57.

[14] *Sunday Times* v. *UK*, para 49.

[15] *Silver* v. *UK* (1983) 5 EHRR 347, paras 87-88 (prison orders and instructions), *Malone* v. *UK* (1985) 7 EHRR 14, paras 66-8 (Home Office guidelines on the tapping of telephones) *Govell* v. *UK* (judgment 14 January 1998) see [1999] EHRLR 121 (internal police guidelines).

[16] In the French text of the Convention, which is equal in authenticity to the English, "prescribed by law/*prévues par la loi*" and "in accordance with the law/*prévue par la loi*" are (i) essentially identical and (ii) contain in their language the concept of foresight.

[17] *Silver* v. *UK*. To like effect, see *Lüdi* v. *Switzerland* (1993) 15 EHRR 173.

action taken in reliance upon it will not be sufficiently foreseeable to amount to a law for Convention purposes. In effect, the requirement of foreseeability is a reference to the protection of the rule of law itself, in that it proscribes any interference with rights save in relation to a set of knowable norms, which are not applied arbitrarily, but in a sufficiently predictable fashion to give them the character of law at all.

If the law, and its scope, are known, then courts have it in their power to prevent secret, arbitrary or unreviewable actions. If the scope of the law is uncertain, then public authorities may act in ways which the courts are unable to restrain. For example, in *Amann* v. *Switzerland*,[18] a businessman (who sold depilatory devices) had a call from a woman in the former Soviet Embassy in Berne. The call was intercepted by the Federal Public Prosecutor's office, which made an entry in its security index, noting that Mr Amann was a businessman, a contact with the Russian Embassy, and that espionage was established. The ECHR held that this was an interference with Mr Amann's Article 8 rights, and was not "in accordance with the law" because the Swiss legal provisions relied upon did not contain specific and detailed provisions on the gathering, recording, storing or destruction of the data to comply with the requirement of foreseeable application of the law, or to permit proper safeguards against abuse. Notwithstanding the existence of a domestic legal basis for it, the interference was held not to be "in accordance with the law".[19]

Thus, administrative rules by themselves are unlikely to constitute law. But if the decision-maker makes public administrative practices which clarify the way in which an otherwise over-wide statutory discretion will be used, this may be sufficient to make a rule or regulation sufficiently knowable to have the qualities of a law. In the *Silver* case, the prison rules governing interference with prisoners' correspondence were not, on their own, sufficiently precise to enable the subjects of the rules to know how they would be applied. But, read with the notices to

---

[18] (2000) 30 EHRR 843.

[19] There are some dicta in recent English case-law to like effect. See *R* v. *Secretary of State for the Home Department ex p Pierson* [1998] AC 539 at 573G-575D, 587C-598A, and *R* v. *Secretary of State for the Home Department ex p Simms* [1999] 3 WLR 328 especially per Lord Steyn at 340. See, however, the discussion of *R* v. *Secretary of State for Health ex parte C* (2000) I FLR 656, (discussed below), and Stephen Grosz's article discussing this case in the May 2000 *Law Society Gazette*, LSG 97 (17).

the prisoners informing them of the content of Orders and Instructions, the criterion of sufficient foreseeability was satisfied.[20] Again, the Convention chimes with the sentiments underlying the common law:

> [Law] may be notified, *viva voce*, by officers appointed for that purpose, as is done with regard to proclamations, and such acts of parliament as are appointed to be read in churches and other assemblies. It may lastly be notified by writing, printing, or the like; which is the general course taken with all our acts of parliament. Yet, whatever way is made use of, it is incumbent on the promulgators to do it in the most public and perspicuous manner; not like Caligula, who (according to Dio Cassius) wrote his laws in a very small character, and hung them upon high pillars, the more effectually to ensnare the people.[21]

Though the sentiment of the common law and the Convention is the same, a positivist legal tradition in the domestic court in the *Silver* case meant that the House of Lords had not been prepared to consider the "legality" of the use of the prison rules by reference to the criterion of knowability. Nonetheless, the concept of foreseeability must take colour from its context. In some contexts (interception of communications is an example) the Court may accept that complete foreseeability is unattainable. For example, given the national security implications, an element of secrecy may be necessary as to whether particular individual telephones may be subject to surveillance. In *Malone* v. *UK*[22] the Court accepted that an individual was not entitled to such transparency that he could foresee that his telephone would be tapped and so adapt his behaviour accordingly.

Given that practice in individual cases will not be known, the law must provide sufficient safeguards to ensure that the executive is accountable, and that there are safeguards against the abuses of power which the law has conferred. Thus, the law must be sufficiently clear to inform citizens of the types of circumstances in which public authorities are empowered to take such secret measures. In *Malone*, the Court held that in the absence of a comprehensive statutory code governing such activities, UK law was too vague to satisfy the requirement of legality:

[20] *Silver* v. *UK*, para 95; see too *Leander* v. *Sweden* (1987) 9 EHRR 433.
[21] See Blackstone *Commentaries on the Laws of England* (1765) Volume 1.
[22] (1985) 7 EHRR 14, paras 67-8.

... the law must be sufficiently clear in its terms to give citizens an adequate indication as to the circumstances in which and the conditions on which public authorities are empowered to resort to this secret and potentially dangerous interference with the right to respect for private life and correspondence.[23]

Sufficient certainty

Generally

A further principle of the Convention is that a law must be sufficiently certain to enable citizens to know when restrictions may be placed on their freedom, and secondly to enable them accurately to gauge the consequences of their actions.

Such precision is important because, as American judges have observed, the vice of a vague law is that it may inhibit citizens from a far wider zone of activities than would in fact prove to be prohibited if the boundaries were clearly marked.[24] In *Stromberg* v. *California*[25] the Supreme Court stated:

> The maintenance of the opportunity of free political discussion to the end that government may be responsible to the will of the people and that changes may be obtained by lawful means, an opportunity essential to the security of the Republic, is a fundamental principle of our constitutional system. *A statute which upon its face, and as authoritatively construed, is so vague and indefinite as to permit the punishment of the fair use of this opportunity is repugnant to the guarantee of liberty contained in the Fourteenth Amendment.* (Emphasis added)

But, as lawyers know better than most, precision is not always easy to attain. Especially in sensitive areas such as freedom of expression, it may be difficult for the law to create a formula sufficiently sensitive to balance competing interests. It may not be easy to fine-tune the legal response to such situations by resort only to black-letter law or seeking absolute rules in established precedents. If the law is drawn too rigidly, that which was intended as a guide may become a strait-jacket.

---

[23] Ibid at para 67, 69-80. See also *Huvig* v. *France* (1990) 12 EHRR 528 and *Halford* v. *UK* (1997) 24 EHRR 523, para 49.

[24] *Grayned* v. *City of Rockford* (1972) 408 US 104, 108-9 (anti-noise bye-law not unconstitutionally vague).

[25] 283 US 3 59 (1931) at p. 369.

Certainty and development in the common law

Absolute certainty in the common law would require rigid adherence to the doctrine of precedent. Consequently, at first sight a requirement for legal certainty may appear to be incompatible with the very existence of the common law, which is intended to be capable of flexible adaptation to novel situations. However, the Court has not interpreted the requirement for certainty so rigidly as to prevent the incremental development of judge-made law. In the case of *Sunday Times* v. *UK*,[26] the Court accepted that absolute certainty as to the application of the law to a particular case was neither necessary nor attainable:

> . . . whilst certainty is highly desirable, it may bring in its train excessive rigidity and the law must be able to keep pace with changing circumstances. Accordingly, many laws are inevitably couched in terms which, to a greater or lesser extent, are vague and whose interpretation and application are questions of practice.

In that case, the Sunday Times argued that the House of Lords had introduced a new principle into the English common law of contempt, which they could not have anticipated, which was not sufficiently clear (because the reasoning of their Lordships differed) and so was not one upon which they could have based their conduct. After close analysis of the speeches of the Law Lords, the Court held that:

> . . . the applicants were able to foresee, to a degree that was reasonable in the circumstances, a risk that publication . . . might fall foul of the principle.

There are limits, however, to the degree of vagueness which is acceptable if common law norms can be characterised as laws for the purposes of the Convention. In *Harman* v. *UK*[27], the Commission declared admissible an application in which it was claimed that the domestic courts had created a wholly new category of contempt of court. (The case settled and there was no substantive hearing).

The degree of certainty necessary to regulate conduct

Article 7 of the Convention provides that no one shall be punished for an offence unless it was known to the law at the time when it was

---

[26] (1979-80) 2 EHRR 245 at para 49.
[27] (1984) 38 DR 53.

committed. Again, the principle of knowability has roots in the common law. Professor Glanville Williams QC put it in this way:

> "Englishmen are ruled by the law, and by the law alone," wrote Dicey. "A man may with us be punished for breach of law, but he can be punished for nothing else." In its Latin dress of *Nullum crimen sine lege, Nulla Poena sine lege* – that there must be no crime or punishment except in accordance with fixed, predetermined law – this has been regarded by most thinkers as a self-evident principle of justice ever since the French Revolution. The citizen must be able to ascertain beforehand how he stands with regard to the criminal law; otherwise to punish him for breach of that law is purposeless cruelty. . . . *Observe how the principle is not satisfied merely by the fact that the punishment inflicted is technically legal. The Star Chamber was a legal tribunal, but it did not exemplify the rule of law in Dicey's philosophy. "Law" for this purpose means a body of fixed rules; and it excludes wide discretion even though that discretion be exercised by independent judges. The principle of legality involves rejecting "criminal equity" as a mode of extending the law.*[28] (Emphasis added)

In Strasbourg, however, the Court adopts the same pragmatic standard in considering the degree of certainty which is necessary to enable punishment for a wrong to be lawful (under Article 7) as it imposes on limitations to an individual's positive rights to act. In *Wingrove* v. *UK*[29] and *Müller* v. *Switzerland*,[30] cases involving freedom of expression, the Court accepted that the concepts of blasphemy and obscenity were not capable of precise definition.

In *Kokkinakis* v. *Greece* (1993) 17 EHRR 397, the Court recognised that many statutes were imprecise in their wording. It accepted that the need to avoid excessive rigidity and to keep pace with changing circumstances means that many laws are couched in terms which are, to a greater or lesser extent, vague. In paragraph 52 of the judgment, the Court said:

> . . . an offence must be clearly defined in law [but] this condition is satisfied where the individual can know from the wording of the relevant provision and, if need be, with the assistance of the courts' interpretation of it, what acts and omissions will make him liable.

[28] G. Williams *Criminal Law: The General Part* (Sweet & Maxwell 2nd edn. 1961) pp. 575-6.
[29] (1997) 24 EHRR 1.
[30] (1991) 13 EHRR 212.

In a common-law context, the Court rejected the allegation that a finding of rape within marriage contravened the requirement of Article 7 that an offence be known to law. The Court held that the law had developed to such a degree that the likely consequences of such an act were foreseeable: gradual clarification of the criminal law by judicial decision did not contravene Article 7 provided the development was consistent with the essence of the offence and was reasonably foreseeable.[31]

The distinction between acceptable and unacceptable degrees of certainty is, however, a fine one. In *Steel & Others* v. *UK*,[32] the Court accepted that "breach of peace" and being "bound over" to keep the peace following such breach were sufficiently precise to amount to knowable legal requirements, though it accepted that the expression "to be of good behaviour" was "particularly imprecise". In similar (but not identical) circumstances, the Commission has held there to be an infringement of Article 10 where hunt saboteurs who had shouted at hounds but had not breached the peace were bound over to keep the peace because their conduct was *contra bonos mores*. The Court held that a requirement to "be of good behaviour" was insufficiently precise to enable the subjects of the order to foresee what would constitute a contravention of it. Accordingly it was not a lawful infringement of the right to freedom of expression in Article 10.[33] The distinction between the two cases would seem to be that whereas in *Steel* the complainants had been convicted of a breach of the peace, and so might reasonably foresee what conduct was said to be unacceptable, the complainants in *Hashman* had committed no offence and so had no lawful standard by which to judge the behaviour which the local magistrates would regard as sufficiently "good". The common law alone ought to have achieved this result. See Glanville Williams:

> Punishment in all its forms is a loss of rights or advantages consequent on a breach of law. When it does not have this quality it degenerates into an arbitrary act of violence that can produce nothing but bad social effects. Opinions about what people ought to do are almost as numerous as human beings, but opinions about what people are legally obliged to do should be capable of being ascertained by legal research.[34]

---

[31] *SW & CR* v. *UK* (1996) 21 EHRR 363, paras 33-4.
[32] (1999) 28 EHRR 603.
[33] *Hashman & Harrup* v. *UK* (2000) 30 EHRR 241.
[34] *Supra* n. 28.

The incorporation of the Convention will, however, assist in concentrating judicial minds on the essential qualities of a law, and make it easier to articulate the basis for requiring a clear, ascertainable law.

The competing values of certainty and flexibility are reflected in constitutional cases from other jurisdictions. Recently, the Court held that a prohibition on "political activities" was not too vague to contravene the legal requirement for certainty.[35] A similar prohibition on "political campaigning" by civil servants has been held not to be unconstitutionally vague by the Supreme Court of Canada.[36] In a recent Privy Council decision in a constitutional appeal from Mauritius, *Dharmarajen Sabapathee v. The State*,[37] it was held that a statutory provision which criminalised the "trafficking" of drugs was not too imprecise a prohibition to enable citizens to understand those transactions which fell within and those which fell outside the ordinary meaning of the expression. Thus, it could not be said that the provision was so vague as to give rise to decisions which were arbitrary and unfair or unconstitutional. Lord Hope, giving the judgment of the Court, referred to the jurisprudence of the European Court of Human Rights to like effect.

Nonetheless, in both the United States and Canada, statutes can, and have, been declared to be "void for vagueness", if they fail to provide an "intelligible standard" for the application of the prohibition.[38]

Certainty and the interpretation of statutory discretions

Many legal provisions confer discretions on public authorities. In order to fulfil the legal requirement of certainty, a law which confers a discretion must give sufficient indication as to the scope of the discretion.[39] The method by which and the extent to which that indication must be given will vary according to the circumstances of the case, but the Court will not be satisfied by rules which give the executive an overbroad discretion as to when interference with fundamental rights is permissible, appropriate or necessary:

---

[35] *Rekvenyi* v. *Hungary* [1999] EHRLR 114.

[36] *Osborne* v. *Canada* [1991] 2 SCR 69.

[37] Privy Council Appeal No 1 of 1999, transcript pp. 7-11.

[38] See generally discussion at para 33.7(c) of Peter Hogg, *Constitutional Law of Canada* (3rd edn. Carswell) In *re Blainey and Ontario Hockey Association* (1986) 54 OR (2d) 513 CA, for example, an exemption from a Human Rights Code for sex-segregated sport was struck down because it "prescribe[d] no limits and provide[d] no guidelines".

[39] *Silver* v. *UK, supra* n. 3..

> . . . it would be contrary to the rule of law for the legal discretion granted to the executive to be expressed in terms of unfettered power. Consequently, the law must indicate the scope of any discretion conferred on the competent authorities and the manner of its exercise with sufficient clarity, having regard to the legitimate aim of the measure in question, to give the individual adequate protection against arbitrary interference.[40]

The Court may, however, impose a stricter standard in circumstances such as cases of secret surveillance where the law itself is less likely to provide a procedure for scrutiny of the basis for decision-making than in more transparent situations where a degree of judicial scrutiny is easier to achieve. In *Olsson* v. *Sweden*,[41] the Court accepted the Applicants' submission that the Swedish legislation governing the decision as to whether to take children into care was admittedly rather general in its terms and conferred a wide measure of discretion on the State. On the other hand, such proceedings were by their nature so variable that it would be impossible to frame a law which covered every eventuality, and the discretions in question were open to judicial review at various levels. In those circumstances, the Court was satisfied that the procedures in that case were sufficiently certain to protect against arbitrary action and were "in accordance with the law".

The concern for accountability to both the courts and the legislature which arises in this context is the same as that which has underpinned anxiety (in a domestic context since at least the 1920s) in relation to "Henry VIII" clauses in legislation.[42] If Parliament gives the executive an over-broad discretion, this puts the purposes for which and the method by which those powers are used beyond the supervision of the courts and prevents citizens from knowing whether an action is or is not "in accordance with the law".

The concern for legality contained in the common law but reinforced by the Convention is an aspect of the fundamental protection of Article 6.

---

[40] *Malone* v. *UK*, para 68 and see *Kopp* v. *Switzerland* (1999) 27 EHRR 91 paras 71-2.

[41] (1988) 11 EHRR 259, paras 30-1, 60-3.

[42] Which Parliament itself now attempts to regulate through, in particular the House of Lords' Delegated Powers Deregulation Committee. See Erskine May, *Parliamentary Practice* (22nd edn., pp. 467-8, 592-3, 578, 624).

Protection against arbitrary action: proper purposes and procedural guarantees

The object which underlies these interlocking principles is to ensure that there is one rule for all, that power is not exercised arbitrarily or for an improper purpose, and that minimum safeguards exist against the abuse of power.[43] The Court will, therefore, apply a definition of law which has at least an element of autonomous "Strasbourg" meaning and imply a procedural, as well as substantive content into the definition of a lawful action.

As to the purpose for which ostensible legal authority can be used, in *Ashingdane* v. *UK*,[44] the Court considered that the question of whether detention of a person of unsound mind was lawful for the purposes of Article 5(1)(e) extended not just to the fact of deprivation of liberty but also to the manner of its execution. There must be a relationship between the grounds for the deprivation of liberty and the place of detention. Thus detention can only be "lawful" if it is in a hospital, clinic or other appropriate institution authorised for that purpose.

This arguably goes beyond the requirement that a legal power be used for a proper purpose in domestic cases such as *Padfield* v. *Ministry of Agriculture:*[45] it is not merely a limit on the purpose for which the legal power can be used, but creates positive requirements as to how action under it must be executed so as to give effect to the purpose underlying its use. In *Tsirlis & Kouloumpas* v. *Greece,*[46] the Court emphasised that the concept of "lawful detention" in Article 5 of the Convention required restrictions on freedoms to conform to the substantive and procedural rules of national law, and that these must be sufficient to protect individuals from arbitrary use of it.

The text of Article 5 of the Convention contains explicit due-process guarantees: it requires that no person may be deprived of their liberty unless the detention is "lawful" and "in accordance with a procedure which is prescribed by law". But in considering "lawfulness" in the context of the other Articles also, the Court will seek such procedural guarantees as it regards as inherent in the concept of "lawful" action.

---

[43] This was clearly a concern underlying the decision on tapping of all the phones in a lawyer's office under an order which required respect for legal privilege in *Kopp* v. *Switzerland* (*supra* n. 5). See also *Valenzuela Contreras* v. *Spain* (judgment 30 July 1998, para 46).

[44] (1985) 7 EHRR 528, para 44.

[45] [1968] AC 997.

[46] (1998) 25 EHRR 198, paras 55-6.

In one case, the Court found a violation where revenue authorities operated a pre-emption procedure where they believed there to be a sale at an undervalue. This procedure flouted the requirement in Article 1 Protocol 1 that the conditions for deprivation of possessions be "provided for by law" because it:

> operated arbitrarily and selectively, and was scarcely foreseeable, *and it was not attended by basic procedural guarantees.*[47] [My emphasis]

In two French "telephone-tapping" cases,[48] the Court articulated positive procedural requirements necessary to render an infringement of rights "lawful". It stated that the rules for so serious an infringement of rights as telephone tapping must

> afford safeguards against various possible abuses. For example, the categories of people liable to have their telephones tapped by judicial order and the nature of the offences which may give rise to such an order are nowhere defined. Nothing obliges a judge to set a limit on the duration of telephone tapping. Similarly unspecified are the procedures for drawing up the summary reports containing intercepted conversations; the precautions to be taken in order to communicate the recording intact and in their entirety for possible inspection by the judge . . . and by the defence, and the circumstances in which records may be erased or the tapes be destroyed. . .

The Court will consider not merely the existence of procedural guarantees, but also whether they are sufficient in practice to give practical effect to the requirement for legal mechanisms to insure against unlawful infringements of rights. In *RMD* v. *Switzerland*,[49] a prisoner on remand was moved from prison to prison and across a number of Swiss cantons. Though each canton had a procedure through which the legality of the detention may be challenged, the procedure ceased and had to be re-started each time the prisoner left one canton and was imprisoned in another. The Court held that though legal procedures were theoretically available, the procedural difficulties involved in using them were so great as to mean that the theoretical legal remedy was not

---

[47] *Hentrick* v. *France* (1994) 18 EHRR 440, para 42.
[48] *Huvig* v. *France & Kruslin* v. *France, supra* n. 23 and *Kopp* v. *Switzerland, supra* n. 23.
[49] (1999) 28 EHRR 225.

an effective method of challenging the detention, and there was therefore a violation of Article 5(4).

The common law of England ought to provide such guarantees sufficiently. In *Ong Ah Chuan* v. *Public Prosecutor of Singapore*[50] Lord Diplock (giving the decision of the Privy Council) said that it was a misuse of language to describe as a law something which did not contain within it the fundamental rules of natural justice which were inherent in the common law.

The incorporation of the Convention will reinforce the impetus for courts to scrutinise the face of domestic law to ensure that this requirement is met. If they do not, their efforts may be challenged in Strasbourg. The Court will require signatory states to provide such positive safeguards under the law as are necessary to protect against arbitrary interferences with the rights contained in the Convention, and to give *effet utile* to Article 6.

AREAS OF POTENTIAL CHANGE IN ENGLISH LAW

A positive concept of legality

Throughout this chapter, I have emphasised continuities between the common law concept of legality and that contained in the Convention. There are also, however, discontinuities and incompatibilities, which the courts will have to address.

The first is the English legal tradition of treating the Crown as a legal person which can do anything which is not expressly forbidden. This has a profound (and, in my view, undemocratic) cultural effect: there is an unspoken assumption that the executive has some inherent power to act for (its view) of the common good, and courts operate a relatively low level of review of the legality of executive action, at least by central government departments.

It is true that in two important recent cases, the House of Lords has analysed the common-law concept of "legality" in a rigorous way: *R* v. *Secretary of State for the Home Department ex p Pierson*[51] and *R* v. *Secretary of State for the Home Department ex p Simms*.[52] *Simms*

---

[50] [1981] AC 648 at 670F-671A.
[51] [1998] AC 539 at 573G-575D, and 587C-598A.
[52] [1998] AC 539 and [1999] 3 WLR 328 respectively.

concerned prison rules made under section 47(1) Prisons Act 1952 which restricted face-to-face interviews between prisoners and journalists. The House of Lords held that, literally construed, the rules did permit rules restricting such interviews, but that a blanket ban curtailed fundamental rights, and was therefore *ultra vires,* because a power to curtail fundamental rights cannot be implied without the use of express words or necessary implication.

However, there remains a difference between the English concept of a "legal" basis for executive interference with rights and that identified in the Strasbourg case-law. *R* v. *Secretary of State for Health ex parte C,*[53] concerned a challenge to the legality of an index which the Department of Health made available to employers, of people about whom there might be doubts as to their suitability to work with children. There is no statutory basis for this index, whose existence is regulated only by Departmental Circular. The Court of Appeal held that the Crown, as a corporation with legal personality, had "the same capacities and liberties" as a natural person, but could not infringe private rights of others without lawful authority. Since no one had a right to a job (justiciable under Article 6 of the Convention), the index was not unlawful.

The concept of legality used in this decision is the Diceyan idea that the Crown can do anything which is not made illegal by some countervailing private right. Using the Convention concept of legality, however, the "negative freedom" for the Crown to do what it likes is unlikely to provide a sufficient positive legal basis to allow interference with rights (for example, under Article 8 of the Convention). It was that approach to the power to monitor which had been used by the domestic court in *Malone* v. *Metropolitan Police Commissioner,*[54] and found wanting by the ECtHR in *Malone* v. *UK,*[55] which required a positive, foreseeable permission for the State to interfere with rights, rather than an assumption that it could do so unless forbidden.

It is interesting to contrast the decision in *ex parte C* with the decision in *Amann* v. *Switzerland,*[56] and to ask whether *ex parte C* would have been decided in the same way if the *Amann* decision had been brought to its attention. It is unlikely that it would have been so

[53] (2000) I FLR 658.
[54] [1979] 1 Ch 344.
[55] (1984) 7 EHRR 14.
[56] *Supra* n. 18.

decided, and in future cases, the domestic court would have been obliged to take *Amann* into account by virtue of section 2 of the Human Rights Act 1998.[57]

One effect of the incorporation of the Convention into English law, therefore, may be to shift our constitutional thinking, so that those exercising executive power, and those scrutinising it analyse the issue not in terms of the Crown's liberty to act (in a negative sense), but seek instead a positive legal basis for state interference with citizens' freedoms.

Certainty and legality

If the Convention concept of legality is taken seriously, domestic courts may scrutinise legal instruments more closely to determine whether they are sufficiently certain to meet the Convention standard of legality. For example, in *McEldowney* v. *Forde* [1971] AC 632, the House of Lords had to decide whether a regulation containing a ban on "organisations . . . describing themselves as 'republican clubs' or any like organisation howsoever described" was so vague and uncertain as to render the regulation invalid for uncertainty. It decided that the regulation was not ultra vires.

With the enactment of the Human Rights Act 1998, such a regulation will have to withstand scrutiny under Article 11 of the Convention (right to freedom of association) and possibly also Article 10 (right to free speech). Restrictions on such rights must be "prescribed by law". If the Convention concept of "prescribed by law" is taken sufficiently seriously, it is unlikely that so vague a proscription would be held to be sufficiently certain to constitute a valid legal basis for such a ban affecting these fundamental rights.

Questions of accessibility and accountability

Modern legislation often requires executive bodies to have regard to guidance or to Codes of Practice.[58] Where these are published and easily available (for example, the Code of Practice made under section 53 of the Disability Discrimination Act 1995), there will be no questions of accessibility: indeed, such documents are often more accessible than the underlying statutory provisions. But some operational policies

---

[57] See Stephen Grosz [May 2000] *Law Society Gazette*, LSG 97 (17).

[58] For example, the School Standards and Framework Act 1998 makes extensive use of this method of legislating.

or procedures may be difficult to obtain, or even be unpublished. With the advent of freedom of information legislation and the continuing development of the Internet, fewer reasons will exist for not ensuring that the rules by which public bodies operate are easily available to everyone. One possible development, therefore, is that courts will expect a high level of "accessibility" before they are prepared to say that a rule is sufficiently available to constitute a law.

There will be questions (as there were in the *Silver* case) as to the degree of intelligibility which is necessary on the face of the legislation to give it the requisite standard of accessibility; how much can be "filled in" by resort to guidance; and how easily available that guidance or policy or operational documents must be to give statutory discretions (which would otherwise be insufficiently fettered to constitute law) the status of "laws" on the Strasbourg standard.

Accessibility of law is important. It deserves to be taken seriously. Decision-makers, and those affected by the decisions, are entitled to know the basis upon which decisions affecting them are to be made. As Lord Steyn said in *Simms*:[59] "The structure of the law matters. It is necessary to find the exact location of this case on the map of public law".

Additionally, if courts, and applicants, search for accessible legal standards, the emerging doctrine of a "right to reasons" may be brought forward a stage: the requirement that restrictions on Convention rights are "prescribed by a [foreseeable] law" may mean that courts look for the basis upon which executive decisions were taken – or at least, the basis of their reasoning – to have been published in advance.

A difficult example, discussed in the media, is the provision in the Social Security Act 1986 which (among several hundred other provisions) substantially reduced the level at which survivors' pensions, earned by workers' contributions to the State Earnings Related Pension Scheme (SERPS), would be paid with effect from 2001. Though the statute was passed, no steps were taken to notify those making SERPS contributions that the provision which they believed themselves to be making for their survivors was not, in fact, in place. They were thus unable to modify their behaviour accordingly and had no reason to seek legal advice. There was no mention of the impending (reduced) benefit levels in DSS explanatory leaflets until 1996, and then the

---

[59] *Supra* n. 19.

change was not highlighted. In a domestic context, it is clear that there is a statutory basis for this deprivation. But it may be argued in Strasbourg that the provision permitting this deprivation of possessions (albeit in primary legislation) was insufficiently accessible to the persons affected by it, in the circumstances of the case, to constitute a "lawful" deprivation on the Strasbourg standard of legality.[60]

Discretion and foreseeability

Another modern trend is primary legislation which leaves wide discretions for ministers to make such rules as they see fit, or as they may consider necessary, without a precise statement of the objects for which the powers may be exercised. One example is Sections 19 and 20 of the Immigration and Asylum Act 1999, which give extremely wide discretions to ministers to pass or receive personal information across national boundaries to or from defined "specified persons" for "specified purposes". This enables ministers, untrammelled by the legislature, categories or persons for defined purposes, but also to broaden the categories of persons and data which can be transmitted, without positive legal safeguards akin to those introduced (as a result of the *Malone* case) by the Interception of Communications Act 1985. In paragraphs 4.1-4.14 of the *Asylum and Immigration Bill: Human Rights Compliance: JUSTICE's evidence to the House of Commons Special Standing Committee, March 1999.* JUSTICE questioned whether the uses of personal information permitted by these sections (then Clauses 11 and 12) could be said to be "prescribed by law" and "necessary in a democratic society".

A ministerial statement of compatibility under section 19 of the Human Rights Act 1998 was given to these clauses, on the basis that those using the Act would not use or disclose information in a way which was incompatible with common law duties of confidence, the Data Protection Act 1998 or Article 8 of the Convention. Until orders under these sections are made by which such "specified" uses of data are permitted, it is difficult to see how the legislation can be sufficiently certain for a minister to say with confidence that the infringements of Article 8(1) which it will permit will meet the Strasbourg standard of being "prescribed by law". Regulations made under these clauses may be open to challenge on the basis that they

---

[60] See reference to Blackstone, *supra* n. 7.

do not have a sufficiently certain legal basis to permit them to have been made.

In relation to "Henry VIII" clauses, if the Parliamentary Deregulation and Contracting Out Committees do not adequately ensure that legislation is not unduly delegated, the courts may be prepared to declare any use of a statutory instrument made under such inappropriately wide powers to be unlawful, and/or to make a Section 10 declaration in respect of the parent power.

Certainty and flexibility and the common law

The point of the common law is that it can develop incrementally to meet changing social standards. On the other hand, certainty is also an essential legal value, necessary to enable people to regulate their conduct, and to enable courts to determine and enforce individual rights. If the concept of legality were used to require absolute foreseeability, it could inhibit the development of common law torts by courts which would otherwise develop common law or equitable concepts to give effect to their own positive obligations under section 6 of the Human Rights Act 1998.[61]

It is possible that arguments will develop, in private law cases, as to whether a particular development of the common law to give effect to some protected Convention right goes too far, so that one party finds itself penalised or criticised for acting in a way which, it alleges, could not reasonably have been foreseen. The Human Rights Act 1998 has heralded a revolution in legal reasoning: Lord Cooke of Thorndon said during the parliamentary debates that hereafter "the common law approach to statutory interpretation will never be the same again".[62] Judges may sometimes be caught between the Scylla of the requirement for reasonable legal certainty and the Charybdis of sections 2 and 3 of the Human Rights Act, which will require them positively to develop the common law creatively in bold, purposive judgments to give effect to the positive obligations of the Convention.

However, developments in the common law and statutory interpretation to give effect to the Convention concept of legality should not

---

[61] However, the courts show no signs thus far of having been so inhibited: see (e.g.) *Douglas & Others* v. *Hello! Ltd* (*The Times*, 16 January 2001).

[62] *Hansard* HL, 3 November 1997, cols. 1272-3.

take its citizens by surprise. "Parliament does not legislate in a vacuum. Parliament legislates in a European liberal democracy, founded on the principles and traditions of the common law".[63] The courts will need the Convention concept of legal certainty if they are to develop the common law in accordance with the common European legal traditions from which it emerged. Legal accountability is at the centre of the European concept of democracy. Freedom from state interference except as clearly permitted by a defined, accessible and foreseeable legal power is essential to the guarantees of rights set out in the Convention; and enforceable legal standards are inherent in Article 6 of the Convention and the rule of law.

[63] Per Lord Steyn in *Simms* above.

Identifying the Principles
of Proportionality

Michael Fordham and Thomas de la Mare

INTRODUCTION

1. In this chapter[1] we will ask what the approach should be in the United Kingdom to the concept of proportionality and the margin of appreciation under the Human Rights Act 1998 ("the 1998 Act"). However, we think it impossible sensibly to answer that question in the abstract, or by reference to the 1998 Act and case-law of the European Court of Human Rights ("the Strasbourg Court") alone. In order to understand how judges will and should react, we think it essential to search first for clues throughout the pre-existing legal culture into which the 1998 Act is being delivered.

2. The principle of proportionality is at the heart of the European legal order and increasingly recognised as a key component in the rule of law. It provides a systematic approach to judicial review of a measure (normally, a decision or rule), adopted by a public authority, restricting a basic right. It is a concept with three important, general features:

1. It identifies a logical template of *questions* to be addressed.
2. It provides for an *intensive review* by the courts as to the way in which those questions are to be asked and answered.
3. It involves placing upon the public authority an important *onus*, of satisfying itself and the Court that there are proper answers.

3. Alongside proportionality is to be found a concept which we will call, generically, "latitude" or "the margin" (Strasbourg jurisprudence speaks of a "margin of appreciation", and domestic law has begun to speak of a "discretionary area of judgment"). The idea of latitude, or a

---

[1] Our internal cross-references use <5> (meaning "see paragraph 5") and <P2> (for the principles on pp. 28–29).

margin, represents the public authority's room for freedom of choice. Proportionality does not turn government officials into robots, nor judges into government officials. It does not dictate that there is only one measure which could be adopted, one objective pursued, or one means of its pursuit. The Court does not assume the role of a primary decision-maker, with the function of delineating policy or imposing preferences. The concept of the margin (or latitude) has three main features.

1. It recognises that public authorities will have some *freedom* of choice or appraisal, when answering the questions posed by the proportionality template.
2. It serves as a reminder that intensive review by the Court is still intensive *review*: the judge is asking "is the measure justified?", not "would I have adopted it ?"
3. It introduces an idea of *variability*: margins can differ in their width, depending on the nature of the power and subject-matter.

PROPORTIONALITY: SUGGESTED PRINCIPLES

P1. Proportionality introduces this **four-question template**:
 Q1 *Legitimacy*. Is the measure adopted to pursue a legitimate aim?
 Q2 *Suitability*. Can it serve to further that aim?
 Q3 *Necessity*. Is it the least restrictive way of doing so?
 Q4 *Means/ends fit*. Viewed overall, do the ends justify the means?[2]

P2. The starting-point is always to identify and respect the **legislative mandate**: any supreme instrument stating: (1) what measures are permissible; (2) what objectives are legitimate; or (3) how wide the authority's margin is.

P3. Q1-Q4: (1) operate together and not in mutual isolation; (2) may not each appear to be in play (if obviously satisfied); and (3) can each involve its own margin.

P4. Alongside them is a concept of **pressing need**, both in a *threshold* sense (a problem whose resolution satisfies Q1) and an *overall* sense (informing Q2-Q4).

---

[2] So, if prevention of rape is a permissible aim (*legitimacy*), which can (*suitability*) and can only (*necessity*) be furthered by forced castration, the question is then one of overall cost and benefit (*means/ends fit*).

P5. Q1 and Q4 involve a **value-judgment inquiry**: (1) identifying the competing *interests* (rights and objectives); (2) *weighting* their relative importance; (3) asking whether, in principle and in the circumstances, any can properly take *precedence*.

P6. Q2-Q3 involve protecting individuals from ineffective and unnecessary regulation.

P7. The four-question template (and value-judgment inquiry) should be used by public authorities because: (1) good public administration requires a disciplined and focused reasoning process; which (2) will protect the public authority from judicial interference.

P8. The Court is entitled to scrutinise, with reference to the four-question template and value-judgment inquiry: (1) the public authority's **reasoning process** (questions it asked); and (2) its **substantive conclusions** (answers it arrived at).

P9. Scrutiny of substantive conclusions involves setting the appropriate *margin* (and so *intensity of review*), which depends on the nature of: (1) *the right infringed* (how fundamental ?); (2) *the objective pursued* (how compelling ?); (3) *the measure and decision-maker* (what status ?); (4) *the context of the dispute* (how sensitive ?).[3]

P10. The *onus* is on the public authority to demonstrate an appropriate reasoning process and justified conclusions. The Court should insist on: (1) *evidence* (operative rationale); and not (2) *submission* (subsequent rationalisation).

WEDNESBURY REVIEW

4. As proportionality is the central feature in the legal order of Europe, so *Wednesbury* ([1948] 1 KB 223) has been the central feature of public law in England and Wales. Although Lord Greene MR was summarising principles which were "well understood" (see 228), the name of the case caught on (and has proved impossible to shake off) as synonymous

---

[3] *Not* (5) *The nature of the judicial proceedings.* In reality, judges may be influenced by whether the issue is raised in a mode of litigation apt for an intensive (e.g. fact-assessing) review. But it is impossible to see this as proper: if required to effect a given level of scrutiny, the Court should modify or switch the litigation mode.

with the deferential standard of domestic substantive review. As we shall later show, domestic common law has developed more mature and active doctrines of substantive review. We use the term *Wednesbury* deliberately, to describe the passive, old-fashioned principle.

5. Importantly, the Court will always have started by asking whether there is any relevant *legislative mandate* (see e.g. *Hammersmith* <44>). The supreme legislative instrument in a normal domestic case is an Act of Parliament. Under principles of legality (*ultra vires*) the public authority will be held to any *statutory objective* for which alone the power may be used, whether this is express or implied as a matter of legislative intent.[4] Similarly, the Court will be astute to identify the width of the *statutory margin*. In the words of Professor Wade:[5]

> in a system based on the rule of law, unfettered governmental discretion is a contradiction in terms. The real question is whether the discretion is wide or narrow, and where the legal line is to be drawn. For this purpose everything depends upon the true intent and meaning of the empowering Act.

6. *Wednesbury* Review operates, first, on the level of review of the *reasoning process*. It requires that a public authority asks itself the right questions and takes account of relevant considerations (see Lord Greene MR at 229). It does not tend to prescribe any particular logical sequence (or template) of relevant questions, provided that the authority's chosen sequence was logical. As Sedley J said in *R* v. *Parliamentary Commissioner for Administration, ex p Balchin* ([1998] I PLR I at 13E–F), *Wednesbury* unreasonableness is apt to mean "an error of reasoning which robs the decision of logic". Here, as elsewhere, *Wednesbury* is dominated by recognition of a *margin*. Beyond certain matters which the Court identifies (usually from the statute) as relevant or irrelevant as a matter of legal duty, the authority is given freedom to decide for itself:

---

[4] E.g. *R* v. *Secretary of State for Foreign and Commonwealth Affairs, ex p World Development Movement Ltd* [1995] 1 WLR 386 (express) and *Padfield* v. *Minister of Agriculture Fisheries & Food* [1968] AC 997 (implied).

[5] Cited with approval by Lord Bridge in *R* v. *Tower Hamlets London Borough Council, ex p Chetnik Developments Ltd* [1988] AC 858 at 872B-F.

There is, in short, a margin of appreciation within which the decision-maker may decide just what considerations should play a part in his reasoning process.[6]

Similarly, the *weight* to be attributed to a relevant consideration is conventionally a matter for the authority, subject only to unreasonableness:

it is entirely for the decision maker to attribute to the relevant considerations such weight as he thinks fit, and the courts will not interfere unless he has acted unreasonably in the *Wednesbury* sense.[7]

7. It can certainly be a conventional reviewable error for the public authority to fail to take account of, and balance against the intended aim, any rights and interests affected. Examples include *R* v. *Secretary of State for the Home Department, ex p Chahal* [1995] 1 WLR 526 (where the Court of Appeal accepted (at 533A-534F) that, by reference to the principle of proportionality, the Secretary of State owed in a deportation context an important duty to balance the competing interests of national security and the rights and interests of the deportee); also *International Trader's Ferry* [1998] 3 WLR 1260, 1272H (where Lord Slynn emphasised, as a matter of domestic *Wednesbury* Review, that the Chief Constable had carried out a carefully considered balancing exercise). And it is noteworthy that in *R* v. *O'Kane and Clarke, ex p Northern Bank Ltd* [1996] STC 1249 (at 1269e-f), when granting judicial review of a notice for the production of bank documents, Ferris J chastised the tax inspectors, who "appear to have had no regard to the burden thereby imposed on the recipients or to the proportionality of that burden and the benefit which is sought to be obtained".

8. It is with review of *substantive conclusions* that *Wednesbury* is normally associated. The doctrine identifies abuses of power. But it is driven by the concept of a wide *margin*. Some domestic judges have begun to speak of this as a "margin of appreciation",[8] though even

---

[6] *R* v. *Somerset County Council, ex p Fewings* [1995] 1 WLR 1037 per Simon Brown LJ at 1050A.

[7] *Tesco Stores Ltd* v. *Secretary of State for the Environment* [1995] 1 WLR 759 per Lord Keith at 764H.

[8] See e.g. *R* v. *Commissioner of Police of the Metropolis, ex p P* (1996) 8 *Admin LR* 6 per Simon Brown LJ at 14G; *R* v. *Chief Constable of Sussex, ex p International Trader's Ferry Ltd* [1998] 3 WLR 1260 per Lord Slynn at 1268F. An analysis of the doctrine of the margin of appreciation before the European Court of Human Rights is at <34–38>.

recent case-law uses a range of phrases including "the range of reasonable decisions open to a decision maker", the "field of judgment", the "sphere" and the "area of judgment".[9]

9. Such is the margin that the *Wednesbury* principle is notoriously weak in its *intensity of review*. Lord Greene MR spoke (at 229) of "something so absurd that no sensible person could ever dream that it lay within the powers of the authority" and "a decision . . . so unreasonable that no reasonable authority could ever have come to it". Such formulations, and those from a long line of subsequent cases, have meant that a principal skill of the English advocate is to clothe the merits of a grievance with one of the many and less ambitious-sounding grounds for judicial review. It is only recently that more straightforward language has refreshingly been endorsed by Lord Cooke in *R* v. *Chief Constable of Sussex, ex p International Trader's Ferry Ltd* [1998] 3 WLR 1260 (at 1289B-C), namely "whether the decision in question was one which a reasonable authority could reach". But the fact remains, as Henry LJ said in *R* v. *Lord Chancellor, ex p Maxwell* [1997] 1 WLR 104 (at 109B, E) that: "In making such a challenge, the applicant has a mountain to climb . . . Decisions so unreasonable as to warrant interference jump off the page at you".

10. Turning to where the *onus* lies, the *Wednesbury* test places the burden on the person challenging the measure to demonstrate that it is substantively unreasonable.[10] Moreover, this burden has to be borne in a legal culture in which often: (1) the public authority has not been required to give reasons; (2) the Court has been reluctant to draw adverse inferences;[11] and so (3) advocates have been able to construct arguments as to how (as a matter of *submission* rather than *evidence*) the decision could be reasoned with the result that it is to be seen as *reasonable*.

---

[9] See (respectively): *Boddington* v. *British Transport Police* [1998] 2 WLR 639, 666B; *R* v. *Manchester Crown Court, ex p McDonald* [1999] 1 WLR 841, 851A; *R* v. *Legal Aid Board, ex p Parsons* [1999] 3 All ER 347, 354a; *R* v. *Criminal Cases Review Commission, ex p Pearson* [1999] 3 All ER 498, 523.

[10] See e.g. *R* v. *Birmingham City Council, ex p O* [1983] 1 AC 578 per Lord Brightman at 597C-D.

[11] See especially *R* v. *Secretary of State for Trade and Industry, ex p Lonrho Plc* [1989] 1 WLR 525 at 539H-540B.

11. Without doubt, the orthodox *Wednesbury* doctrine is to be sharply contrasted with proportionality. But it is worth pointing to two reasons why, even were proportionality to be introduced, it would be dangerous not to retain the fall-back of *Wednesbury.* (1) There are contexts where proportionality may be inapt, whether because of the nature of the "measure" (e.g. administrative inaction or delay) or the context (e.g. a case where no "right" is being restricted). An ever-present safety-net entitling the Court to intervene in cases of substantive unreasonableness, but with a built-in respect for the primary decision-maker, is a desirable principle and should continue to be available to the courts. (2) *Wednesbury* has served as an important umbrella under which the seeds of other candidate principles of substantive review (such as substantive unfairness, inconsistency, inequality, error of fact, uncertainty) have been nurtured and so begun to take root. Recognition of a new ground for judicial review is eased by being able to identify and reinterpret cases where the (now independent) vice previously served as a hallmark of irrationality.

12. Weak may be the intensity of review, and heavy the onus on the applicant, but the *Wednesbury* principle has nevertheless provided an important minimum degree of scrutiny. Indeed, it can be seen to have done so in relation to substantive conclusions on each of the four questions which make up the *four-question template.*

Q1. As to *legitimacy,* in several cases the Court has rejected as inappropriate an objective which the public authority was seeking to pursue. Alongside holding authorities to statutory objectives as a matter of legislative mandate, the Court will intervene in a case where an aim is characterised by the Court as to constitute an improper purpose or motive. Examples are *R* v. *London Borough of Ealing, ex p Times Newspapers Ltd* [1987] IRLR 129 (where the council's decision to ban Murdoch newspapers from its libraries so as to show solidarity with print workers was overturned as introduced for an impermissible political purpose); and *Wheeler* v. *Leicester City Council* [1985] AC 1054 (where the Court overturned a ban on the use of council land by a rugby club about to tour South Africa, imposed in pursuit of the council's anti-apartheid policy).

Q2. A recent *suitability* example may be *R* v. *Islington London Borough Council, ex p Reilly* (1999) 31 HLR 651, where Richards J held a local authority's housing policy to be unreasonable because, on analysis, it was (at 666) simply "incapable of producing a fair assessment of applicants' respective housing needs".

Q3. A good *necessity* example is *Northern Bank* [1996] STC 1249 (at 1269f-g):

> A justification for the inspector setting out his maximum require-ment of a single notice was said to be that this is the only means of putting in place effective criminal sanctions against falsification or destruction of documents under s.20BB. I do not accept this, partic-ularly where the recipient of the notice is a party such as a bank which is likely to be particularly careful about retention of records. But if there were thought to be a need for protection I see no reason why this could not be achieved by the method suggested by the bank in this case. . . ..

Q4. As to *means/ends fit*, an overall concept of proportionality is clearly evident in a line of cases where judicial review has been granted in relation to excessive sanctions.[12] "Clearly", as Lord Lowry said in *Brind* (at 762D), *Wednesbury* unreasonableness applies to a decision "which suffers from a total lack of proportionality".

13. The fact remains that substantive review has been dominated by judicial restraint. But why? The need for circumspection is powerfully illustrated by *Roberts* v. *Hopwood* [1925] AC 578, where the House of Lords (upholding the district auditor) were willing to characterise as unreasonable a local borough council's minimum wage policy designed to promote sex equality. This was the same duty to "act reasonably" (see e.g. 613) which Lord Greene was later to describe in *Wednesbury*. In a memorable passage casting a lengthening shadow, and which has caused modern judges to cringe,[13] Lord Atkinson said (at 594) that the council had wrongly:

> allowed themselves to be guided . . . by some eccentric principles of socialistic philanthropy, or by a feminist ambition to secure the equality of the sexes in the matter of wages in the world of labour.

---

[12] See e.g. *R* v.*Barnsley Metropolitan Borough Council, ex p Hook* [1976] 1 WLR 1052; *R* v. *St Albans Crown Court, ex p Cinnamond* [1981] QB 480, 485D.
[13] See e.g. *Pickwell* v. *Camden London Borough Council* [1983] QB 962, 986H.

This is a corrosive illustration of the potential dangers of allowing the (unelected) judiciary to scrutinise the justification for measures adopted by (often elected) public authorities.

14. It is inescapable that the very fact of a substantive unreasonableness doctrine, *wherever* the threshold is to be found, will involve the Court in a degree of *value-judgment*. The realism of Thomas J in the New Zealand Court of Appeal in *Waitakere City Council* v. *Lovelock* [1997] 2 NZLR 385 is admirable (at 400, 401):

> The strongest quality demanded by so many Judges and lawyers of *Wednesbury* unreasonableness is that it provide an objective measure for assessing the unreasonableness of an authority's decision. But it never was capable of providing an objective test. The subjective element inherent in a substantive determination whether a decision is unreasonable or not is too patent to be overwhelmed by repetition or semantics . . . [A] Court is ultimately required to make a value judgment in determining whether the decision in issue is so unreasonable that no reasonable body could have made it.

15. It has doubtless been because of the desire to draw a self-disciplined line as to the extent to which judges should be making value-judgments, that traditional *Wednesbury* Review has stopped short of a proportionality doctrine. Hence the *Brind* case ([1991] 1 AC 696), where the House of Lords upheld a government ban which bizarrely fought terrorism by requiring the voices of certain TV and radio interviewees to be overdubbed by actors. It is striking, and after so short a time-span, how moderate now appears Junior Counsel (David Pannick)'s question (see 762G and 766F): "Could the minister reasonably conclude that his direction was necessary?". But their Lordships were reluctant to ask even this. Fearing that a higher intensity of review would overstep the proper limits of the judicial role, they declined to recognise proportionality as a principle warranting the grant of judicial review, with Lord Lowry (at 764G-766B) reasserting unreasonableness in language so strikingly deferential that it has since dominated many a public authority's skeleton argument ever since.

16. Lord Lowry's concluding comments (at 766G-767G), to which we will return <64>, are so ringing and revealing that we set them out at length:

In my opinion proportionality and the other phrases are simply intended to move the focus of discussion away from the hitherto accepted criteria for deciding whether the decision-maker has abused his power and into an area in which the court will feel more at liberty to interfere. The first observation I would make is that there is no authority for saying that proportionality in the sense in which the appellants have used it is part of the English common law and a great deal of authority the other way. This, so far as I am concerned, is not a cause for regret for several reasons: 1. The decision-makers, very often elected, are those to whom Parliament has entrusted the discretion and to interfere with that discretion beyond the limits hitherto defined would itself be an abuse of the judges' supervisory jurisdiction. 2. The judges are not, generally speaking, equipped by training or experience, or furnished with the requisite knowledge and advice, to decide the answer to an administrative problem where the scales are evenly balanced, but they have a much better chance of reaching the right answer where the question is put in a *Wednesbury* form. The same applies if the judges' decision is appealed. 3. Stability and relative certainty would be jeopardised if the new doctrine held sway, because there is nearly always something to be said against any administrative decision and parties who felt aggrieved would be even more likely than at present to try their luck with a judicial review application both at first instance and on appeal. 4. The increase in applications for judicial review of administrative action (inevitable if the threshold of unreasonableness is lowered) will lead to the expenditure of time and money by litigants, not to speak of the prolongation of uncertainty for all concerned with the decisions in question, and the taking up of court time which could otherwise be devoted to other matters. The losers in this respect will be members of the public, for whom the courts provide a service. . . . It finally occurs to me that there can be very little room for judges to operate an independent judicial review proportionality doctrine in the space which is left between the conventional judicial review doctrine and the admittedly forbidden appellate approach. To introduce an intermediate area of deliberation for the court seems scarcely a practical idea, quite apart from the other disadvantages by which, in my opinion, such a course would be attended.

LUXEMBOURG REVIEW

17. The Treaties of the European Union and their associated secondary legislation are primarily concerned (alongside conferring key areas of limited legislative competence upon the EC institutions) with the enforcement in Member States of certain fundamental freedoms, essentially of an economic nature (e.g. free movement of goods, workers, services and capital). As Community law has matured, these economic freedoms have been shaped into directly enforceable individual *rights*. They have been accompanied by the development of other rights from Treaty provisions (e.g. those preventing sex and nationality discrimination).

18. The Treaties and associated legislation constitute instruments of supreme legislative status <P2>. They frequently indicate in broad terms on what basis individual rights conferred by the Treaty or its secondary legislation can be limited. For instance, Article 30 (ex Article 36) EC and Article 39(3) (ex Article 48(3)) EC provide that such rights can be subjected to limitations on grounds of public policy, public security or public health. These limited exceptions have been supplemented by the European Court of Justice ("the Luxembourg Court")'s case-law with a series of court-fashioned "objective justifications" that apply in the case of indirectly discriminatory measures or other measures with market partitioning effect.

19. Since the landmark 1970 case of *Solange* [1970] ECR 1125 the Luxembourg Court (under pressure from the German courts) has guaranteed the effective protection of fundamental human rights, generally taken to be the rights protected by the European Convention on Human Rights. Observance of fundamental rights by EC institutions and Member States acting within areas of law with an EC dimension has been secured by judicial inventiveness as a fundamental condition of legality. In *Solange*, proportionality simultaneously emerged (in a very German formulation) as a key "general principle of law" designed to ensure the protection of such basic human rights from unjustifiable interference. Since then the range of the proportionality principle has been extended and it has been used rigorously and routinely by the Luxembourg Court.

20. Why might the EC jurisprudence be relevant under the Human Rights Act? Because: (1) this is a rich source providing an excellent illustration of the *four-question-template* in action; (2) the case law provides helpful indications as to how to approach the variable intensity of review likely to be applied in cases involving tensions between various state and private interests; (3) the EC law has a special fundamental human rights component; (4) there will doubtless be a desire to avoid a mismatch in the approach in purely domestic cases and those involving an EC component; and (5) domestic judges have had considerable experience dealing with the principle of proportionality in an EC context (and any successes and failures are likely to be transposable to other forms of proportionality test).

21. The proportionality principle is in play in two different modes of proceedings which come before the Luxembourg Court. The first mode we will call *Direct Review*.

(1) Here, the Luxembourg Court is reviewing (under Article 230[14] (ex 173) EC proceedings) the measure of an EC institution, usually the Council or Commission. The cases illustrate the tension between the Community interest (e.g. in properly organised, stable, agricultural markets) and the individual interest (e.g. trading or property rights).

(2) The principle of proportionality is of sufficient importance to have been enshrined in Article 5 (ex 3b) of the EC Treaty, which provides that: "Any action by the Community shall not go beyond what is necessary to achieve the objectives of the Treaty."

(3) The operation of this principle reflects the *four-question template*. See e.g. *R* v. *Ministry of Agriculture Fisheries and Food, ex p FEDESA* [1990] ECR I -4023 (at 4063 para 13):

By virtue of [the proportionality] principle, the lawfulness of the prohibition of an economic activity is subject to the condition that [Q2] the prohibitory measures are appropriate and [Q3] necessary in order to achieve [Q1] the objectives legitimately pursued by the legislation in question; where there is a choice between several appropriate

---

[14] Review on grounds of "lack of competence, infringement of an essential procedural requirement, infringement of the Treaty or of any rule of law relating to its application, or misuse of powers".

measures recourse must be had to the least onerous, and [Q4] the disadvantages caused must not be disproportionate to the aims pursued.

(4) As to review of the EC institution's *reasoning process* it is plain that the Luxembourg Court requires some form of coherent reasoning on the application of the proportionality principle in the body of the decision itself. As AG Jacobs stated in the case of *Werner Faust* [1991] ECR I-4905 (at para 45):

> the Commission has made no serious attempt to justify the size of the additional amount. Given that the measures had to be "strictly necessary", one would expect some justification for the size of the amount to be stated in the contested regulations. However, the preambles to the regulations contain no indication whatever of the basis on which the additional amount was calculated or of the reasons why such an amount was necessary. Nor has any such justification been advanced in the present proceedings. Instead the Commission has sought to rely essentially on the argument that it was entitled to impose such a high levy because it could have taken the more severe step of prohibiting imports altogether.

(5) As to review of the EC institution's *substantive conclusions*, the Luxembourg Court will scrutinise the substantive position as to all four questions: (Q1) legitimacy (see e.g. *Wuensche Handelsgesellschaft* v. *Federal Republic of Germany* [1984] ECR 1995, para 24); (Q2) suitability (see *Crispoltoni* v. *Fattoria autonoma Tabacchi di Citta id Castello* [1991] ECR I-3695, paras 18 to 20); (Q3) necessity (see *National Dried Fruit Trade Association* [1988] ECR 757, para 32); and (Q4) overall means-ends fit (see e.g. *Werner Faust* [1991] ECR I-4905).

(6) As to the latitude or margin (and so *intensity of review*), although tending to prefer analysing the problem in terms of "manifest error" rather than using phrases like the "margin of appreciation" or "discretionary area of judgment", the Luxembourg Court has nevertheless acknowledged in terms that there is room for choice (or "discretion") as to both objectives and appropriateness of their pursuit. See e.g. *FEDESA* (at para 14):

> However, with regard to judicial review of compliance with those conditions it must be stated that in matters concerning the common

agricultural policy the Community legislature has a discretionary power which corresponds to the political responsibilities given to it by Articles 40 and 43 of the Treaty. Consequently, the legality of a measure adopted in that sphere can be affected only if the measure is manifestly inappropriate having regard to the objective which the competent institution is seeking to pursue.

In a similar vein, in the *Working Time Directive* case, [1996] ECR I-5755 the Court said at page 5811 that:

As to judicial review . . . the Council must be allowed a wide discretion in an area which, as here, involves the legislature in making social policy choices and requires it to carry out complex assessments. Judicial review of the exercise of that discretion must be limited to examining whether it has been vitiated by manifest error or misuse of its powers, or whether the institution concerned has manifestly exceeded the limits of its discretion.

(7) The width of the "discretion" will depend on the particular context with which the Court is concerned. One commentator has persuasively identified the following factors as affecting in particular the intensity of review of EC measures: (i) the extent of any power of appraisal; (ii) the restrictive effect of the measure and the type of interest affected; (iii) the objective of the measure and the type of interest it seeks to protect; (iv) the availability of less restrictive means asserted in fact or in policy; (v) the treatment of comparable products or producers; (vi) the extent of actual hardship suffered; (vii) the duration of the measures; (viii) the urgency of the situation; (ix) the technicality of the subject matter/degree of expertise required.[15]

(8) As to *onus*, the case-law clearly imposes the burden of justification once a prima facie case is shown (either by showing some impact upon a protected EC or fundamental right). Moreover the above reasoning of AG Jacobs in *Werner Faust* [1991] ECR I-4905 together with the precise terms of Article 253 (ex Article 190) EC indicates that what is required is *evidence* and not *submission*, since

---

[15] Takis Tridimas, "Searching for the Appropriate Standard of Scrutiny", in Ellis (ed.) *The Principle of Proportionality in the Law of Europe* (Hart Publishing, 1999) pp.76-7.

the reasons are to be given by EC institutions contemporaneously with the measure in question.

22. The second mode of relevant proceedings which come before the Luxembourg Court and where proportionality is in play we will call *Referred Review.*

(1) Here, the Luxembourg Court is delineating (primarily on an Article 234 (ex 177) EC reference for preliminary ruling) the principles which the national court should apply in reviewing (in domestic judicial review or related proceedings) a measure of a domestic public authority. The Luxembourg Court is acting as an advisory Court. It is the national court, to whom the case is referred back, which is required to scrutinise the legality of measures adopted by national authorities, applying the legal principles to the facts. Moreover, it is the national court which remains in control of whether to grant a remedy.

(2) The content and application of the proportionality principle is formulated in exactly the same way as under Direct Review, though often Q4 (means-ends fit) is subsumed in Q3 (necessity). A typical formulation is that found in *Kraus* [1993] ECR I-1663 (para 32) where what was said to be required of a measure was that it:

> pursued a [Q1] legitimate objective compatible with the Treaty and was justified by pressing reasons of public interest . . . It would however also be necessary in such a case for application of the national rules in question to be [Q2] appropriate for ensuring attainment of the objective they pursue and [Q3] not to go beyond what is necessary for that purpose.

(3) The Luxembourg Court tends to apply a high *intensity of review,* being particularly anxious to investigate less restrictive ways in which legitimate social objectives can be achieved: see e.g. *Conegate* v. *Customs and Excise Commissioners* [1986] ECR 1007; and *De Peijper* [1976] ECR 613. This is seemingly because: (a) the cases referred to typically centre on alleged infringements of individual rights expressed to be fundamental to the Treaty; (b) strong notions of necessity and/or justification are called for in such contexts, by reference to relatively narrow grounds whether identified legislatively (e.g. public health, public policy, national security) or judicially (e.g.

consumer protection); and (c) the margin is often hemmed in by detailed secondary legislation.

(4) However, a noticeable trend is that where fundamental treaty freedoms are interfered with for general social policy reasons, the Luxembourg Court is willing to grant an increasingly wide discretion to the domestic legislators. Thus, in *Schindler* [1994] ECR I-1039 para 63 the Luxembourg Court, when reviewing United Kingdom gaming/lottery regulations, stated that the social policy context of the disputed measure did "justify national authorities having a sufficient degree of latitude to determine what is required to protect the players".

(5) As to the *onus* on the public authority, and the need for *evidence* rather than *submission*, the general position is that the justification is required not only to be identified, but also communicated, at the time of the measure. As the Luxembourg Court stated in *Heylens* [1987] ECR 4097, para 17:

> Effective judicial review, which must be able to cover the legality of the reasons for the contested decision, presupposes in general that the court to which the matter is referred may require the competent authority to notify its reasons. But where, as in this case, it is more particularly a question of securing the effective protection of a fundamental right conferred by the treaty on community workers, the latter must also be able to defend that right under the best possible conditions and have the possibility of deciding, with a full knowledge of the relevant facts, whether there is any point in their applying to the courts. Consequently, in such circumstances the competent national authority is under a duty to inform them of the reasons on which its refusal is based, either in the decision itself or in a subsequent communication made at their request.

23. In any case of *Referred Review*, the Luxembourg Court's role is to advise the national court as to the principles to be applied. Those delineated principles will also fall to be applied by domestic courts in future cases where they are considered to be sufficiently clear not to warrant any further advice. How have domestic judges responded to the proportionality principle?

(1) Domestic courts readily identify and pose the *four-question template*. A recent example is *International Trader's Ferry (ITF)*

[1998] 3 WLR 1260, where *legitimacy* (Q1) was not in dispute (see 1275D), and where Lord Slynn concluded (at 1277D):

> I am satisfied, as was the Court of Appeal, that the Chief Constable has shown here that what he did in providing police assistance was proportionate to what was required. To protect the lorries, in the way he did, was a [Q2] suitable and [Q3] necessary way of dealing with potentially violent demonstrators. To limit the occasions when sufficient police could be made available was, in the light of the resources available to him to deal with immediate and foreseeable events at the port, and at the same time to carry out all his other police duties, necessary and in no way [Q4] disproportionate to the restrictions which were involved.

(2) An example of proportionality principles informing review of the *reasoning process* is the *Diane Blood* case [1999] Fam 151, where judicial review was ultimately granted because the respondent authority had failed to recognise that (184G):

> In coming to its decision the authority was required to take into account that to refuse permission to export [sperm] would impede the treatment of Mrs Blood in Belgium and to ask whether in the circumstances this was justified.

(3) Cases such as *Else* [1993] QB 534 indicate the importance (for the public authority) of being seen (in *evidence*) to consider and eliminate, on reasoned grounds, alternative courses of action. This case, together with the quotation from *First City Trading* (below), shows that the case for proportionate action should be made out by *evidence* as opposed to submission.

(4) It is uncontroversial that the *onus* lies on the public authority to justify the measure: see *ITF* (Lord Slynn) at 1274D.

(5) As to review of substantive conclusions, a question which has concerned domestic judges is to what extent in truth they are simply to conduct *Wednesbury* Review. Some encouragement for such a stance is evident in *ITF* (Lord Slynn) at 1277C:

> In [*Brind*] the House treated *Wednesbury* reasonableness and proportionality as being different. So in some ways they are though the distinction between the two tests in practice is in any event much less

than is sometimes suggested. The cautious way in which the European Court usually applies this test, recognising the importance of respecting the national authority's margin of appreciation, may mean that whichever test is adopted, and even allowing for a difference in onus, the result is the same.

Lord Cooke said (at 1288G-H):

> on the particular facts of this case the European concepts of proportionality and margin of appreciation produce the same result as what are commonly called *Wednesbury* principles. Indeed in many cases that is likely to be so.

(6) No doubt the *result* will often be the same under proportionality or *Wednesbury* Review, but the former is undoubtedly a more structured principle and often capable of higher intensity review. It is doubtful whether Kennedy LJ's statement in *ITF* in the Court of Appeal ([1997] 3 WLR 132, 148E) truly reflects the general law, namely that:

> It is European law as well as domestic law that no court will interfere with his decision unless it can be shown that he was plainly wrong.[16]

The leading case[17] is the decision of Laws J in *R* v. *MAFF, ex p First City Trading* [1997] 1 CMLR 250, at 278 paras 68 to 69 (emphasis added):

> It is not the court's task to decide what it would have done had it been the decision-maker, who (certainly in the case of elected Government) enjoys a political authority, and carries a political responsibility, with which the court is not endowed. The court's task is to decide whether the measure in fact adopted falls within the range of options legally open to the decision-maker. In the nature of things it is highly unlikely that only one of the choices available to him will

---

[16] Applied, most recently, in *R* v. *MAFF, ex p Geiden* 30 September 1999 unreported (Owen J).

[17] See too *R* v. *Secretary of State for the Home Department, ex p Arthur H Cox Ltd* [1999] EuLR 677 (EC proportionality not to be equated with *Wednesbury*, but wide "margin of appreciation" in present context); *R* v. *MAFF, ex p Astonquest* [1999] *EuLR* 141, 147G-148C; cf. *SIAC Constructions Ltd* v. *Mayo County Council* [1999] *EuLR* 535; and cf. *R* v. *MAFF, ex p Bell Line* [1984] 2 CMLR 502.

pass the test of objective justification: and the court has no business to give effect to any preference for one possible measure over another when both lie within the proper legal limits. In this sense it may be said that the decision-maker indeed enjoys a margin of appreciation. The difference between *Wednesbury* and European review is that in the former case the legal limits lie further back. I think that there are two factors. First, the limits of domestic review are not, as the law presently stands, constrained by the doctrine of proportionality. Secondly, at least as regards a requirement such as that of objective justification in an equal treatment case, the European rule requires the decision-maker *to provide a fully reasoned case*. It is not enough merely to set out the problem, and assert that within his discretion the Minister chose this or that solution, constrained only by the requirement that his decision must have been one which a reasonable Minister might make. Rather the court will test the solution arrived at, and pass it only if substantial factual considerations are put forward in its justification: considerations which are relevant, reasonable and proportionate to the aim in view. But as I understand the jurisprudence the court is not concerned to agree or disagree with the decision: that would be to travel beyond the boundaries of proper judicial authority, and usurp the primary decision-maker's function. *Thus Wednesbury and European review are different models - one looser, one tighter of the same juridical concept, which is the imposition of compulsory standards on decision-makers so as to secure the repudiation of arbitrary power."*

(7) This approach has been further elaborated on by the Court of Appeal in *R v. Secretary of State for Health, ex p Eastside Cheese Company (a firm)* [1999] EuLR 968, where (in the context of a dispute arising in a free movement of goods context, also with an arguable right to property dimension) the Court of Appeal stated that:

[I]t is clear that the national legislature has a considerable margin of appreciation, especially in legislating on matters which raise complex economic issues connected with the Community's fundamental policies. . . The margin of appreciation for a decision-maker (which includes, in this context, a national legislature) may be broad or narrow. The margin is broadest when the national court is concerned with primary legislation enacted by its own legislature in an area where a general policy of the Community must be given effect in the particular economic and social circumstances of the member state in question. The margin narrows gradually rather than abruptly with changes in the character of the decision-maker and the scope of what has to be decided (not, as the Secretary of State submits, only with the latter) . . . This appeal must be approached on the basis that the Secretary of State, in making the emergency control orders on 20 and 21 May 1998, was not entitled to the broad margin of appreciation which might be accorded to primary legislation enacted by a national legislature. He is however entitled to the narrower margin of appreciation appropriate to a responsible decision-maker who is required, under the urgent pressure of events, to take decisions which call for the evaluation of scientific evidence and advice as to public health risks, and which have serious implications both for the general public and for the manufacturers, processors and retailers of the suspect cheese.

(8) Because of the prime and direct status of European legislation on the domestic legal order, and the relationship between the Luxembourg Court and national courts, it is the role of the domestic judge to *apply* the Luxembourg principles and decide whether the measure has been shown to be justified. It has taken time for domestic judges to become comfortable with an enhanced Euro-driven role of scrutinising the activities of public authorities. However, the direct responsibility for applying the rigorous standards of Luxembourg proportionality is reflected in the case-law. *Eastside Cheese* again:

> In principle the decision on proportionality has to be taken by the national court which is seized of an issue on Article 36, subject of course to any possible reference to the Court of Justice . . . The judge's task was (so far as Article 36 was concerned) to see whether the exercise of the Secretary of State's power under section 13 of the 1990 Act had been objectively justified and had been shown not to be disproportionate. . . The test is more demanding than that of "manifest error" and is also more demanding than that of *Wednesbury* unreasonableness.

(9) What the cases recognise is that: (a) EC proportionality is more exacting, both in terms of standards and intensity than *Wednesbury* Review; but (b) the same result may often be produced under both tests, particularly when (as is frequently the case) the subject matter

of the dispute is the proportionality of economic regulation in an area where the Member State has a wide, residual, legislative discretion. We leave the last words on the point to the Harry Street Lecture by Advocate General Jacobs:[18]

> Although it is sometimes said that the [*Wednesbury*] test and the Community law principle are similar in their operation, the better view seems to be that Community law imposes a more exacting standard, and one that is more fully articulated. It provides for an explicit weighting of interests, and is therefore perhaps better suited to the review of legislative measures for which *Wednesbury* was not of course intended. At the same time proportionality provides a flexible test: it allows for account to be taken of fundamental rights of the individual, and of fundamental public interests. . . It seems to me a rational and well-structured test, which provides useful guidance to courts, and which may even reflect the way in which administrative measures are (or ought to be) arrived at.

24. We mention separately EC discrimination law (sex and nationality). Here, under the governing principle of *objective justification*, proportionality serves as the means by which purported justifications for indirectly discriminatory behaviour is reviewed. *Legitimacy* (Q1) is evident in cases like *Enderby* v. *Frenchay Health Authority* [1994] 1 All ER 495 (where the court recognised demonstrable changes in market forces but not imperatives of collective negotiations as potential justifications for indirectly discriminatory differences in pay). The law is encapsulated by the classic test of proportionality in a sex discrimination case, namely *Bilka Kaufhaus* [1986] ECR 1607:

> It is for the national court, which has sole jurisdiction to make findings of fact, to determine whether and to what extent the grounds put forward by an employer to explain the adoption of a pay practice which applies independently of a worker's sex but in fact affects more women than men may be regarded as objectively justified economic grounds. If the national court finds that the measures chosen by Bilka correspond to a [Q1] real need on the part of the undertaking [Q2] are appropriate with a view to achieving the objectives pursued and are [Q3] necessary to that end, the fact that the measures affect a far

---

[18] F.G.Jacobs, "Public Law – The Impact of Europe" [1999] PL 232, 239.

greater number of women than men is not sufficient to show that they constitute an infringement of Article 119.

It will be noted that this formulation contains no express reference to the overall means-ends fit (Q4), but such a balancing exercise (as in the EC free movement of good cases) is evident in the application by the Luxembourg Court of a rigorous necessity test (Q3), a good example of a concept of necessity deployed in an overall sense <P4>. The *Bilka Kaufhaus* test can apply to both legislative sex discrimination (i.e. sponsored by state legislation) or purely private discrimination.[19] The *onus* will be on the state or employer, and not on the person discriminated against. As explained by Evelyn Ellis,[20] there was formerly a unified and strictly applied test (i.e. a high *intensity of review*). In "horizontal" areas the test remains strict. However, subsequent cases such as *Nolte* [1995] ECR I-4265 and *Lewark* [1996] ECR I-243 demonstrate the increasingly "broad margin of discretion" granted to Member States implementing indirectly discriminatory legislative measures in fields such as social security, employment relations policy. As such, a measure of deference to political bodies (no doubt, partially under the guise of "subsidiary" in an unharmonised field) has been reintroduced.

25. Separate mention is also due of cases before the Luxembourg Court which involve fundamental human rights.

(1) What is apparent here is an intense (albeit variable) review, whether in a Direct Review (where the rights tend to be confined to property issues and due process) or Referred Review context (where a wider range of human rights issues arise). In general the rights receive serious, intensive investigation and protection using the proportionality principle. This intensity is generally evident in the form of focus on each of the four limbs of the EC proportionality test, an abandonment of the language of manifest error, and a careful comparative approach analysing interferences in terms of their effects on the "substance of the right" in a way immediately familiar to ECHR lawyers: see e.g. *Hauer* [1979] ECR 3727; *Nold* [1974] ECR 491, para 14.

[19] See, most recently, *Barry* v. *Midland Bank Plc* [1999] 3 All ER 974 (HL), 984e-j.
[20] E. Ellis, "The Concept of Proportionality in EC Sex Discrimination Law" in *The Principle of Proportionality in the Law of Europe* (Hart Publishing, 1998).

(2) Although it has been suggested that the EC's avowed protection of fundamental rights is illusory or intended primarily to gain the acceptance of its supremacy doctrine, the truth is more nuanced and certainly complicated by the fact that: (a) very many EC fundamental rights cases involve an assertion of the relatively weak right to property or associated right to trade in precisely the sort of regulatory circumstances (usually the Common Agricultural Policy) which Article 1 Protocol 1 of the Human Rights Convention contemplates interference being justified; (b) the EC freedoms may themselves to a degree encapsulate fundamental rights (e.g. the right of association/ free movement/equal pay and non-discrimination) in tension with competing rights; and (c) an overly assertive human rights role risks conflict with the Strasbourg Court.

(3) Nevertheless, the Luxembourg Court's anxious concern for human rights has been especially evident in: (a) cases involving civil penalties or forfeiture of deposits imposed by Member States or Community organs (both giving rise to property Convention right issues), where a stricter approach has been discerned: e.g. *E.D. & F. Man Sugar* [1985] ECR 2889 and the cases that have followed it; and (b) cases on the imposition of criminal penalties by Member States in order to enforce EC law or in areas of activity touched by EC law: see e.g. *Pastoors* [1997] ECR I-285. The Luxembourg Court has also struck down or "sympathetically interpreted" measures for infringement of the principle of freedom of expression (see e.g. *Oyowe and Traore* [1989] ECR 4285) or of an applicant's right to privacy (*X* v. *Commission* [1994] ECR I-4737, paras 18 to 21 concerning the legitimacy of the Commission's AIDS testing practices), as well as legion cases (e.g. *Ahlstroem* v. *Commission* [1993] 4 CMLR 407) for failure to respect Article 6 due process rights.

STRASBOURG REVIEW

26. Under the law of the European Convention on Human Rights, the primary instrument of supreme legislative status <P2> is the Convention itself. The Convention contains a *code* of protected rights, including those of life (Article 2), liberty (Article 5), privacy (Article 8), religion (Article 9), speech (Article 10), assembly (Article 11) and property (Article 1 of Protocol 1).

27. The Convention specifies, as a matter of *legislative mandate* <P2> on what bases[21] the protected rights may be interfered with. The bases, in addition to general emergency powers (Article 15), are:

Article 2 – deprivation of life, only by a court-imposed death penalty or the use of force which is:

> no more than absolutely necessary (a) in defence of any person from unlawful violence; (b) in order to effect a lawful arrest or to prevent the escape of a person lawfully detained; (c) in action lawfully taken for the purpose of quelling a riot or insurrection;

Article 5 – deprivation of liberty, only by lawful arrest and detention;

Article 8 – interference with private and family life, only as is:

> necessary in a democratic society in the interests of national security, public safety or the economic well-being of the country, for the prevention of disorder or crime, for the protection of health or morals, or for the protection of the rights and freedoms of others;

Article 9 – limitations of freedom of religion and belief, only as are:

> necessary in a democratic society in the interests of public safety, for the protection of public order, health or morals, or for the protection of the rights and freedoms of others;

Article 10 – restrictions (or formalities, conditions or penalties) on freedom of speech, only as are:

> necessary in a democratic society, in the interests of national security, territorial integrity or public safety, for the prevention of disorder or crime, for the protection of health or morals, for the protection of the reputation or rights of others, for preventing the disclosure of information received in confidence, or for maintaining the authority and impartiality of the judiciary;

Article 11 – restrictions of freedom of peaceful assembly and association, only as are:

---

[21] A precondition is that the mode of restriction be "provided by law" (Article 2); "prescribed by law" (Articles 5, 9-11); "in accordance with the law" (Article 8) or "provided for by law" (Article 1 Protocol 1).

necessary in a democratic society in the interests of national security or public safety, for the prevention of disorder or crime, for the protection of health or morals or for the protection of the rights and freedoms of others;

Article 1 Protocol 1 – deprivation of possessions or control of property, only "in the public interest" or "in accordance with the general interest or to secure the payment of taxes or other contributions or penalties".

28. These express provisions show that the question of *legitimacy* (Q1) is primarily controlled by the (often rather detailed) wording of the Convention itself. This is reinforced by Article 18 which provides that permitted restrictions may only be applied for the prescribed purposes. The provisions also give clues, through the existence and nature of the specified objectives, as to the kind of latitude (or *margin*) that public authorities may have in deciding whether to introduce measures which restrict such rights. What the Convention does *not* do, is to spell out (any more than do the EC Treaties) a doctrine of proportionality. That has been left to the Strasbourg Court (as to the Luxembourg Court under the EC Treaties <19>), the entry point largely being the Convention phrase "necessary in a democratic society".

29. The essential role of the Strasbourg Court is one of *Long-Stop Review*. The Court was established to ensure observance by the state parties (Article 19) and its jurisdiction extends to "all matters concerning the interpretation and application of the Convention" (Article 32(1)). Unlike the Luxembourg Court, it does not conduct a Direct Review <21> (European Court reviewing the legality of measures of European institutions), nor a Referred Review <22> (European Court advising national court of principles applicable in pending proceedings).[22] Instead the Court is either receiving a complaint by one state against another (Article 33) or, much more usually, an individual application from the victim of an alleged violation (Article 34). It is the latter scenario which has given rise to the Strasbourg case-law. The Court will be asking whether there has been a violation of the Convention (see Article 41). *But the Strasbourg Court does not expect to be the primary judicial decision-maker, even as to that question.* For the Convention is designed and intended to be operated on the level of

---

[22] The Court has jurisdiction to give advisory opinions at the request of the Committee of Ministers, on questions of interpretation of the Convention (Article 47).

domestic national law. The state parties have agreed to secure to everyone in their jurisdiction the Convention rights (Article 1); the victim is required to exhaust domestic remedies before making an application to the Strasbourg Court (Article 35(1)); and, most importantly of all, a person whose Convention rights have been violated "shall have an effective remedy before a national authority" (Article 13). In other words, the *application* of the Convention and the principles of justification which it produces is expected to be a matter for the domestic court. The Strasbourg Court can be expected to delineate those principles and to provide a "long-stop" remedy where national law has been found to be inadequate (see Article 41). In doing so, the Strasbourg Court will ask whether there has been a violation, but this is a secondary (and fall-back) review: *the primary judicial review of the national authority should be by the national court.*

30. Proportionality principles are a key feature of the Strasbourg case-law. They enter the frame by virtue of the concept of *necessity* found in the Convention ("no more than absolutely necessary"; "necessary in a democratic society") <27>. From the starting-point of necessity as a threshold question it can operate in an overall sense <P4>. As the Strasbourg Court held in *Sunday Times* v. *United Kingdom* (1979) 2 EHRR 245 (at para 59) the phrase "necessary in a democratic society" implies a "pressing social need", so that the question for the Court becomes (para 62):

> whether the interference complained of corresponded to a pressing social need, whether it was proportionate to the legitimate aim pursued, and whether the reasons given by the national authorities to justify it are relevant and sufficient.

In *Olsson* v. *Sweden* (1988) 11 EHRR 259 the Strasbourg Court said:

> According to the Court's established case-law, the notion of necessity implies that an interference corresponds to a pressing social need and, in particular, that it is proportionate to the legitimate aim pursued.

The test "no more than absolutely necessary" (Article 2 <27>) has been held by the Strasbourg Court to involve a "stricter and more compelling test of necessity" and, in turn, a test of "strict proportionality": see *McCann* v. *United Kingdom* (1995) 21 EHRR 97 (paras 149-50).

31. The *four-question template* <P1> is undoubtedly in play in Strasbourg Review.

Q1 (*legitimacy*) is the "legitimate aim" referred to in *Sunday Times* and *Olsson* <30>. It is largely dealt with by the Convention's express code of objectives. Even where these express provisions appear open-textured, the Strasbourg Court will intervene if it detects a wholly illegitimate aim: see e.g. *Shoenberge & Durmaz* v. *Switzerland* (1988) 11 EHRR 202.

Q2 (*suitability*) is evident in the requirement, articulated by the Strasbourg Court in *Sunday Times* and *Olsson* (above), that the interference must "correspond" to a pressing social need. Examples of measures which were incapable of vindicating the objective pursued and so unjustified include *Observer and Guardian* v. *United Kingdom* (1991) 14 EHRR 153 para 68 (where injunctions were unjustified once the book had been published outside the United Kingdom) and *Weber* v. *Switzerland* (1990) 12 EHRR 508 (unjustified fine for disclosing information already in the public domain).

Q3 (*necessity*) obviously fits with "necessary in a democratic society". It is illustrated by *Campbell* v. *United Kingdom* (1992) 15 EHRR 137 (where a blanket rule permitting routine searching of correspondence to legal advisers was too wide – a narrower measure permitting interference only where abusive practices were suspected would adequately fulfil the pressing social need).

Q4 (*means/ends fit*) is implicit in the passages from *Sunday Times* and *Olsson* ("proportionate to the legitimate aim pursued"). It is illustrated by cases like *F* v. *Switzerland* (1988) 10 EHRR 411 (where the paternalistic justifications for banning F from marrying, namely to protect him and others from himself, were held to be fundamentally incapable of justifying this restriction) and *Nasri* v. *France* (1996) 21 EHRR 458 (where deportation, albeit justifiable as necessary in principle in many cases, involved an excessively heavy burden on the particular facts). It is also squarely visible in those cases where the Strasbourg Court asks "is the substance of the right being interfered with": see e.g. *Campbell* v. *United Kingdom* (1992) 15 EHRR 137 paras 41 and 60; *Jacubowski* v. *Germany* (1995) 19 EHRR 64; *Johansen* v. *Norway* (1996) 23 EHRR 33.

32. Strasbourg Review places the *onus* squarely on the public authority, to establish justification, by means of *evidence*. Illustrations are *Kokkinakis* v. *Greece* (1993) 17 EHRR 397 (where no evidence was presented by Greece to show that the Applicant was in fact guilty of the conduct complained of, namely attempting to convert other individuals "by improper means", the interference with his freedom of religion therefore being held to be unjustified); also *Barthold* v. *Germany* (1985) 7 EHRR 383 (where the necessity for the measures was required to be "convincingly established" by the State).

33. The Strasbourg Court has a need for a particular kind of evidence in the cases with which it deals, namely that of the "European consensus" as to whether a problem exists and, if so, what solutions can and should be adopted to solve it. As we will demonstrate below, the proportionality of measures adopted in any one state must be set against the practice of other Member States. Some applicants, and some respondent authorities, will be able to provide this material. Often, third party interventions are the most useful way of addressing this wider perspective: see e.g. *Lingens* v. *Austria* (1981) 4 EHRR 373.

34. When the Strasbourg Court is setting the *intensity of review* (of substantive conclusions) it uses the (now familiar) phrase, "the margin of appreciation". When used in this context, it is a phrase to be approached from a recognition of the Long-Stop Review role of the Strasbourg Court <29>. For the margin is *two-dimensional*: its first plane involves the deference of court to public authority; its second involves the deference of international court to state authorities (public authority and court). The presence of the first dimension (judge-to-administrator deference) is clear from expressions such as this, from *Soering* v. *United Kingdom* (1989) 11 EHRR 439 (para 89):

> inherent in the whole of the Convention is a search for the fair balance between the demands of the general interest of the community and the requirements of the protection of the individual's human rights.

The presence of the second dimension (international deference) is clear from this key passage in *Handyside* v. *United Kingdom* (1976) 1 EHRR 737 (paras 48-50):

> By reason of their direct and continuous contact with the vital forces of their countries, state authorities are in principle in a better position than

the international judge to given an opinion on the . . . "necessity" of a "restriction" or "penalty" . . . it is for the national authorities to make the initial assessment of the reality of the pressing social need implied by the notion of "necessity" in this context. Consequently, Article 10(2) leaves to the contracting states a margin of appreciation. This margin is given both to the domestic legislator ("prescribed by law") and to the bodies, judicial amongst others, that are called upon to interpret and apply the laws in force. Nevertheless, Article 10(2) does not give the contracting states an unlimited power of appreciation. The Court . . . is responsible for ensuring the observance of those states' engagements, is empowered to give the final ruling on whether a "restriction" or "penalty" is reconcilable with the freedom of expression . . . The domestic margin of appreciation thus goes hand in hand with a European supervision. Such supervision concerns both the aim of the measure challenged and its necessity; it covers not only the basic legislation but also the decision applying it, even one given by an independent court.

35. It is extremely difficult to extract from the Strasbourg case-law on the margin of appreciation a picture involving only the first of its two dimensions, namely that of proper deference from court to public authority. Yet this dimension alone will provide relevant guidance to any domestic court reviewing domestic measures for incompatibility with Convention rights. The most helpful exercises which can be undertaken are: (1) to analyse *relative* width of the margin in different cases, by reference to the *factors* which inform that width; and (2) to consider the role which the Strasbourg Court expects of a domestic court for the purposes of compliance with Article 13 (right to an effective remedy before a national tribunal).

36. Turning to the first exercise, an analysis of the *factors* which have led the Strasbourg Court to identify a (*relatively*) wide or narrow discretion in particular cases <P9>, we would draw attention to the following:

(1) *The right infringed.* The Convention sets up a broad hierarchy of rights of varying degrees of absoluteness. The very wording of the right conferred and exceptions to which it is subject will necessarily affect the intensity of review when an interference is demonstrated. Thus, there is the stricter test of proportionality (higher intensity, narrower margin) discernable from the Article 2(2) test ("no more than absolutely necessary") seen in *McCann* v. *United Kingdom*

(1995) 21 EHRR 97. Similarly, the absence of scope to interfere with the holding of religious beliefs (as compared with manifestation of those beliefs) is implicit in Article 9(2). Even within a particular Article, aspects of a right will receive particular emphasis and keen protection. Thus, the role of the press in facilitating the receipt and communication of information is often given particular importance in Article 10 cases (see *Lingens* v. *Austria* (1981) 4 EHRR 373; *Goodwin* v. *United Kingdom* (1996) 22 EHRR 123); and in *Dudgeon* v. *United Kingdom* (1982) 4 EHRR 149 the Court stated that the right to private sexual relations was of such importance as to require "particularly serious reasons" in order to justify any interference (see also *Smith and Grady* v. *United Kingdom* (1999) 29 EHRR 493, para 89). Equally, cases such as *Golder, Campbell* and *Silver* all confirm the importance of the sanctity of correspondence with legal advisers under Articles 6 and 8. At the other end of the scale, the proportionality test applied in cases involving alleged infringements with the (weak) Article 1 Protocol 1 right to property is relatively undemanding and closely parallel to the (low) intensity to that applied by the Luxembourg Court: see e.g. *Lithgow* v. *United Kingdom* (1986) 8 EHRR 329; *Buckley* v. *United Kingdom* (1996) 23 EHRR 101.

(2) *The extent of the interference.* As a general proposition, the more substantial the interference with the right in question, the harder it will be for the state to provide "sufficient and relevant" justification. Criminal penalties will attract greater examination than civil ones. Careful attention must be paid to the effect of the interference: for example, in *Handyside* the contested books were confiscated but could be reprinted with amendments. This is evidently a less drastic interference than that at issue in *Muller* v. *Switzerland* (1991) 13 EHRR 212, para 43 where the forfeiture of the artist's *original* paintings was thought to present special difficulties. See also *Smith and Grady* (1999) 29 EHRR 493, para 90 commenting on "the exceptionally intrusive character" of some of the infringements.

(3) *The objective pursued: competing rights.* Where a Convention right, for instance the right to freedom of expression, comes into conflict with another Convention right, for instance the right to a fair trial, the State's initial views or assessments as to how a balance between the rights should be struck will carry significant weight and receive a degree of deference. However, even in this scenario the State

UNIVERSITY OF WOLVERHAMPTON
Harrison Learning Centre

Customer ID: WPP6292285B

Title: Understanding human rights principles
ID: 76224563T7
Due: 09/12/2016 23:59

Total items: 1
Total fines: £6.00
18/11/2016 10:27
Issued: 6
Overdue: 5

Thank you for using Self Service.
Please keep your receipt.

Overdue books are fined at 40p per day for
1 week loans, 10p per day for long loans.

must take care to avoid absolutist protection to one right over the other: see e.g. *Sunday Times* (1979) 2 EHRR 245 (where the then United Kingdom contempt rules were found to be an excessive restriction); and query whether, after *Observer and Guardian* v. *United Kingdom* (1991) 14 EHRR 153, para 60 (emphasising the need for great care in prior restraint cases, but rejecting the argument in favour of any such restraint), the rule in *Bonnard* v. *Perryman* suffers from such absolutism. The only exception is where a Convention right which is subject to exceptions conflicts with one which is absolute.

(4) *The objective pursued: competing interest.* Clearly the nature of the competing interest, even if not amounting to a Convention right, will affect the nature of the balance and the degree of intensity of review applied. For instance, the prevention of crime is generally treated as an important competing interest. Equally, other economic and social rights with a strong policy content (e.g. right to good housing, right to adequate benefits etc.) should receive a wide measure of latitude. However, the prevention of littering or foul language in public places would occupy a lesser status. Further, the "objectivity" of the competing interest is of clear importance as *Sunday Times* (1979) 2 EHRR 245 clearly illustrates. In that case the Strasbourg Court drew a distinction between the greater objectivity of the notion of "maintaining the authority and impartiality of the judiciary" and the less objective "protection of morals". The precision of the former interest led to a stricter review of the State's activities, the latter led to a wider margin; see also *Muller* v. *Switzerland* (1991) 13 EHRR 212. The upshot is that the State's actions in areas of moral and religious sensibility are subject to less intense review. Indeed, the Court has shown itself particularly sensitive (many would argue excessively sensitive) to religious sensibilities: see *Wingrove* v. *United Kingdom* (1996) 24 EHRR 1; and *Otto Preminger Institut* v. *Austria* (1995) 19 EHRR 34. However, where such reasoning conflicts with a strongly protected right, such as that to private sexual relations, intense review results nevertheless: see e.g. *Dudgeon; Modinos* v. *Cyprus* (1993) 16 EHRR 485.

(5) *Competing interest: extent of the evidential basis.* Where the evidence tendered to support the existence of a competing interest is slender, the intensity of review will be greater. In other words, where

the existence of a threshold problem is marginal, the intensity of review as to its existence and proposed solution is that much greater. Thus, in *Hertel* where there was no evidence that the remarks attributed were causing any harm to the interests protected by the injunction, the restraint was found to be disproportionate; see also *Vereinigung Demokratischer Soldaten Osterreichs and Gubi* v. *Austria* (1995) 20 EHRR 56; *Sidoropoullos and Others* v. *Greece* (10 July 1998); and *Smith and Grady* (1999) 29 EHRR 493, paras 97 to 99.

(6) *The context of the dispute: issues of justiciability.* The justiciability of an issue affects the degree of intensity of review. Assertions of "national security" receive considerably more sensitive, "hands off" handling provided that adequate procedural safeguards are put in place: see, e.g. *Leander* v. *Sweden* (1987) 9 EHRR. This notion that substantively non-justiciable material should, in order to be proportionate, be subject to substantial procedural safeguards is an important recurrent theme that is evident in other areas such as the protection of children, adoption and so on: see *Olsson* v. *Sweden* (1988) 11 EHRR 259; *W* v. *United Kingdom* (1987) 10 EHRR 29.

(7) *The existence of positive obligations.* Where the complaint is that the State has breached its positive obligation to protect individuals from interference with their Convention rights, a lesser intensity of review is applied. The Strasbourg Court has held on several occasions that positive duties can be discharged by the State in a variety of ways and the choice of means made is largely a matter for the State: see e.g. *Winer* v. *United Kingdom* (1986) 48 D&R 154. Given the structure of the Convention rights the assertion of positive obligations on the State often coincides with less justiciable subject-matter. The Strasbourg Court treats these positive obligations with a much lighter hand: see e.g. *Osman* v. *United Kingdom* [1999] 1 FLR 193, paras 116 and 121. Exceptionally, as in *D* v. *United Kingdom* (1997) 24 EHRR 423 (a case involving the deportation of an AIDS sufferer in the terminal stages of the illness to a country which did not have the medical facilities to prevent a rapid decline in his condition) a violation was found (albeit of Article 3 rather than Article 2).

(8) *The nature of a democratic society.* The fact that the restraints must be necessary in a democratic society affects the nature of review in that interference premised upon notions that conflict with or under-

mine the pluralistic, tolerant and inclusive nature of such society will be especially hard to justify: see e.g. *Klass* v. *Germany* (1978) 2 EHRR 214, para 42; *Smith and Grady* (1999) 29 EHRR 493, para 89.

(9) *The extent of a common European standard.* The extent of congruity in the practice of the Member States was historically a most important factor (potentially diminished since the expansion in the number of Convention signatories) though not, as *Handyside* demonstrates, conclusive. This notion, taken together with that of a democratic society, is key in keeping Convention rights alive as constantly changing, increasingly sophisticated tools of individual protection that tend to evolve over time. The existence of a consensus militates in favour of any practice departing from it; the absence of such consensus means that greater latitude will be allowed to the government in question: see, for instance, *Modinos* v. *Cyprus* (1993) 16 EHRR 485 (in the Commission Report); and the cases on transsexuality such as *Rees* v. *United Kingdom* (1986) 9 EHRR 56; *Cossey* v. *United Kingdom* (1990) 13 EHRR 622; *B* v. *France* (1993) 16 EHRR 1; and *Sheffield and Horsham* (1998) 27 EHRR 163. These cases illustrate the role the European consensus plays in the ongoing development of the case-law. *Smith and Grady* (27 September 1999) paras 103-104 highlight the role of comparative evidence and experience (even if not founding a consensus) in testing governmental assertions and justifications.

37. Turning to the second exercise, the role which the Strasbourg Court expects of a domestic court for the purposes of compliance with Article 13 is a matter given fresh impetus by *Smith and Grady* (1999) 29 EHRR 493. In a key passage the Court stated:

As was made clear by the High Court and the Court of Appeal in the judicial review proceedings, since the Convention did not form part of English law, questions as to whether the application of the policy violated the applicants' rights under Article 8 and, in particular, as to whether the policy had been shown by the authorities to respond to a pressing social need or to be proportionate to any legitimate aim served, were not questions to which answers could properly be offered. The sole issue before the domestic courts was whether the policy could be said to be "irrational"... [N]otwithstanding any human rights context, the threshold of irrationality which an applicant was required to surmount was a high one. This is, in the view of the Court, confirmed by the judgements of the High Court and the Court of Appeal themselves. . . Nevertheless, both courts concluded that the policy could not be said to be beyond the range of responses open to a reasonable decision-maker and, accordingly, could not be considered to be "irrational". In such circumstances, the Court considers it clear that, even assuming that the essential complaints of the applicants before this Court were before and considered by the domestic courts, the threshold at which the High Court and the Court of Appeal could find the Ministry of Defence policy was placed so high that it effectively excluded any consideration by domestic courts of the question of whether the interference with the applicants' rights answered a pressing social need or was proportionate to the national security and public order aims pursued, principles which lie at the heart of the Court's analysis of complaints under Article 8 of the Convention.

38. What is the thrust of this critique? On one level it is as much about the articulation of standards and in particular the domestic court's failure to systematically apply the Strasbourg Court's own *Sunday Times/Olsson* test <30>. It makes a compelling case that Article 13 requires the application of an express four-stage proportionality test. On a second level, it is really about intensity of review and the minimum level of such review that is compatible with the discharge of Convention obligations. While the Strasbourg Court did not articulate the level or intensity of review it considers appropriate, it is plain that what was on offer was defective. This indicates that any national test that fails to review the *weight* attached to fundamental rights and competing interests cannot discharge the standards set out in the *Sunday Times/Olsson* test.

CONSTITUTIONAL REVIEW

39. Just as Strasbourg judges are inspired and informed by the existence or not of a European consensus, so too domestic judges are increasingly influenced by comparative material. Through association with the Convention, the law and practice of other Convention states will obviously be highly material and in high profile cases will be adduced before domestic courts just as it is in Strasbourg. However, two other inter-

locking sources of comparative material are likely to have an especially strong effect in shaping the judges' approach to shaping and applying a proportionality test, namely: (a) experience of applying proportionality in Privy Council constitutional cases; and (b) reference to comparative Commonwealth constitutional material.

40. Two recent examples of proportionality in Privy Council constitutional cases will suffice. The first case is *De Freitas* v. *Permanent Secretary of Ministry of Agriculture Fisheries Lands and Housing* [1998] 3 WLR 675. At issue was the constitutionality of section 10(2)(a) of Antigua and Barbuda's Civil Service Act which prohibited civil servants from expressing opinions on controversial matters and so interfered with their constitutional right to freedom of expression. The reasoning (Lord Clyde for the Privy Council) is a model application of the proportionality test.

(1) The plain wording of the section [Q1] had a legitimate objective, namely the maintenance of the neutrality of civil servants; [Q2] the restraint imposed was rationally connected with that objective; but [Q3] it failed the hurdle of necessity or [Q4] a fair balance as a blanket ban was clearly excessive. This was bolstered by the Strasbourg case of *Vogt* v. *Germany* (1995) 21 EHRR 205.

(2) The Court of Appeal of the Eastern Caribbean Supreme Court had proceeded from such reasoning to rescue the section by implying words to the effect that restraint would only be required "when his forbearance from such publication is reasonably required for the proper performance of his official functions". This solution was also rejected by the Privy Council, not just on grounds of legal certainty, but because the remaining restraint was overly wide (ie. offending [Q3] the principle of necessity). His Lordship dealt with the case as follows:

> Even if the subsection, with or without the supplementary provision sought to be implied by the Court of Appeal, satisfied the first of the two requirements already referred to, namely that it was a restraint upon the freedom of civil servants "reasonably required for the proper performance of their functions", it would still have to satisfy the second requirement of being "reasonably justifiable in a democratic society". . . . [In] *Nyambirai v National Social Security Authority* [1996] 1 LRC 64 . . . Gubbay CJ . . . saw the quality of

reasonableness in the expression "reasonably justifiable in a democratic society" as depending upon the question of whether the provision under challenge "arbitrarily or excessively invades the enjoyment of the guaranteed right according to the standards of a society that has a proper respect for the rights and freedoms of the individual". In determining whether a limitation is arbitrary or excessive he said that the court would ask itself: "whether: (i) the legislative objective is sufficiently important to justify limiting a fundamental right; (ii) the legislative measures designed to meet the objective are rationally connected to it; and (iii) the means used to impair the right or freedom are no more than is necessary to accomplish the objective". Their Lordships accept and adopt this threefold analysis of criteria.

41. The second Privy Council case is *Thomas* v. *Baptiste* [1999] 3 WLR 249 and is in a similar vein. The case involved an appeal against the order for their execution after very substantial periods in custody; one of the focal points of challenge were instructions relating to the exercise by the applicants of their right to apply to an international human rights body (the UNHRC). In examining the instructions Lord Millett (for the majority of the Privy Council) stated:

> [T]he instructions were disproportionate because they curtailed the prisoners rights further than was necessary to deal with the mischief created by the delays in the international appellate processes. It would have been sufficient to prescribe an outside period of (say) 18 months for the completion of all such processes. This could apply whether the petitioner made only one application or applied successively to more than one international body or made successive applications to the same body. It was unnecessary and inappropriate to provide separate and successive time limits for each application and for each stage of each application. This had the effect of drastically and unnecessarily curtailing the time limits within which the first such body could complete the processes.

42. These cases illustrate that: (1) the four-question template <P1> is in operation in Constitutional Review in the Privy Council; (2) it is seemingly applied to a respectable degree of intensity; and (3) it is applied with reference to comparative constitutional material dealing with concepts such as proportionality, "necessary in a democratic society", "pressing social need" and so on.

43. Finally, a very brief mention of comparative constitutional and rights-oriented material.

(1) As indicated in *De Freitas* the Canadian Charter of rights and freedoms offers a sophisticated and developed proportionality test, most famously expounded in the case of *R* v. *Oakes* (1986) 26 DLR (4th) 200. The position is summarised in *RJR-MacDonald Inc* v. *Attorney General of Canada* [1995] 3 SC 199 (concerning the Canadian tobacco advertising ban), para 60:

> Section 1 of the Charter guarantees the rights and freedoms set out therein "subject only to such reasonable limits prescribed by law as can be demonstrably justified in a free and democratic society". It is well established that the onus of justifying the limitation of a Charter right rests on the party seeking to have that limitation upheld, in this case the Attorney General. In *Oakes*, this Court set out two broad criteria as a framework to guide courts in determining whether a limitation is demonstrably justified in a free and democratic society. The first is that the objective the limit is designed to achieve must be of sufficient importance to warrant overriding the constitutionally protected right or freedom. The second is that the measures chosen to achieve the objective must be proportional to the objective. The proportionality requirement has three aspects: the measures chosen must be rationally connected to the objective; they must impair the guaranteed right or freedom as little as possible; and there must be proportionality between the deleterious effects of the measures and their salutary effects.

(2) In *Ross* v. *New Brunswick School District No. 15* [1996] 1 SCR 825, at 872 (per La Forest J) the Canadian Supreme Court emphasised the need that the proportionality principle be "applied flexibly, so as to achieve a proper balance between individual rights and community needs". The *MacDonald* case too clearly emphasises the need for flexible, variable application of the proportionality, with greater deference being paid in the case of "socio-economic legislation". In all cases the burden of proving justification for an interference rests squarely on the State: see *Andrews* v. *Law Society of British Columbia* (1989) 56 DLR (4th) 1 at 21 per McIntyre J.

(3) As *De Freitas* again indicates, this jurisprudence has been most influential on emergent constitutional democracies confronted with constitutional and human rights reasoning for the first time. For instance the South African Supreme Court (per Sachs J) has framed the problem in this way in *Coetzee* v. *The Government Of The Republic Of South Africa* [1995] 4 LRC 220, 239-40:

The more profound the interest being protected, and the graver the violation, the more stringent the scrutiny; at the end of the day, the court must decide whether, bearing in mind the nature and intensity of the interest to be protected and the degree to which and the manner in which it is infringed, the limitation is permissible. The President of this Court has outlined the basic balancing process in the following words:

"The limitation of constitutional rights for a purpose that is reasonable and necessary in a democratic society involves the weighing up of competing values, and ultimately an assessment based on proportionality. . . The fact that different rights have different implications for democracy, and in the case of our Constitution for 'an open and democratic society based on freedom and equality', means that there is no absolute standard which can be laid down for determining reasonableness and necessity. Principles can be established, but the application of those principles to particular circumstances can only be done on a case by case basis. This is inherent in the requirement of proportionality, which calls for the balancing of different interests. In the balancing process, the relevant considerations will include the nature of the right that is limited, and its importance to an open and democratic society based on freedom and equality; the purpose for which the right is limited and the importance of that purpose to such a society; the extent of the limitation, its efficacy, and particularly where the limitation has to be necessary, whether the desired ends could reasonably be achieved through other means less damaging to the right in question. In the process regard must be had to provisions of Section 33(1), and the underlying values of the Constitution, bearing in mind that, as a Canadian Judge has said, 'the role of the Court is not to second-guess the wisdom of policy choices made by legislators'. (*S v Makwanyane and Another* 1995(6) BCLR 665 (CC), at 708D-G per Chaskalson P).

If I might put a personal gloss on these words, the actual manner in which they were applied in *Makwanyane* (the Capital Punishment case) shows that the two phases are strongly interlinked in several respects: firstly, by overt proportionality with regards to means, secondly by underlying philosophy relating to values and thirdly by a general contextual sensitivity in respect of the circumstances in which the legal issues present themselves.

(4) The comparative materials have a great wealth of exposition of and explanation of the proportionality standards, both in theory and in application. Perhaps most crucially, they adopt (as the cases above hint) a highly sophisticated and experienced approach as to *margin* or *intensity* of review. This material is likely to prove invaluable in assessing the legitimacy of the objective justification for restricting Convention rights when confronted with Strasbourg authorities weakened by its "international court" "margin of appreciation" approach <34, 60>.

INTENSIVE DOMESTIC REVIEW

44. Domestic law has matured beyond passive *Wednesbury* Review <4-16> to produce modes of scrutiny far more akin to proportionality. There have been five strands to the legal weave. The first strand is the recognition of *flexibility* in the doctrine of substantive unreasonableness, and so the notion of a *variable* intensity of review. This came, ironically, in the form of recognition of a special judicial restraint in cases involving the application of government policy (and no reference to fundamental rights).[23] Such contexts are readily recognisable (even were fundamental rights in play) as indicating a wide margin. Lord Bridge summarised the position (*Hammersmith* at 597E-H) in this way:

The restriction which the *Nottinghamshire* case . . . imposes on the scope of judicial review operates only when the court has first determined that the ministerial action in question does not contravene the requirements

[23] *R* v. *Secretary of State for the Environment, ex p Nottinghamshire County Council* [1986] AC 240; *Hammersmith & Fulham London Borough Council* [1991] 1 AC 521; also *Council of Civil Service Unions* v. *Minister for the Civil Service* [1985] AC 374 per Lord Diplock at 411D-F.

of the statute, whether express or implied, and only then declares that, since the statute has conferred a power on the Secretary of State which involves the formulation and the implementation of national economic policy and which can only take effect with the approval of the House of Commons, it is not open to challenge on the grounds of irrationality short of the extremes of bad faith, improper motive, or manifest absurdity. Both the constitutional propriety and the good sense of this restriction seem to me to be clear enough. The formulation and the implementation of national economic policy are matters depending essentially on political judgment. The decisions which shape them are for politicians to take and it is in the political forum of the House of Commons that they are properly to be debated and approved or disapproved on their merits. If the decisions have been taken in good faith within the four corners of the Act, the merits of the policy underlying the decisions are not susceptible to review by the courts and the courts would be exceeding their proper function if they presumed to condemn the policy as unreasonable.[24]

45. The second strand is the recognition by the common law of certain fundamental rights as having a special status. Most recently, in *R* v. *Lord Chancellor, ex p Lightfoot* [2000] 2 WLR 318, the Court of Appeal has endorsed this "hallmark" of "constitutional rights", from the judgment of Laws J at first instance in the same case ([1999] 2 WLR 1126, 1136F-G):

that special class of rights which, in truth, everyone living in a democracy under the rule of law ought to enjoy. Access to justice is one. Freedom of the person, of speech, thought, and religion are others. They are largely articulated in the principal provisions of the European Convention on Human Rights.

---

[24] In *O'Connor* v. *Chief Adjudication Officer* [1999] 1 FLR 1200 (at 1210H-1211B), Auld LJ has doubted whether this approach, once called "Super-*Wednesbury*" (*Smith* [1996] QB 517 (DC) at 533G) involves "a notion of 'extreme' irrationality", since "good old *Wednesbury* irrationality is about as an extreme form of irrationality as there is". He suggests that the special restraint may be attributable to practical considerations of a "heavy evidential onus" borne by applicants, their difficulty in producing "all the relevant material bearing on legislative and executive policy behind an instrument" and the court's reluctance "to form a view on the rationality of a policy based on political, social and/or economic considerations outside its normal competence".

The reference to the Convention reflects a line of cases culminating in *R* v. *Secretary of State for the Home Department, ex p McQuillan* [1995] 4 All ER 400, where Sedley J said (at 422f-j):

> the principles and standards set out in the Convention can certainly be said to be a matter of which the law of this country now takes notice in setting its own standards. . . Once it is accepted that the standards articulated in the [Convention] are standards which both march with those of the common law and inform the jurisprudence of the European Union, it becomes unreal and potentially unjust to continue to develop English public law without reference to them.

46. The third strand is the doctrine of "anxious scrutiny", used for identifying abuses of power. This was inspired by the first two strands (flexibility <44> and fundamental rights <45>) and by comments regarding the need in a fundamental rights case for "the most anxious scrutiny" or "close scrutiny" in *Bugdaycay* [1987] AC 514 (at 531F and 537H) and then (ironically) in *Brind* (at 749A, 751E-F and 757C). The doctrine was considered in many cases, culminating in the adoption by the Court of Appeal in *R* v. *Ministry of Defence, ex p Smith* [1996] QB 517 (at 554D-G, 563A and 564H-565B), endorsed and applied on countless occasions since[25], of David Pannick QC's formulation ("the *Smith* test") that:

> The court may not interfere with the exercise of an administrative discretion on substantial grounds save where the court is satisfied that the decision is unreasonable in the sense that it is beyond the range of responses open to a reasonable decision-maker. But in judging whether the decision-maker has exceeded this margin of appreciation the human rights context is important. The more substantial the interference with human rights, the more the court will require by way of justification before it is satisfied that the decision is reasonable in the sense outlined above.

---

[25] Two Court of Appeal references (*R* v. *Secretary of State for the Home Department, ex p Canbolat* [1997] 1 WLR 1569, 1579E-F; *R* v. *Secretary of State for the Home Department, ex p Ahmed* [1999] Imm AR 22, 41) and two House of Lords (*R* v. *Secretary of State for the Home Department, ex p Stafford* [1999] 2 AC 38, 47G; *R* v. *Secretary of State for the Home Department, ex p Simms* [1999] 3 WLR 328, 340C, 353D) suffice.

47. The fourth strand is the recognition that the *onus* of providing the substantial justification lies on the public authority. There have been two relevant aspects of the case-law. First, it is inherent in the *Smith* test that the public authority is required to provide the "justification", without which the measure will not be upheld. As Hooper J (dissenting, though not on this point) said in the Divisional Court in the "Bloody Sunday" case (*R v. Lord Saville, ex p A* [1999] 4 All ER 860): "In effect the burden is on those who seek to uphold the decision". Secondly, the courts have been astute to avoid an unsatisfactory mismatch between judicial review and habeas corpus, where it has always been the case that the burden has been on the respondent authority, observing that in fundamental rights cases the same position applies for all practical purposes in judicial review too.[26]

48. An important question then arises. Can the *Smith* test <46> (with the public authority's onus <47>) produce a sufficiently intensive review to satisfy proportionality principles ?

(1) A convergence of principle had certainly been countenanced, even pre-*Smith*. In *McQuillan* [1995] 4 All ER 400, Sedley J made this tantalising comment (at 422j-423a):

> the standard of justification of infringements of rights and freedoms by executive decision must vary in proportion to the significance of the right which is at issue. Such an approach is indeed already enjoined by *ex p Bugdaycay* . . . in relation to a predominant value of the common law – the right to life – which, as it happens, the European Convention reflects. Whether this in itself is a doctrine of proportionality I do not now pause to ask; if it is, the House of Lords has long since contemplated its arrival with equanimity.

(2) Ironically, the case which most strongly suggests that the *Smith* test is unpromising, as a model of intensive review apt to embrace proportionality, is *Smith* itself. For in that case the test bore no fruit. The Court of Appeal strongly indicated that it did not think that the ban on gays in the military could withstand the scrutiny of the European Court of Human Rights, as it ultimately did not (*Smith and Grady*, (1999) 29 EHRR 493. Yet the Court felt inhibited, even

---

[26] See *R v. Oldham Justices, ex p Cawley* [1997] QB 1, 19B; *R v. Barking Havering and Brentwood Community Healthcare NHS Trust* [1999] 1 FLR 106, 115E.

under the new test, from intervening. Its approach strongly indicated a deliberately lower intensity of review than Strasbourg proportionality, and it is no surprise that the Strasbourg Court has said so in
Smith and Grady <37>. For proportionality fans, either *Smith* misap-
plied its own test, or some stronger test is necessary.

(3) There are signs that a modified test of substantive unreasonableness *can* be recognised and applied as a genuine high-intensity
review. It has been recognised that the Court is called on to scrutinise
the *weight* to be given to competing interests, by sharp contrast with
traditional *Wednesbury* Review <6>. This insight is embedded in a
stunning passage from the judgment of Laws J in *Chesterfield
Properties Plc* v. *Secretary of State for the Environment* [1998] JPL 568,
579-80 (emphasis added):

> *Wednesbury* . . . is not, at least not any longer, a monolithic standard of
> review. Where an administrative decision abrogates or diminishes a
> constitutional or fundamental right, *Wednesbury* requires that the deci-
> sion-maker provide a substantial justification in the public interest for
> doing so. . . The identification of any right as "constitutional",
> however, means nothing in the absence of a written constitution unless
> it is defined by reference to some particular protection which the law
> affords it. The common law affords such protection by adopting,
> within *Wednesbury*, a variable standard of review. There is no question
> of the court exceeding the principle of reasonableness. It means only
> that reasonableness itself requires in such cases that *in ordering the
> priorities which will drive his decision, the decision-maker must give a
> high place to the right in question. He cannot treat it merely as something
> to be taken into account, akin to any other relevant consideration; he must
> recognise it as a value to be kept, unless in his judgment there is a greater
> value which justifies its loss.* In many arenas of public discretion, the
> force to be given to all and any factors which the decision-maker must
> confront is neutral in the eye of the law; he may make of each what he
> will, and the law will not interfere because the weight he attributes to
> any of them is for him and not the court. But where a constitutional
> right is involved, the law presumes it to carry substantial force. Only
> another interest, a public interest, of greater force may override it. The
> decision-maker is, of course, the first judge of the question whether in
> the particular case there exists such an interest which should prevail.

(4) The best illustration of the *Smith* test as a high-intensity review is probably *R* v. *Lord Saville, ex p A* [1999] 4 All ER 860.[27] There, the Court of Appeal carried out a detailed critique of the reasons given by the "Bloody Sunday" tribunal for a denial of anonymity which it was feared would threaten the safety of testifying soldiers. Two features of the judgment of the Court are revealing. First, there was this recognition of the rigours of the *Smith* test, as a matter of *words*:

> when a fundamental right such as the right to life is engaged, the options available to the reasonable decision maker are curtailed. They are curtailed because it is unreasonable to reach a decision which contravenes or could contravene human rights unless there are suffi-ciently significant countervailing considerations. In other words it is not open to the decision maker to risk interfering with fundamental rights in the absence of a compelling justification. Even the broadest discretion is constrained by the need for there to be countervailing circumstances justifying interference with human rights. The courts will anxiously scrutinise the strength of the countervailing circum-stances and the degree of the interference with the human right involved and then apply the test accepted by the Lord Chief Justice in *Smith* which is not in issue.

Secondly, and unlike *Smith* itself, there was the conversion from words to *action*. The Court's conclusions were the clear product of an examination in detail of the reasoning process of the tribunal (including its value-judgment inquiry) and the *substantive conclu-sions*. The Court identified no fewer than six matters which it was not satisfied had been accorded "sufficient significance" (undoubt-edly intensive review extending to questions of *weight*), before coming to the conclusion that no decision was possible other than the grant of anonymity. Along similar lines is the important recent case of *R* v. *Secretary of State for the Home Department, ex p Turgut,* [2000] Imm AR 306.

(5) Perhaps the most compelling illustration of an intense review model, embraced as a maturing common law standard reared from

---

[27] Another example is *R* v. *North and East Devon Health Authority, ex p Coughlan* [2000] 2 WLR 262, where the Court of Appeal granted judicial review (*inter alia*) because, applying the *Smith* test, they regarded the authority's decision as an unjustified infringement of the applicant's right to respect for her home.

Wednesbury, involves a flashback to the short-lived judgment of Laws J in the *Child B* case ([1995] 1 FLR 1055). That case concerned the denial of further chemotherapy for a ten-year-old child. Laws J granted judicial review, ordering the health authority to reconsider, because he was not satisfied that they had justified their decision to the Court. The case had been presented as *Wednesbury* Review, but Laws J had expressed to Counsel "the greatest doubt whether the decisive touchstone for the legality of the respondents' decision was the crude *Wednesbury* bludgeon" (see 1058H). His judgment described the emergent principle from *Brind* and *Bugdaycay*, by reference to a concept of *objective justification* (at 1060B-E) (emphasis added):

> The principle is that certain rights, broadly those occupying a central place in the European Convention on Human Rights and obviously including the right to life, are not to be perceived merely as moral or political aspirations nor as enjoying a legal status only upon the international plane of this country's Convention obligations. They are to be vindicated as sharing with other principles the substance of the English common law. Concretely, the law requires that where a public body enjoys a discretion whose exercise may infringe such a right, it is not to be permitted to perpetrate any such infringement *unless it can show a substantial objective justification on public interest grounds.* The public body itself is the first judge of the question whether such a justification exists. The court's role is secondary as Lord Bridge said [in *Brind*]. Such a distribution of authority is required by the nature of the judicial review jurisdiction, and the respect which the courts are certainly obliged to pay to the powers conferred by Parliament upon bodies other than themselves. But the decision-maker has to recognise that he can only infringe such a fundamental right by virtue of an objection of substance put forward in the public interest.

The question which Laws J posed was whether the explanation put forward by the health authority reasonably constituted a justification on substantial public interest grounds (see 1061G), identifying the unfulfilled burden (at 1065B) of explaining "the priorities that have led them to decline to fund the treatment".

(6) The Court of Appeal cleared the decks and heard the *Child B* case on appeal the same day ([1995] 1 WLR 898). They overturned

Laws J, on the basis that (per Sir Thomas Bingham at 906G-H) "it would be totally unrealistic to require the authority to come to court with its accounts and seek to demonstrate that if this treatment were provided for B then there would be a patient C who would have to go without treatment". Absent from the judgments in the Court of Appeal was any analysis of the implications of *Brind* and *Bugdaycay* for the general test of irrationality or the onus of proof. This is perhaps unsurprising, given the speed with which the case had to be dealt and the fact that Counsel were evidently not equipped to assist with the "anxious scrutiny" implications. What the Court of Appeal might well now say is that, although Laws J's general approach was sound for anxious scrutiny cases, the special sensitivities in a scarce medical resources context called for a wide margin (especially in view of the potentially competing rights of other patients). Ironically, two of the judges in the Court of Appeal in *Child B* were soon to preside over *Smith* ([1996] QB 517: Simon Brown LJ in the Divisional Court and Sir Thomas Bingham MR in the Court of Appeal), where the argument explored the developing doctrine from *Bugdaycay* and *Brind*, which Laws J had been articulating. To complete the conundrum, the judgments of neither Laws J nor the Court of Appeal in *Child B* were cited to either Court in *Smith*.

49. The fifth and final strand is the most powerful. It has become known as "the principle of legality". The idea is simple: sources of public authorities' power should be construed as not permitting unjustified restrictions on fundamental rights, except where primary legislation deliberately authorises such restrictions. These have been the principal landmarks.

(1) *R* v. *Secretary of State for the Home Department, ex p Leech* [1994] QB 198, where the Court of Appeal struck down a Prison Rule entitling the governor to censor correspondence between a prisoner and his solicitor as ultra vires the statutory rule-making power. Influenced by Strasbourg case-law, the Court interpreted the power ("to make rules for the regulation and management of prisons") as authorising an intrusion on the right to communicate in confidence with a solicitor, being part of the "constitutional right" (see 210A) of access to a court, but *only* to the extent that the intrusion was "the minimum necessary to ensure that the correspondence is in truth

bona fide legal correspondence" (at 217G). The Home Office had not discharged the *onus* of satisfying the test (214D-E).

(2) *R* v. *Lord Chancellor, ex p Witham* [1998] QB 575, where the Divisional Court struck down as ultra vires the Lord Chancellor's Order imposing substantial fees, including on litigants in person, for commencing legal proceedings. The Divisional Court interpreted the wide enabling power ("may by order under this section prescribe the fees to be taken") as not authorising interference with the constitutional right of access to the Court. The approach in *Witham* has been endorsed by the Court of Appeal in *R* v. *Lord Chancellor, ex p Lightfoot* [2000] 2 WLR 318, but refined to make clear that deliberate authority in primary legislation may arise by necessary implication and not merely express words.

(3) *R* v. *Secretary of State for the Home Department, ex p Pierson* [1998] AC 539, where Lord Browne-Wilkinson stated this "principle of legality" (at 575D):[28]

> A power conferred by Parliament in general terms is not to be taken to authorise the doing of acts by the donee of the power which adversely affect the legal rights of the citizen or the basic principles on which the law of the United Kingdom is based unless the statute conferring the power makes it clear that such was the intention of Parliament.

50. The most compelling application of the principle of legality is to be found in the speech of Lord Steyn (with whom Lords Browne-Wilkinson and Hoffmann agreed) in *R* v. *Secretary of State for the Home Department, ex p Simms* [1999] 3 WLR 328. There, the House of Lords held to be unlawful the Home Secretary's policy and prison governors' decisions preventing journalists from visiting prisoners in the cause of their protestations of innocence. Lord Steyn construed the (wide and unambiguous) enabling power by reference to the principle of legality, in this way (at 340F-H):

> Literally construed there is force in the extensive construction put forward. But one cannot lose sight that there is at stake a fundamental

---

[28] See too *R* v. *Secretary of State for the Home Department, ex p Stafford* [1999] 2 AC 38, 48C-D.

or basic right, namely the right of a prisoner to seek through oral interviews to persuade a journalist to investigate the safety of the prisoner's conviction and to publicise his findings in an effort to gain access to justice for the prisoner. In these circumstances even in the absence of an ambiguity there comes into play a presumption of general application operating as a constitutional principle as Sir Rupert Cross explained in successive editions of his classic work: *Statutory Interpretation*, 3rd edn. (1995), pp.165-6. This is called "the principle of legality": *Halsbury's Laws of England*, 4th edn. reissue, vol.8(2) (1996), pp.13-14, para 6. Ample illustrations of the application of this principle are given in the speech of Lord Browne-Wilkinson, and in my speech, in [*Pierson* at] 573G-575D, 587C-590A. Applying this principle I would hold that [the standing orders] leave untouched the fundamental and basic rights asserted by the applicants in the present case.

On this basis, the policy and decisions were unlawful, because the Home Office had failed to establish a case of pressing need under the test in *Leech* (see 339G).

51. As a mode of intensive domestic review, the principle of legality is a solution of breathtaking skill. It involves the use, rather than any modified *irrationality* principle, of concepts of *legality*. Instead of holding the measure to be unjustified by reference to common law (i.e. judge-made) standards of abuse of power, the measure is ultra vires as a matter of *legislative mandate* <P2, P5>, by reference to the proper scope of the legislatively-conferred power (as presumed to be limited). Such considerations trump those which engage the substantive unreasonableness threshold, as Lord Bridge recognised in *Hammersmith* <44>. In essence, the principle is identifying a legislatively-mandated margin, whereby no power (however wide the enabling provision) may be used to bring about an unjustified restriction of a fundamental right. The limiting feature is the situation where Parliament, being legislatively supreme, has provided for the intrusion, again as a matter of legislative mandate.

52. The principle of legality seen in *Simms* hardens the *Smith* test <46> to produce a high-intensity review to match that contemplated in the Strasbourg Review and Constitutional Review. *Simms* uses a Strasbourg proportionality hallmark (pressing social need) <30>. Importantly, it is

apt to inform review of *reasoning process* <P8>: see *Ex p LM*.[29]. As to review of *substantive conclusions*, *Simms* points to a wide and general use of a high-intensity proportionality test. In particular, we suggest that:

(1) *Simms* does not contemplate the use of the pressing social need test solely in a *threshold* sense but in an *overall* sense <P4>. Hence the parallel with *Leech*, where the test had been used to mean "the minimum necessary" to achieve the (admittedly legitimate) objective.

(2) *Simms* contemplates a high-intensity test in cases of *any fundamental right*. Although *Simms* and *Leech* are freedom of speech cases (in which area the common law has traditionally mirrored the Strasbourg case-law), it is clear from *Witham* and *Pierson* <49> that the principle of legality will apply to cases involving other fundamental rights. A pressing social need test has been considered helpful in cases involving other such rights: see e.g. *Ex p LM* (above), where the pressing social need test was applied in the context of disclosure of information to the police in infringement of the right to privacy (Article 8). Whether "pressing social need" will be apposite in all fundamental rights contexts is open to question. But to the extent that other high-intensity formulations (drawn perhaps from the Strasbourg law) are more apt, the principle of legality is sufficiently broad and flexible to embrace these.

(3) Perhaps most controversially, *Simms* contemplates a high-intensity test in relation to *the exercise of power*. There was pre-*Simms* case-law suggesting a two-staged approach: (a) that the *Leech* test applied to the question whether power *existed* to interfere with the fundamental right; but that if so (b) an irrationality test applied to the question whether the exercise of power in the particular case was a justified interference.[30] It is difficult to see how this (potentially artificial) distinction can withstand *Simms*. In the first place, *Simms* was itself a case of the lawfulness of the exercise of a power (concerning

---

[29] *R* v. *A Local Authority, ex p LM* [2000] 1 FLR 612 (error in failing to apply pressing social need test), following *R* v. *Chief Constable of North Wales, ex p Thorpe* [1999] QB 396. Cf. *R* v. *Advertising Standards Authority, ex p City Trading Ltd* [1997] COD 202 (ASA not obliged to apply pressing social need test).

[30] This seems to have been the approach of the Court of Appeal in *R* v. *Broadmoor Special Hospital, ex p S* [1998] COD 199 (concerning a policy of searching mental health patients). See too *Broadmoor Special Health Authority* v. *Robinson* [1999] QB 957 (whether implied power to seize manuscript of a book).

the Secretary of State's policy and decisions by prison governors). Secondly, Lord Steyn deliberately placed the *Leech* principle alongside the *Smith* test (at 340B-D) in engaging and defeating a submission, based on United States case-law, in favour of a wide margin (or generous "measure of judicial deference owed to corrections officials"). Thirdly, the following observation of Lord Hoffmann in *Simms* (at 341F-H; emphasis added) is consistent only with a wide version of the principle of legality, as a general high-intensity proportionality principle, akin to Constitutional Review <39-43>:

> the importance of the principle of legality in a constitution which, like ours, acknowledges the sovereignty of Parliament. Parliamentary sovereignty means that Parliament can, if it chooses, legislate contrary to fundamental principles of human rights. The Human Rights Act 1998 will not detract from this power. The constraints upon its exercise by Parliament are ultimately political, not legal. But the principle of legality means that Parliament must squarely confront what it is doing and accept the political cost. Fundamental rights cannot be overridden by general or ambiguous words. This is because there is too great a risk that the full implications of their unqualified meaning may have passed unnoticed in the democratic process. In the absence of express language or necessary implication to the contrary, the courts therefore presume that even the most general words were intended to be subject to the basic rights of the individual. *In this way the courts of the United Kingdom, though acknowledging the sovereignty of Parliament, apply principles of constitutionality little different from those which exist in countries where the power of the legislature is expressly limited by a constitutional document.*

53. The principle of legality fits with the Forsyth theory, which has it that all grounds of judicial review are part of an "ultra vires" doctrine.[31] The idea is that judges are doing no more than enforcing standards of public administration which Parliament intended when conferring powers. The main criticism of what is undoubtedly a neat trick, is the intellectual dishonesty of peddling "presumptions" as to what

---

[31] For the academic battlelines, see Christopher Forsyth, "Of Fig Leaves and Fairy Tales: the *Ultra Vires* Doctrine, the Sovereignty of Parliament, and Judicial Review" (1996) 55 *Camb LJ* 122; and Paul Craig, "*Ultra Vires* and the Foundations of Judicial Review" (1998) 57 *Camb LJ* 63.

Parliament is to be "taken as intending", to mask the truth of judge-created standards. For present purposes, we merely note three things. First, that, to the extent that it is a desirable aim that judges be encouraged to be more proactive in scrutinising the substance of measures, the reality in the case of the more cautious judge may be that 'legality' serves as a useful comfort blanket. Secondly, that it is unmistakeable and inevitable that Human Rights Act Review will involve the application of a principle of illegality/vires <55-56>. Thirdly, that *whatever the juridical basis for proportionality*, the proof of the pudding is in (a) the framework of overt questions posed and (b) the rigour with which they are answered.

HUMAN RIGHTS ACT REVIEW

54. The Human Rights Act 1998 brings the European Convention on Human Rights directly into domestic law. As Lord Ackner said in *Brind* that it would ([1991] 1 AC 696, 763A), incorporation brings into domestic law the principle of proportionality. Inevitably, judges will be besieged with Strasbourg authorities. But Counsel should be wary of their unfocused use. A warning shot is *R v. North West Lancashire Health Authority, ex p A* (1999) 2 CCLR 419, where the Court of Appeal said that the deployment of generalised propositions from Strasbourg case-law as to rights and sexual identity contributed nothing to the resolution of the issues, but were positively unhelpful, cluttering up consideration of what were adequate and more precise domestic principles and authorities.

55. In human rights cases in domestic courts, the 1998 Act, and those articles of the Convention which it incorporates, is the instrument of supreme legislative status <P2>. The scheme of the 1998 Act does three main things.

(1) It enacts in statutory form, as *codified rights*, "the Convention rights" set out in Schedule 1, including: Article 2 (life), Article 5 (liberty), Article 8 (privacy), Article 9 (religion), Article 10 (speech), Article 11 (expression), Article 12 (assembly) and Article 1 Protocol 1 (property). The codified rights are henceforth part of the law of the land.

(2) It enacts a *rule of interpretation* (section 3), which requires primary and subordinate legislation to be read and given effect, "so far as it is possible to do so", "in a way which is compatible with the Convention rights". Statutory protection of the codified rights will only yield to the *legislative mandate* of other primary legislation, which it is not "possible" to read or give effect to in any other way. In such a case a special remedy (the declaration of incompatibility) may be ordered by the Court (section 4).

(3) It enacts an *illegality rule* (section 6) which makes it "unlawful for a public authority to act in a way which is incompatible with a Convention right". Again, this yields only to the *legislative mandate* of the provisions of (or made under) other primary legislation, which primary legislation it is not "possible" to read or give effect to in any other way (section 6(2)).

56. There is a striking parallel between the structure of the 1998 Act and the position which common law intensive review had reached under *Simms* <50-52>. The crux is and remains whether *Simms* "pressing social need" involves a sufficiently high-intensity review to test whether "action is incompatible with a Convention right". *If it does*, then there is here a stunning 1998 Act-common law fit.

(1) The 1998 Act codifies the Convention rights, but in substance the same rights were afforded primary status (indeed, "constitutional" status) under a common law marching with the Convention <45>.

(2) Both the 1998 Act and *Simms* approach the problem from the point of view of statutory legality, rather than common law abuse of power. The difference is that *Simms* tackles the power at *source*, by construing the enabling power (by reference to which the public authority is acting) to involve an *internal restriction* (no power to permit unjustified restrictions of protected rights); whereas the 1998 Act contains an *external prohibition*,[32] by banning any exercise of power (whatever the source) which unjustifiably restricts rights. In

[32] For an example of unlawfulness by reference not to the enabling statute but an "external" statutory prohibition, see *Apple Fields Ltd* v. *New Zealand Apple & Pear Marketing Board* [1991] 1 AC 344 (levy imposed under the Apple and Pear Marketing Act 1971 falling foul of restrictions contained in the Commerce Act 1986).

both cases the measure is "ultra vires" (internally or externally). The difference between statutory *inhibition* (*Simms*) and statutory *prohibition* (section 6) is subtle. It is difficult to see any practical difference in effect between the two techniques.

(3) Both the 1998 Act and *Simms* involve deferring to primary legislation which cannot be read or applied so as to preserve the protected rights from unjustified interference. If, as a matter of express words or necessary implication (cf. *Lightfoot* <49(2)>), primary legislation requires or allows the infringement of rights, then the Court cannot intervene, save to draw attention to the clash, for which the 1998 Act provides an express remedy (section 4).

(4) There is then this twist. Section 3 of the 1998 Act calls the Court to a mode of interpretation of any relevant enactment, including the *source* power, which is compatible with the Convention rights. *If* it is the case that *Simms* establishes a respectable mode of statutory interpretation by which source power can be construed to prohibit any unjustified interference with protected rights, then it follows that the work of section 6 is already done. And if the nature of the particular source power is such that it *cannot* be so construed, because it expressly or by necessary implication permits or requires the interference with rights, then section 6 cannot help. In other words, on this analysis, section 6 is the braces to section 3's belt.

57. Looked at in this way, the comments of Lord Hoffmann in *Simms* about the effect of that case (set out above <52>) are compelling, as are his observations about the 1998 Act:

> The Human Rights Act 1998 will make three changes to this scheme of things. First, the principles of fundamental human rights which exist at common law will be supplemented by a specific text, namely the European Convention on Human Rights and Fundamental Freedoms. But much of the Convention reflects the common law: see *Derbyshire County Council v Times Newspapers Ltd* [1993] AC 534, 551. That is why the United Kingdom Government felt able in 1950 to accede to the Convention without domestic legislative change. So the adoption of the text as part of domestic law is unlikely to involve radical change in our notions of fundamental human rights. Secondly, the principle of legality will be expressly enacted as a rule of construction in section 3

and will gain further support from the obligation of the minister in charge of a Bill to make a statement of compatibility under section 19. Thirdly, in those unusual cases in which the legislative infringement of fundamental human rights is so clearly expressed as not to yield to the principle of legality, the courts will be able to draw this to the attention of Parliament by making a declaration of incompatibility. It will then be for the sovereign Parliament to decide whether or not to remove the incompatibility.

None of these are changes of *substantive judicial intervention.* But if Lord Hoffmann is right that the 1998 Act does not make any such change, this is *not* because the 1998 Act is weak, but because under *Simms* (properly understood and applied) it could finally be said that *the common law is strong.*

58. Whether or not *Simms* can already be regarded as embracing a sufficiently high-intensity test for the purposes of section 6 is a fascinating question. However, its practical significance is limited to (a) whether the changeover to the 1998 Act will involve an abrupt "jolt" or whether the law is already in smooth transition; and (b) whether there is a divergence of principle between cases under section 6 of the 1998 Act and rights cases outside it.

59. In the final countdown, and whatever the common law position, three main things will be required for proportionality principles to operate properly under the Human Rights Act. The first requirement is that there must be *labels connoting a culture of high-intensity review.*

(1) The *Smith* test <46> (reasonableness and justification) is not a safe basis for the law. It fails in terms of lack of a systematic analysis and in terms of intensity of review. It may have been that the *Smith* test could have been used as the platform for developing high-intensity principles. But *Smith* was always an incremental step in the law's development, and its limitations have been exposed by the Strasbourg Court. It had two main problems. First, "reasonableness" and "justification" in the *Smith* test <46> left entirely unidentified the coherent set of questions and practical rigour with which to test them. Secondly, the application of the test in *Smith* itself could not be reconciled with high-intensity proportionality. Ironically, it was the application of the *Smith* test in other cases, like *Bloody Sunday* <48(4)>, that was far closer to the mark.

(2) It does not follow that common law developments should be discarded and the labours of those responsible for its more progressive trends devalued. There are concepts which may well prove helpful in communicating the kind of scrutiny required by section 6 of the 1998 Act. We suggest that there are three useful and interrelated notions. The first is (of course) *proportionality* itself, familiar to domestic judges from Luxembourg Review, Strasbourg Review and Constitutional Review. Here, a useful guide is the judgment of Laws J in *First City Trading* <23(6)>. Secondly, there is the concept of *pressing social need*, a strong theme in Strasbourg Review, from cases like *Sunday Times* <30>, but deployed by the common law. Here, a useful guide is *Leech* and *Simms* <49(1), 50>. Thirdly, there is the concept of *objective justification*, familiar from EC discrimination law <24>, but which echoes in general Luxembourg Review (see *First City Trading* <23(6)>) and Intensive Domestic Review, where the useful guide is the decision of Laws J in *Child B* <48(5)>. True, that decision did not survive long (in a pre-*Smith* culture) <48(6)>. But in the brave new world of the 1998 Act, the vice of Laws J's judgment (that it did not reflect *Wednesbury* Review) becomes its virtue.

60. The second requirement is that there be *a proper framework of questions and considerations.*

(1) No matter what the phrases with which intensive Human Rights Act Review becomes associated, that review will need to be focused on an appropriate set of questions. Otherwise, the law risks being trapped by linguistics or cast adrift on catch-phrase. This was why *Smith* was only ever a starting-point. It is simply not sufficient to say to judges that they must "look carefully" to see that a measure is "proportionate" or "justified", any more than to "look carefully" to see that it is "reasonable" or "rational".

(2) It is vital, whatever the basis of appropriate high-intensity review, that there should be <53> overt proportionality reasoning deployed by both public authority and reviewing court. What are the all-important terms of reference ? We commend again the *four-question template* <P1> and, with it, the *value-judgment inquiry* <P5>. These should inform public authorities and the courts, as to the methodology and reasoning for testing the justification of a measure.

61. The third requirement is that there be a recognition of a *variable latitude enjoyed by public authorities.* The law must always reflect the existence of some *latitude*, and do so in a way which recognises *variable* standards of review (and so variable widths).

(1) What the domestic judges should not do is to "*read-across*" the "margin of appreciation" *as applied by the Strasbourg Court* in individual cases. The "margin of appreciation" described by that Court has a second (international) dimension of deference <34>, consistent with the Strasbourg Court's role as an international court conducting Long-Stop Review <29>.

(2) The impermissibility of *reading-across* is supported by reference to various sources. First, there is the recognition by the Strasbourg Court itself of the special dimension of international deference built into the margin of appreciation which it applies, in cases like *Handyside* <34>. Secondly, there is the wealth of juristic opinion, from which we single out one example:

> The margin of appreciation doctrine as it has been developed in Strasbourg will necessarily be inapt to the administration of the Convention in the domestic courts for the very reason that they are domestic; they will not be subject to an objective inhibition generated by any cultural distance between themselves and the state organs whose decisions are impleaded before them.[33]

Thirdly, there is the 1998 Act itself, which carefully provides (section 2(1)(a)) that domestic courts are to "take into account" (*not*, apply or be bound by) decisions of the Strasbourg Court. Fourthly, there are *Hansard* statements which speak of emphasising domestic features to any case and of the margin of appreciation conferred on the domestic *court*. Notably these two passages:[34]

> The courts will often be faced with cases that involve factors perhaps specific to the United Kingdom which distinguish them from cases considered by the [Strasbourg Court] . . .
> The doctrine of the margin of appreciation means allowing this

---

[33] Sir John Laws, "The Limitations of Human Rights" [1998] PL 254 at 258.
[34] Lord Irvine LC (19 January 1998) 484 HL 1270, 1271; Jack Straw MP (3 June 1998) 313 HC 398, 404. See Francesca Klug, "The Human Rights Act 1998, *Pepper* v. *Hart* and All That" [1999] PL 246 at 251-252.

country a margin of appreciation when it interprets our law and the actions of our Government . . . Through incorporation we are giving a profound margin of appreciation to British courts to interpret the Convention . . .

Fifthly, there are judicial comments such as those of Buxton LJ in *R v. Stratford Justices, ex p Imbert* (1999) 2 Cr.App.R 27:[35]

> The application of the doctrine of the margin of appreciation would appear to be solely a matter for the Strasbourg Court. By appealing to the doctrine that court recognises that the detailed content of at least some Convention obligations is more appropriately determined in the light of national conditions. . .. The English judge cannot therefore himself apply or have recourse to the doctrine of the margin of appreciation as implemented by the Strasbourg Court.

(3) Although domestic judges should not read-across the margin of appreciation as described by the Strasbourg Court, there will need to be *some* doctrine of a "margin". Otherwise, the Court will risk arrogating to itself the role of primary policy- and decision-maker. Moreover, although the doctrine of the "margin of appreciation" as articulated by the Strasbourg Court is "half-wrong" (insofar as it has its second dimension of international deference) it is also "half-right" (insofar as it has its first dimension of judicial deference) <34>. It is interesting to see how Buxton LJ continued his observation in *Imbert*:

> The English judge cannot therefore himself apply or have recourse to the doctrine of the margin of appreciation as implemented by the Strasbourg Court. He must, however, recognise the impact of that doctrine upon the Strasbourg Court's analysis of the meaning and implications of the broad terms of the Convention provisions: which is the obvious source of guidance as to those provisions, and a source that in any event the English court will be obliged, once section 2(1)(a) of the 1998 Act has come into force, to take into account.

(4) As to how to "unpick" from the Strasbourg jurisprudence the relevant nutrients as to setting the latitude or margin, we have identified

[35] Note too *R v. Secretary of State for the Home Department, ex p Adan* [1999] INLR 362, 379A-B ("margin of appreciation" as an expression "not happily chosen" to apply to third country approaches to the Refugee Convention, "given the expression's association with the ECHR jurisprudence").

and conducted in outline two legitimate exercises <35-38>: (a) the factors which lead to *relative* width or narrowness of the margin; and (b) the Strasbourg picture of how the domestic Court should scrutinise measures (for the purposes of Article 13). Commonwealth and comparative approaches should also greatly assist in this regard.

(5) It may be that domestic judges will remain attracted to the phrase "margin of appreciation". We see nothing wrong in a judge recognising and seeking to delineate *a* margin of appreciation, *provided* that it is not a read-across of *the* margin of appreciation delineated by the Strasbourg Court. The phrase is a good one: it attributes a positive characteristic to the public authority's role rather than a negative (weak) aspect to the Court's; the word "margin" is apt to convey the sense of both *latitude* and its *variable width*; and "appreciation" is apt to include questions of judgment and appraisal, as well as matters of discretion. Moreover, the practical reality is that "margin of appreciation" is a phrase already used by domestic judges, including in the context of Luxembourg Review (where it is plainly not a read-across from Strasbourg case-law) <23(5)-(7)>, as well as in domestic intensive review <6, 8, 46>.[36] The waters around the Strasbourg "margin of appreciation" may be cloudy with international deference, but it may suffice to run new bathwater, as with the name "*the discretionary area of judgment*" without throwing out the baby.

(6) We have identified factors from Strasbourg Review which inform questions of relative width of the margin <36>. We suggest the following as some illustrations of how the margin will fall to be set under Human Rights Act Review. Cases involving strong political, social policy, regulatory, and resources overtones are likely to be subject to a wide margin, most particularly where the only impact felt is upon a weak Convention right (e.g. property or association). Conflict between such objectives and strong, central rights, particularly those the courts are well-equipped to deal with (liberty, speech, privacy) are likely to retain a narrow margin, especially in contexts with which the Court is familiar (e.g. immigration law, criminal law). A very narrow margin is likely in cases involving central rights but in a private law context (i.e. where section 3 construction or

---

[36] Lord Templeman was evidently attracted to the phrase in *Brind*: see [1991] 1 AC 696, 751C.

section 6 infringement arise as a collateral issue) or in a "horizontal effect" manner (most obviously with the right to privacy at home or work) with the potential for judicial view-substitution. Due deference will be paid to expertise, whether democracy-based policy-making or health and science specialisms.

(7) This sort of approach is strongly in evidence in the reasoning of the Court of Appeal in *R* v. *Secretary of State for the Home Department, ex p Turgut* [2000] Imm AR 306. The Court combined a number of factors, such as the nature of the rights and interests at stake (the right to life and/or avoidance of ill-treatment), the comparative ability of the Court to take the decision (as good, the courts having the same materials available), and the conduct of the decision-making process to arrive at the conclusion that the Secretary of State's "discretionary area of judgment" was "a narrow one".

62. In establishing these three key requirements <59-61>, there is a great advantage to doing so by reference to rigorous but *pre-existing* principle. Judges (like anyone else) are more likely to respond to encouragement – suggestions of how previous sketches can be made use of, rather than insisting on a return to the drawing-board with nothing but blank paper. Use of existing principle and illustration gives judges not merely the inspiration of a distant call, but the equipment of map and compass. Perhaps most importantly, it provides a path to the development of *converged legal principle*. It is strongly desirable that there be an integrated approach, to Human Rights Act Review and the other forms in which domestic judges have to consider justification for measures restricting basic rights (whether Luxembourg Review, Intensive Domestic Review, Constitutional Review). Such consistency is surely achievable. We would suggest, then, that the dynamic common law can be deployed in a way which enables substantially the same approach as under Human Rights Act Review to apply for Intensive Domestic Review where the 1998 Act is not directly in play: for example, where the Court recognises a basic right albeit not a codified (Convention) right (see section 11) or where a measure is under challenge other than by the "victim".

63. Some comments about *evidence*. It is inevitable that there will be close forensic examination by domestic judges of the reasoning and evidence said to justify measures which restrict the codified rights. Indeed, such a process has already been set in motion by the decision of the Court of Appeal in *R* v. *Secretary of State for the Home Department, ex p Turgut* [2000] Imm AR 306. More particularly, this should also mean a greater emphasis on contemporaneous documentation, alongside sworn or affirmed explanation. Where a material conflict arises, whose resolution is key to the question of justification, the Court will have to decide what evidence is to be preferred. The public authority's evidence should explain: what rights were identified as going to be restricted?; what was the aim of the restriction?; why was it thought that the restriction would achieve the aim?; what was the pressing need?; what was the consequence of the restriction intended to be?; what alternative measures were considered?; why were they rejected?; why was the restriction felt to be fair overall? The Court will frequently be assisted by collateral evidence, such as was adduced in *Simms* [1999] 3 WLR 328 at 337G-339C ("compelling detail" as to the importance of communications between prisoners and journalists). It will not be uncommon for expert, statistical and comparative material to be adduced in this way. Will there be widespread cross-examination and disclosure in judicial review? We think not. There will be a strong cultural disinclination towards this, if for none other reason than the practical concern of procedural gridlock. The analytical answer is surely this: if the respondent public authority does not present a sufficiently clear and compelling evidential position then the *onus* of showing justification has not been discharged and the matter can be remitted for reconsideration.

64. We set out at the end of this chapter an attempted prescription of "rules" of proportionality under the 1998 Act. We should first revisit Lord Lowry's observations in *Brind*, which we previously set out at length <16>.

(1) Lord Lowry was right as to many of the consequences of the proportionality doctrine: the Court feeling more at liberty to interfere; the need for judges to be equipped by training and experience to tackle the questions which they are required to address; and the practical considerations arising out of a growth in numbers of legal challenges.

(2) There are several answers to Lord Lowry's observation that there was "very little room" between *Wednesbury* and the "forbidden

appellate approach" for proportionality. They are: (a) in some cases an "appellate approach" will, by reason of the subject matter, be the correct one; (b) in those cases not favouring full substitution of view, the proportionality doctrine must find that room; (c) setting narrower and more exacting margins for choice by public authorities properly creates that room by reducing the forbidden ground. As Laws J pointed out in *First City Trading* it is the case that for some special cases this may mean that the options are reduced to one (or even zero); and/or (d) insofar as there is still little space between *Wednesbury* and proportionality, this is because the development of the common law had already become closely aligned with proportionality.

(3) Undoubtedly, judges will be coming far closer to the substantive "merits" of cases. Value-judgments will be even more obvious <14>, and more judicial disagreement (successful appeals; dissenting judgments) will inevitably follow. But in no way is this "an abuse of the judges' supervisory jurisdiction", as Lord Lowry feared. It is part of the vindication of the rule of law and protection of the citizen's rights from unjustified interference. Most importantly, it is a supervision which bears the mark of legislative approval, by means of the 1998 Act.

65. Finally, to clear away all the words, and try to give some concrete indication of what it all means in practical terms, we suggest that: *Smith* <48(2)> would be decided the other way under the 1998 Act; *Brind* <15> would be very differently reasoned, and would probably be decided the other way; Laws J's general approach in *Child B* <48(5)> would fit, albeit that the outcome of the case would probably still be as in the Court of Appeal <48(6)>; good working examples of the kind of result to be expected are the domestic cases of *Bloody Sunday* <48(4)>, *Simms* <50> and *Turgut* <63>, and the international cases of *De Freitas* <40> and *Thomas* v. *Baptiste* <41>.

PROPORTIONALITY UNDER THE 1998 ACT: SUGGESTED RULES

R1. Before deciding to make any measure which may restrict one of the Convention rights (Schedule 1), there are *key questions* which a public authority should address. It should *ask* whether there is a pressing need, in these respects:

Q1 Is the measure adopted to pursue a legitimate aim ?
Q2 Can it serve to further that aim ?
Q3 Is it the least restrictive way of doing so ?
Q4 Viewed overall, do the ends justify the means ?

It should *consider:* (a) what competing interests are at stake; (b) what weight should be given to those competing interests; (c) whether any of them can properly take precedence over another.

R2. The authority should only adopt the measure if, having asked and answered the key questions, the authority considers that the measure is (a) a justified thing to do and (b) the right thing to do.

R3. The authority should record its assessment of all these matters for future reference. Often, it will be appropriate to make immediate disclosure of the reasoning with communication of the measure.

R4. If a measure is adopted without assessing these matters, the authority will usually be well-advised to reconsider afresh whether the measure is appropriate.

R5. If the authority is challenged under the 1998 Act, it will have the burden of explaining to the Court, by way of *evidence*, on what basis (by reference to the key questions) the measure is justified.

R6. In order to test the justification for the measure, the Court will often be assisted by evidence of a broader picture than usually available in litigation.

R7. Only rarely will it be necessary to probe evidence by way of cross-examination and disclosure. If the Court is not satisfied by the evidence presented by the public authority the authority's onus is not discharged and the Court can strike down the measure and/or order it to be reconsidered afresh.

R8. The first task of the Court is to ask whether the authority addressed its own mind to the key questions and, if not, order that the measure be reconsidered afresh.

R9. The second task of the Court is to ask whether the public authority has shown an objective justification for the measure, by means of justified answers to the key questions.

R10. In applying that test of justification, the Court asks whether it considers that the measure was (a) a justified thing to do, but *not* whether it considers that the measure was (b) the right thing to do.

R11. In applying the justification test, the Court should ask itself what height of intensity should be applied in relation to the key questions. The best way to approach this is by asking what width of "margin" (latitude) should be afforded to the authority.

R12. The width of the margin (and so height of intensity) should not be set by "reading across" analyses of the "margin of appreciation" in Strasbourg case-law, though such cases are helpful in identifying relevant factors influencing *relative* width.

R13. The width of the margin generally depends on the nature of: (a) *the right infringed* (how fundamental?); (b) *the objective pursued* (how compelling?); (c) *the measure and decision-maker* (what status?); and (4) *the context of the dispute* (how sensitive?).

R14. In some special high-intensity cases there will in effect be no margin, and only one justified answer. In some special low-intensity cases there is a wide margin and the Court is effectively asking whether the measure is reasonably open to the public authority. In most cases, there will be a margin but not a wide one. The Court is effectively asking whether there was a pressing social need such that the measure is objectively justified.

Determining Civil Rights and Obligations

Javan Herberg, Andrew Le Sueur
and Jane Mulcahy

THE GATEWAY TO ARTICLE 6.1 PROTECTION

This chapter examines the circumstances in which a person may benefit from the protections afforded by Article 6.1 in relation to civil rights and obligations: "In the determination of his civil rights and obligations . . ., everyone is entitled to a fair and public hearing within a reasonable time by an independent and impartial tribunal established by law". As well as the requirement of a fair hearing expressly set out, Article 6.1 includes an implied right of "access to a court" – so that hindrances to initiating proceedings also fall within its ambit.[1] Article 6.1 protections do not, however, arise exclusively in situations of actual or anticipated civil litigation, but apply whenever a public authority is engaged in the activity of determining a person's civil rights or obligations. Decisions taken by planning authorities, regulators and licensing bodies may therefore have to conform to its requirements, or run the risk of challenge.[2]

This chapter is not directly concerned with the content of the protections created by Article 6.1. Rather, the focus is on threshold or gateway questions as to a person's entitlement to claim the protection of Article 6.1 at all.[3] Thus, to fall within the protective ambit of Article 6.1, several conditions are, conventionally, required to be satisfied. There has to be (i) a "contestation" or dispute;[4] (ii) on arguable grounds;[5] (iii) in proceedings which are determinative or "decisive";[6] (iv) of "civil rights and obligations";[7] (v) which are "recognised" by domestic law.[8]

---

[1] *Golder* v. *UK* (1975) 1 EHRR 524; *Airey* v. *Ireland* (1979-80) 2 EHRR 305.

[2] See pp. 116–117.

[3] The distinction between the "civil" and "criminal" aspects of Article 6.1 also falls outside the scope of this chapter.

[4] See p. 93.   [5] See p. 95.   [6] See p. 96.   [7] See p. 1.   [8] See p. 121.

THE CONTEXT OF INCORPORATION

Courts and policy-makers in the UK now that Article 6.1 is given force by the Human Rights Act 1998 are not operating in a vacuum. First, the civil justice system in England and Wales is still adjusting to one of the most radical reform programmes in over a hundred years,[9] the intention of which is as much "to restrict access and to husband the court's resources"[10] as it is to improve access to legal services. It is not immediately obvious that the ideals of Article 6.1 – which takes the fully argued court hearing as the paradigm – sit easily with policies designed to encourage out of court settlements, alternative dispute resolution and summary justice.

The second context is that incorporation of Article 6.1 takes place against the background of existing "fair hearing" and "access to court" rights already recognised and protected by English and European Community law, some of which are "fundamental", in the sense that they may prevail over other laws. The common law has recognised a fundamental right of access to courts[11] and a right to an unbiased tribunal or court at all levels of the legal system,[12] and rules of procedural propriety regulating the decision-making of public authorities, including inferior courts, are now well-established in the principles of judicial review.[13] Where Community law rights are claimed in civil litigation, UK courts and policy-makers are now well used to considering the overriding requirements for "effective remedies", which overlap considerably with Article 6.1. Thus, while some standards demanded

---

[9] Lord Woolf, *Access to Justice: a final report to the Lord Chancellor* (London, HMSO, 1996); the Civil Procedure Rules, in force on 26 April 1999, enacted under the Civil Procedure Act 1997; Access to Justice Act 1999.

[10] Derek O'Brien, "The New Summary Judgment: Raising the Threshold of Admission" (1999) 18 *CJQ* 132.

[11] See e.g. *R* v. *Secretary of State for the Home Department, ex p Leech (No 2)* [1994] QB 198 ("it is a principle of our law that every citizen has a right of unimpeded access to a court", per Steyn LJ); *R* v. *Lord Chancellor, ex p Witham* [1998] QB 575; *R* v. *Lord Chancellor, ex p Lightfoot* [1999] 4 All ER 583; *R* v. *Legal Aid Board, ex p Duncan and MacKinstosh*, [2000] COD 159.

[12] *R* v. *Bow Street Metropolitan Stipendiary Magistrate, ex p. Pinochet Ugarte (No 2)* [2000] IAC 119; *Locabail (UK) Ltd* v. *Bayfield Properties Ltd* [2000] QB 451.

[13] See H. Woolf, J. Jowell and A. Le Sueur, *de Smith's Principles of Judicial Review* (London, Sweet & Maxwell, 1999), chs 6-11.

by Article 6.1 and the approaches of the Strasbourg Court may seem both new and odd,[14] many of the protections it insists upon are already embedded in the values of the UK's legal and administrative systems. It is against this background that we turn to examine the gateway into Article 6.1.

"CONTESTATION"

The French version of the text of Article 6.1 reads "contestations sur ses droits et obligations de caractere civil". There is no counterpart of "contestations" in the English text, but the jurisprudence refers to "dispute" as the English translation.[15]

In order for Article 6 to be applicable, there must be a dispute at the national level that is at least arguably recognised under domestic law.[16] However, the requirement should not be construed too technically.[17] In *Le Compte, Van Leuven and De Meyere* v. *Belgium* the matter of whether or not a "contestation" existed was considered as a preliminary point. The Belgian Government contended that, before a dispute could arise, there must be "two conflicting claims or applications". This submission was not accepted by the European Court. It determined that "contestation" should be given a substantive rather than a formal meaning, not least because it had no counterpart in the English text. Further, and insofar as the word required the existence of a disagreement, that was satisfied on the facts: the professional body had said that

---

[14] See p. 126.

[15] It is perhaps curious that van Dijk translates "contestations" as "determination": Pieter van Dijk, "The interpretation of civil rights and obligations by the European Court of Human Rights – one more step to take" in Franz Matscher and Herbert Petzold (eds.), *Protecting Human Rights: the European Dimension* (Köln, Carl Heymanns Verlag KG, 1990) at 133. No doubt a dispute suggests that there will be a determination, but that determination will not necessarily be decisive of the right in question (see p. 97 below). Nor does a result which is decisive necessarily flow only from a dispute. Nevertheless, *Ringeisen* v. *Austria (No 1)* (1971) 1 EHRR 455 conflates the two: ". . .the French expression 'contestation. . .' covers all proceedings the result of which is decisive for private rights and obligations. The English text, 'determination. . .' confirms this interpretation".

[16] E.g. *Georgiadis* v. *Greece* (1997) 24 EHRR 606, para 30.

[17] *Le Compte, van Leuven and De Meyere* v. *Belgium* (1981) 4 EHRR 1, para 45.

the applicants had committed professional misconduct and the applicants denied that was the case.[18]

The relatively relaxed approach to whether or not a dispute exists was taken one step further in *Moreira de Azevedo* v. *Portugal.*[19] The applicant, who was the victim of a shooting incident, intervened in criminal proceedings relating to the incident. He said his intervention incorporated an implied claim for compensation. However, the Portuguese government insisted that an express application should have been made in order for a dispute to arise. The applicant's argument prevailed. The Court's view was that:

> the right to a fair trial holds so prominent a place in a democratic society that there can be no justification for interpreting Article 6.1. . .restrictively . . . In so far as the French word . . . would appear to require the existence of a dispute, *if indeed it does at all*, the facts of the case show that there was one (our emphasis).[20]

It can be seen that the threshold to asserting a dispute is a low one. However, it was not crossed in the case of *Fayed* v. *UK*.[21] This case is considered in more detail below. Further principles adopted by the European Court in its consideration of whether or not a dispute existed were detailed in *Benthem* v. *Netherlands*.[22]

- A dispute may relate not only to "the actual existence of a right" but also to its scope or the manner in which it may be exercised.[23]
- It may consider both "questions of fact" and "questions of law".[24]
- The dispute must be genuine and of a serious nature.

(That proceedings should be "decisive" is dealt with below).

---

[18] *Le Compte*, para 45

[19] (1990) 13 EHRR 721.

[20] *Moreira de Azevedo*, para 66.

[21] (1994) 18 EHRR 393.

[22] (1985) 8 EHRR 1 at para 32.

[23] In *Benthem*, the actual existence of the right to a licence was disputed: para 33. However, in *Le Compte* the issue was the manner in which the beneficiary of the right could avail himself of it. (He had been suspended, interfering with his right to exercise his medical profession: para 49.)

[24] "Article 6.1 draws no distinction between questions of fact and questions of law. Both categories of question are equally crucial for the outcome of proceedings relating to 'civil rights and obligations'. Hence, the right to a court and the right to a judicial determination of the dispute cover questions of fact just as much as questions of law": *Le Compte*, para 51(b).

"ARGUABLE" RIGHTS

The Court has frequently repeated that there must be an *arguable* right in domestic law as well as an arguable dispute.[25] This is distinct from the question of whether or not the right is a "civil" right for the purposes of the Convention; this latter question "is not to be interpreted solely by reference to the respondent State's domestic law".[26] So, in *Salerno* v. *Italy*[27] (a case concerning payments made to a notaries' pension fund) the European Court stated: "Article 6 paragraph 1. . . extends to 'contestations' (disputes) over (civil) 'rights' which can be said, at least on arguable grounds, to be recognised under domestic law, irrespective of whether they are also protected under the Convention". The Italian Government submitted the case was not arguable because a previous action by Salerno had "by implication" determined that there was no right to repayment of contributions paid to the notaries' fund. However, the European Court decided that there was an arguable right in that the Italian courts had "acknowledged that the applicant's arguments were sufficiently tenable,[28] since they held the action to be admissible".[29]

Nevertheless, the judges of the Court have not been unanimous in the requirement for an arguable right in domestic law. In a concurring opinion in *Salerno* Judge Martens disputed the majority's reasoning on the basis that arguability, on the facts of the case, was immaterial. He stated:

> making the applicability of Article 6 . . . conditional on whether or not the applicant's claim as to (civil) rights and obligations is "arguable" is

---

[25] *Georgiadis* v. *Greece* (1997) 24 EHRR 606, para 30; and see pp. 110–112 below. In *Georgiadis* the Code of Criminal Procedure created a right for a person who had been detained to claim compensation following acquittal, unless it was established that person was "intentionally or by gross negligence" responsible for his detention. The army tribunals held the applicant could not claim because he had been grossly negligent. The European Court held that "it cannot be denied that the outcome of the. . .proceedings was directly decisive for establishing the applicant's right". It went on to hold that the right to compensation was "by its very nature" of a civil character.

[26] *Georgiadis* v. *Greece*, para 34; see generally, p. 121 below.

[27] 12 October 1992, App. No. 11955/86.

[28] Other cases also recite this test: see *Salerno* v. *Italy*, para 4.2 of the concurring opinion.

[29] *Salerno*, paras 14 to 16.

justified – if at all – only where the complaint to the Convention institutions concerns lack of access to a tribunal. . .Where the applicant
protests that the national court which has adjudicated on his claim
lacked independence, was not impartial, denied him a public hearing,
did not decide within a reasonable time or otherwise disregarded principles of a fair hearing there is no room for the "arguability" test.[30]

In any event, Article 6 will not be applicable if the decision at issue is
purely a matter of discretion, since no "right" arises.[31] An alternative
scenario is that a right arises in some circumstances but is subject to
exclusions in others.[32] This is debated, by reference to recent cases, in
the last part of this chapter.

DETERMINATION

Article 6 covers all disputes[33] relating to "civil rights and obligations" as
long as the result is "decisive" of the right/obligation. A tenuous
connection or remote consequence is not enough. Rather "civil rights
and obligations must be the object – or one of the objects – of the

[30] Paragraph 2 of the concurring opinion. The rest of the judgment explains the
genesis of, and unnecessary nature of, the "arguability" test. Having set out the history,
Judge Martens underlines: "In the context of a complaint about lack of access the test,
however open to criticism, may be indispensable in order to enable the Convention
institutions to control whether the applicant is a victim. . .Where the applicant has in
fact had access to a court which has decided on the merits of his claim, such control is
superfluous, with the result that it is not necessary to resort to a test which is open to
serious criticism": para 4.1. He emphasises that "violations of general principles of the
proper administration of justice have nothing to do with the quality of the claim
brought before the courts. The hearing of non-arguable claims must also be fair": para
4.3. Judge Martens went further in his concurring opinion in *Fayed* v. *UK* (1994) 18
EHRR 393, doubting whether there was any point in maintaining the "arguable-claim"
test unless the domestic law clearly and fully excluded such a right: para 7.
[31] E.g. *Masson and van Zon* v. *Netherlands* (1995) 22 EHRR 491, paras 50-2 (there
was no "right" where a public authority merely had an equitable discretion to award
compensation).
[32] E.g. *Powell and Rayner* v. *UK* (1990) 12 EHRR 355 (the applicants did not have a
substantive right because a statutory exclusion prevented them from bringing an action in relation to noise nuisance caused by overflying aircraft: para 36). See further p. 110–112 below.
[33] Proceedings to which the Article applies include those of constitutional courts:
e.g. *Pammel* v. *Germany* (1997) 26 EHRR 100. The nature of the proceedings does not
suffice to remove them from the ambit of the Article: *Pierre-Bloch* v. *France* (1997) 26
EHRR 202. (However, Article 6 did not apply in *Pierre-Bloch* as the right to stand for
election was a political right and not a civil one).

'contestation' (dispute); the result of the proceedings must be directly decisive for such a right".[34]

So, where the labour courts of Austria were unable to examine the dismissal of an employee because the dismissal had already been authorised by an administrative body ("the Board"), the Board's preliminary finding was decisive for the applicant's civil rights and Article 6.1 was applicable.[35] However, the outcome of the proceedings was not decisive in *Hamer* v. *France*.[36] At first sight this case seems similar to *Moreira de Azevedo*, in that the applicant intervened in criminal proceedings and then sought to allege that such intervention gave her a right to compensation. In *Hamer*, though, the Court noted that French law did not absolve the applicant from making a separate claim for financial reparation. At no stage had the applicant claimed damages. Nor had she made known any intention of so doing. The outcome of the criminal proceedings was not therefore decisive of a right, because no right had been asserted. (Similarly, there was no "dispute" over a civil right).[37]

Proceedings relating to a request for a permanent discharge from a psychiatric hospital by a person already provisionally discharged were held by the Commission not to concern a determination of civil rights and obligations.[38] Nor do investigations into a company's affairs under a regulatory system.[39] However, proceedings relating to a preliminary point on liability,[40] costs[41] or the amount of damages[42] are "decisive" for the purposes of Article 6.

---

[34] *Le Compte, van Leuven and De Meyere* v. *Belgium*, para 47.

[35] *Obermeier* v. *Austria* (1990) 13 EHRR 290.

[36] (1996) 23 EHRR 1, para 77.   [37] *Hamer* v. *France*, paras 73 to 79.

[38] Application 10801/84, *L* v. *Sweden*, Report of the Commission, 3 October 1988, para 87. (This decision is perhaps more related to there being no civil right or obligation at issue, the applicant having already been discharged).

[39] *Fayed* v. *UK* (1994) 18 EHRR 393. See also *Saunders* v. *UK* (1996) 23 EHRR 313 where, although the pleadings had not suggested that Article 6.1 was applicable to the proceedings conducted by the Inspectors, the Court nevertheless took the opportunity to restate its previous finding in *Fayed* that the Inspectors' functions were essentially investigative in nature.

[40] *Obermeier* v. *Austria*. The lawfulness of the applicant's dismissal constituted a decisive preliminary question to the proceedings on the revocation of his suspension, and Article 6 therefore applied.

[41] *Robins* v. *UK* (1997) 26 EHRR 527. The costs proceedings, even though separately decided, were a continuation of the substantive litigation and accordingly were part of the determination of civil rights and obligations.

[42] *Silva Pontes* v. *Portugal* (1994) 18 EHRR 156.

The Fayed case

In many cases, there is so obviously a dispute and determination that the Court does not even consider whether these elements are satisfied. Rather, in so far as the applicability of Article 6 is concerned, the Court is more concerned about whether or not the right at issue is a "civil" right.[43] However, as already noted, there are also cases where the failure to show a dispute and/or determination prevents Article 6 coming into play. An example is the case of *Fayed* v. *UK*.[44] The three applicants, brothers including Mohammed Al Fayed, acquired ownership of the House of Fraser in March 1985. In April 1987 the Government appointed two inspectors to investigate the take-over. A report of the investigation was published in March 1990. The applicants complained that, in violation of Article 6.1, the report had determined their civil rights to honour and reputation and had denied them effective access to a court to determine this civil right.

In considering whether the applicants were entitled to a hearing, the European Court emphasised that, in order for Article 6.1 to apply, there must be a dispute over a civil right or obligation, and the result of the proceedings must be directly decisive of such right or obligation. In the Court's view neither requirement was satisfied. The object of the proceedings before the inspectors had not been to resolve any dispute between the applicants and the inspectors, the applicants and the Secretary of State or the applicants and Lonrho (the public company which had opposed the take-over and which had subsequently campaigned against the applicants). Nor did the report determine the applicants' civil right to a good reputation – which right was accepted as a civil right – nor was its result directly decisive for such right.[45] However, the Court found that there was arguably a dispute recognised under domestic law in so far as the applicants alleged that they had no right to a court to bring proceedings in defamation against the inspectors because of the defence of qualified privilege.[46] (The Court found that any interference was justified). The decision of the Court is interesting for several reasons:

---

[43] E.g. *Ringeisen* v. *Austria (No. 1)* (1971) 1 EHRR 455 where, despite reciting the requirement that the proceedings be decisive, the main focus of the Court was on whether the application of rules of administrative law was decisive for the parties' relations in civil law: para 94.

[44] (1994) 18 EHRR 393. [45] *Fayed*, paras 55 to 63. [46] *Fayed*, paras 66 to 68.

- It emphasises that, even though a civil right exists, Article 6.1 will not apply without a dispute that arguably exists in national law, which dispute is directly decisive of such a right.
- However, it also shows that the Court is apparently susceptible to policy arguments in making even this decision, since it "explained" its findings in policy terms. It said that acceptance of the applicants' argument would unduly hamper the effective regulation in the public interest of complex financial and commercial activities since the publication of any report of a similar inquiry was liable to damage the reputation of the individuals whose conduct was being investigated. As a result, investigative proceedings such as those in *Fayed* fell outside Article 6.1.
- It can therefore be questioned as to how far the Court was swayed by such policy considerations. If the definition of dispute in *Le Compte* is applied, all that is necessary is an allegation of professional misconduct which is denied. Arguably, that is analogous to the *Fayed* position.[47]
- As to whether or not such a dispute was sufficiently decisive for the applicants' civil right to a good reputation (rather than such an outcome being a "remote consequence")[48] it could be argued it was so decisive *precisely because* any such publication "is liable to damage the reputation of the individuals whose conduct is being investigated".[49]
- In addition, on the facts of *Fayed*, there was no opportunity to "cure" the determination because any recourse by the applicants against the Inspectors was prevented by the defence of qualified privilege. (Similarly, no further action was taken against the applicants – for example, by the Secretary of State or the Takeover Panel – which

---

[47] The principal question addressed by the Inspectors "can be reduced to whether the Fayed brothers had dishonestly misled the authorities and the public in order to obtain government clearance and acceptance by the [House of Fraser] Board of their bid": para 60. "The Inspectors' published findings – that the applicants had indeed made dishonest representations concerning their origins, their wealth, their business interests and their resources and had thereafter knowingly submitted false evidence to the Inspectors – undoubtedly damaged the applicants' reputations".

[48] *Fayed*, para 56.

[49] This is a more tenuous link than in *Le Compte* where the outcome of the misconduct proceedings was suspension, and the right relied on was the right to exercise a profession. Nevertheless, it is strongly arguable that the outcome complained of in *Fayed* (the damage to reputation) was sufficiently connected with the Inspectors' proceedings: it was certainly not remote.

might have enabled the applicants to advance their case). With hindsight, it is certainly arguable that the report effectively determined the applicants' right to a good reputation without the procedural guarantees of Article 6.1 being respected.[50]

The English courts

There may be proceedings in the English courts where a dispute as such does not arise – for example, a party seeking an advisory declaration – yet it would be surprising if Article 6 did not apply. However, there is every sign that the English courts will follow Strasbourg in the requirement for a determination. In *R* v. *Secretary of State for Health, ex p C*, the Court of Appeal followed *Fayed* in deciding that inclusion in a list of people about whom there are doubts as to their suitability to work with children was not determinative of an individual's rights and obligations.[51] This was despite the fact that the Protection of Children Act 1999 will give a person included in the list the right of appeal to a tribunal (presumably on the basis that the decision to include an individual would fall foul of Article 6 unless such a right was granted).[52]

CIVIL RIGHTS AS "PRIVATE RIGHTS"?

From the early decisions of the European Commission and Court

---

[50] The Court does not seem to have addressed itself to the obvious difference between reports published only to the parties, which form the basis of further proceedings – in which case concerns can be fully addressed in those proceedings– and release to the *public*, without any opportunity of further consideration.

[51] [2000] 1 FLR 627.

[52] Hale LJ, with whom Lord Mustill and Lord Woolf, agreed, stated:

"Inclusion in the Index does have a significant impact upon this appellant's chances of obtaining employment, but it does not interfere with his right to apply for or accept such employment. Indeed, the Index should only be consulted at the stage when the decision has been reached to offer full employment. Inclusion does encourage the prospective employer to become fully informed as to previous relevant events in the applicant's life, but no-one can suggest that those events are not relevant, indeed highly relevant, in this situation. It does not disclose what those relevant events were, unless there is a conviction. It leaves the decision as to whether to pursue the matter and what to make of those events to the prospective employer".

Nevertheless, she expressed "no view" on the lawfulness of the list after the substantive provisions of the Human Rights Act 1998 come into force on 2 October 2000, and noted that "in any event the Department has a solution readily to hand".

onwards, the reference in Article 6.1 to "civil" rights and obligations has been taken, or assumed, to refer to "private" rights and obligations rather than rights and obligations arising in a "public" or "administrative" law context. From the perspective of English courts applying the Human Rights Act, this identification of "civil" with "private" is likely to raise difficult and far reaching issues of interpretation of the ambit of Article 6. These difficulties arise in part from the unfamiliarity, from a common law perspective, of the concept of a body of "civil rights" which excludes from its scope rights arising in public or administrative law, but also from the sheer uncertainty and obscurity of the Strasbourg case-law (as van Dijk has put it, that the case-law is "vague and even unclear" is simply "not a matter of debate").[53] The European Court has resolutely declined to offer any abstract definition of, or conceptual framework for, the term "civil rights and obligations", and has instead proceeded by a piecemeal, case by case development which might be said to be in the worst traditions of the common law were it not for the fact that the concept of "civil" rights so clearly shows a civilian inheritance.[54]

As well as seeking to unravel the Strasbourg case-law , it is important to consider also the likely or possible responses of the English courts to the definitional problems of the concept of a "civil right or obligation". There are a number of reasons for anticipating that, even giving full weight to the statutory injunction contained in section 2 of the Human Rights Act 1998 that the courts "must take into account" the jurisprudence of the Court and Commission, the English courts will be at liberty, should they so choose, to develop an approach which is distinctive from, or at the very least more clearly articulated than, that which emerges from Strasbourg.[55] First, the lack of a clear principled approach in the Strasbourg case-law itself means that the domestic

[53] Pieter van Dijk, "The interpretation of 'civil rights and obligations' by the European Court of Human Rights – one more step to take" in Franz Matscher and Herbert Petzold (eds.), *Protecting Human Rights: the European Dimension* (Köln, Carl Heymanns Verlag KG, 1990) at 133.

[54] Or more respectfully described as "an inductive approach": Anthony Lester and David Pannick (eds.), *Human Rights Law and Practice* (London, Butterworths, 1999), at 4.6.10.

[55] For present purposes, it matters little whether the English courts seek to proceed by elaborating and developing the Strasbourg case-law, or by self-consciously developing a domestic approach offering wider protection for "civil rights and obligations". The former route is certainly open to the courts, given the unsettled nature of the Strasbourg case-law, discussed below.

courts will inevitably be faced with factual situations which cannot be answered by a straightforward application of Convention principles. Secondly, as noted above, in such cases the courts will have to operate within an unfamiliar concept of a "civil" right (as distinct from a public or administrative right), which does not correspond to any pre-existing common law distinction; as we shall see, the distinction does not approximate to the "public/private divide" familiar from the *O'Reilly* v. *Mackman*[56] line of authority. Thirdly, since we believe that the real issue for the English courts will be whether to give a *more* expansionist interpretation of a "civil right or obligation" than that adopted in Strasbourg – i.e. whether to accord to a wider range of rights and inter-ests the protection offered by Article 6.1 – there will be no institutional constraint upon the development of an approach which differs from the Strasbourg case-law.[57] A concept of a civil right which was *narrower* than that of the European Court would risk leaving the United Kingdom in breach of the Convention and would presumably not take "due account" of the Strasbourg jurisprudence as required by section 2 of the Human Rights Act 1998; there is no similar constraint on a concept which is *wider*.

Before turning to the Strasbourg case-law, it is worth anticipating the argument below, and noting the policy tensions which perhaps under-score the cautious approach of the European Commission and Court to the interpretation of the concept of "civil right and obligation", and which stand in the way of a straightforward expansionist interpretation by the domestic courts. The key concern has always been that the protections offered by Article 6.1, where it applies, are relatively far reaching and difficult to satisfy, conferring a greater and more inflexible level of protection than that usually required by domestic principles of natural justice or fairness. The requirement that there be an indepen-dent and impartial tribunal, in particular, immediately "externalises" the decision-making process, requiring that the decision be made or reviewed by a person or body outside the control of the relevant author-ity or organ of the State.

---

[56] [1983] 2 AC 237.
[57] Because, as the Lord Chancellor has (perhaps optimistically) put it, section 2(1) permits the UK courts to depart from existing Strasbourg decisions and "on occasion it might well be appropriate to do so, and it is possible that they might give a successful lead to Strasbourg" (Debate at Committee Stage, 583 HL, Official Report (5th series), cols. 514-15 (18 November 1997).

A "natural"[58] interpretation of Article 6.1 runs the risk, it has been suggested, of conferring these far-reaching procedural protections upon inappropriately wide categories of "discretionary" rights and obligations. And this concern is, it is suggested, all the greater because the European Court by its judgment in *Golder* and following cases gave a liberal interpretation to another aspect of Article 6.1, in holding that it "secures to everyone the right to have any claim relating to his civil rights and obligations brought before a court or tribunal". In other words, the application of Article 6.1 is not restricted to those rights and obligations which national law *permits* to be brought before a court or tribunal.[59] Article 6.1 thus secures the right of *access* to a Court, whatever national law may specify.

It was, it has been suggested, at least partly a reaction to the *Golder* line of cases that led the European Court to balance the expansive autonomous interpretation of a "right or obligation" with a narrowly confined approach to the meaning of a "civil" right, so as to shield from the scope of the Article substantial areas of "public law" decision- making which might not meet the procedural requirements of Article 6. Domestic courts will be faced with the same policy constraints. The "autonomous" *Golder* conception of a "right or obligation" is plainly applicable to domestic interpretation of Article 6.1, so that even where English law does not provide for a judicial "determination" of the claimed right or obligation, Article 6.1 will potentially apply. Accordingly, if the English courts give a wide interpretation to "civil" rights and obligations, it may follow that a wide range of discretionary "public law" decisions are opened up to the requirement that the applicant is entitled to a "fair and public hearing within a reasonable time by an independent and impartial tribunal established by law".

In the final part of this section, we consider whether the English courts need shrink from such a result. We explore the extent to which other mechanisms may be available to forestall or prevent an undesirable formalisation and juridification of decision-making by the undiluted

---

[58] On the face of it, the word "civil", particularly given its juxtaposition to the word "criminal" in the same phrase, might "naturally" be taken to include within its scope all rights and/or obligations which exist under the law of the Contracting State which are not criminal in character: see n. 93 *infra*.

[59] *Golder* v. *UK* (1975) 1 EHRR 524, para 35 et seq; *Sporrong and Lonnnroth* v. *Sweden* (1982) 5 EHRR 35.

application of the Article 6.1 requirements. In particular, we consider
(a) the apparent distinction drawn in the European Court's recent case-
law between "unfettered" discretionary decisions and situations where
the discretionary element of the decision is structured and confined;
and (more importantly) (b) the fact that the Court has increasingly
shown a readiness to take into account the availability and ambit of any
appeal or review from the impugned decision in assessing the overall
compliance of national law with Article 6.1. If, in particular, the availability of judicial review satisfies the requirements of Article 6.1, then a
wider interpretation of "civil rights and obligations" (so as to cover
"public law rights") might have a relatively small practical effect. It is,
however, still uncertain how far judicial review (at least in its traditional
form) can go to satisfy the requirements of Article 6.1. It may be that it
is only if domestic courts are willing to develop and extend "heightened
scrutiny" in cases engaging Convention rights that Article 6.1 will be
satisfied.

The first part of the following section contains a brief survey of the
Strasbourg case-law. There then follows an analysis of the potential
response of the English courts to the interpretative choices which await
them, and the implications of a wide definition of "civil rights".

The Reasoning of the Strasbourg Case-Law

In interpreting the requirement that an application concern a "civil"
right or obligation, the European Court has, from its early decisions,
assumed that "civil" extends (at least) to "private" rights and obligations.[60] The repeated identification of "civil" with "private" makes it
tempting to interpret the two as synonymous, but the Court has
repeatedly declined to attempt a comprehensive interpretation or
abstract definition of the phrase,[61] and has declined to rule out the
possibility that civil rights may include rights which are not
private.[62]

---

[60] See, for example, *Ringeisen* v. *Austria (No. 1)* (1971) 1 EHRR 455 at para 94.

[61] *Benthem* v. *Netherlands* (1985) 8 EHRR 1 at para 35; *Feldbrugge* v. *Netherlands*
(1986) 8 EHRR 425 at para 27 ("Court does not consider that it has to give on this occasion an abstract definition"); *Deumeland* v. *Germany* (1986) 8 EHRR 448 at para 61.

[62] *Konig* v. *Germany* (1978) 2 EHRR 170 at para 95 (not necessary "in the present
case to decide whether the concept . . . extends beyond those rights which have a private
nature . . ."); *Le Compte, van Leuven and De Meyere* v. *Belgium* (1981) 4 EHRR 1 at para

The Court has still, more than twenty years after *Konig* and almost thirty years after *Ringeisen*, declined directly to answer this question of interpretation, and has instead proceeded by seeking to identify ever-increasing categories of case in which, although the dispute is not wholly "private", the protection of "civil" rights and obligations is still engaged as being at least related to "private" rights. Seeking to summarise shortly what is a very complex body of case-law :

(a) "Civil" rights and obligations are not restricted to civil litigation between private individuals.[63]

(b) Whether "civil rights and obligations" are engaged does not turn on categorisation of the right (still less the proceedings) under domestic law: the concept is autonomous, and there may be a determination of a "civil right" even if the law or right does not fall under the "civil law" of the Contracting State.[64] The general principles of domestic law of the Contracting Parties are, however, relevant in interpreting the meaning of the concept under the Convention.[65]

(c) Article 6.1 thus extends to "all proceedings the result of which is decisive for private rights and obligations", even if the form of those proceedings is, according to national law, administrative or otherwise "non-private".[66] Many of the cases have thus turned on the

---

48. The Court probably came closest to identifying civil rights with private rights in *Schouten and Meldrum* v. *Netherlands* (1994) 19 EHRR 432, although even there the identification was tentative and *obiter*; see n. 63 *infra*.

[63] *Ringeisen*, at para 94 (overturning view of the Commission); *Konig*, at para 90.

[64] In the phrase repeated in many cases, "the concept of 'civil rights and obligations' cannot be interpreted solely by reference to the domestic law of the respondent State": *Konig*, at paras 88-9. It is, however, a requirement that there be in issue *some kind* of arguable right under domestic law, even if not (according to domestic law) a civil right: see *Fayed* v. *UK* (1994) 18 EHRR 393, at paras 65 and 67; *Hamer* v. *France* (1996) 23 EHRR 1 at para 73; and see above at p. 95 and below at pp.121–137.

[65] App. 1931/63, *X* v. *Austria*, 2 October 1964 (1964) 7 *Yearbook* 212 at 222; *Ringeisen*, at para 94; *Konig*, at para 88. As noted above, the Court has not, in fact, sought to develop an overarching definition of the concept, whether by reference to the law of the contracting parties or otherwise.

[66] *Ringeisen*, para 94; *Stran Greek Refineries and Stratis Andreadis* v. *Greece* (1994) 19 EHRR 293, para 39. Jacobs and White identify as the "key distinction" the difference between such cases and other cases where a legal relationship between private individuals is not affected, which will fall outside the scope of Article 6 (Francis Jacobs and Robin White, *The European Convention on Human Rights*, 2nd edn. (Oxford,

issue of whether the decision in question is decisive for (or, perhaps, affects) "private rights and obligations", even though the dispute has a public or administrative complexion. The Court has been increasingly ready to recognise that such "private" rights are engaged, even where the dispute is in substance as to a public or administrative decision. For example, in the context of licensing disputes:

(1) *Konig* itself concerned the withdrawal of an authorisation to practise medicine. The Court noted that the applicant's practice, through the operation of a clinic, was a commercial activity, carried on for profit, through contracts made with patients; this "resembles the exercise of a private right in some ways akin to the right of property".[67] Thus, even though the licence was withdrawn pursuant to administrative supervisory powers, the right at stake was a "private" and thus "civil" right.[68]

(2) *Pudas* v. *Sweden*[69] also involved the revocation of a licence, in this case to operate a taxi service on a specified route, the withdrawal taking place as part of an administrative reorganisation. The Court held that the licence was "one of the conditions for the exercise of his business activities":[70] a commercial activity based upon contractual relations between the licence holder and his customers. Thus the right was "civil".[71]

(3) Even a "first time applicant" for a licence may possess a civil right. In *Benthem* v. *Netherlands*,[72] an application for the grant

---

Clarendon Press, 1996) at 130). This distinction, of course, depends on the assumption that civil rights are equivalent to private rights: an assumption which has not (yet) been falsified, as noted above.

[67] *Konig*, at para 92.

[68] See similarly *Le Compte* (above) (suspension rather than withdrawal of licence), at para 48; *H* v. *Belgium* (1987) 10 EHRR 339, where the Court followed similar reasoning in respect of an advocate seeking readmission to the roll (at para 46); *De Moor* v. *Belgium* (1994) 18 EHRR 372 (enrolment of pupil advocate); *Diennet* v. *France* (1995) 21 EHRR 554.

[69] (1987) 10 EHRR 380.

[70] *Ibid.* at para 37.

[71] See similarly, *Tre Traktörer Aktiebolag* v. *Sweden* (1989) 13 EHRR 309 at paras 41-3 (restaurant's licence to sell alcoholic beverages was civil right, notwithstanding that authority entitled to revoke on specified grounds; that the licence was non-transferable; and that it constituted a means of "implementing social policy" within an "essential field of public law"); *Fischer* v. *Austria* (1995) 20 EHRR 349 (tipping licence).

[72] (1985) 8 EHRR 1.

of a statutory licence to operate an installation for the supply of liquefied petroleum gas was rejected (albeit on appeal, thereby "taking away" a right given at first instance). The Court held that this was a determination of the Applicant's civil right, because the grant of a licence was one of the preconditions for the exercise of part of his activities as a businessman. It was noted that the licence had a proprietary character, being closely associated with the right to use possessions in conformity with the law.[73]

(d) Similar reasoning has been employed outside the domain of licensing. The issues of social security and welfare benefits and contributions have been examined by the Court in a series of cases. *Feldbrugge* v. *Netherlands*[74] concerned a dispute over an entitlement to statutory sickness allowance. The Court accepted that there was no common European standard to "classify" such a right as private or public, and it recognised that in Dutch law, the entitlement would be regarded as a "public law right". Yet the Court still held the right to be "civil" in nature since, after conducting a "balancing process", the private law features predominated: the personal and economic nature of the right; the close connection of the right with the contract of employment; and the affinities with insurance under ordinary law.[75] Similar conclusions have been reached in

---

[73] *Ibid*, at para 36. Even an entitlement under national law to object to *another's* licence may constitute a "civil" right: *Zander* v. *Sweden* (1993) 18 EHRR 175 at paras 24-5, 27. The Court held that the Applicants' standing under national law to ask a licensing board to impose conditions (by way of precautionary measures) upon the grant of a licence to dump waste on neighbouring ground meant that they had an arguable right under national law not to have their land polluted; that right was a civil right as it was a facet of their right to their property.

[74] (1996) 8 EHRR 425.

[75] See similarly, *Deumeland* v. *Germany* (1986) 8 EHRR 448: claim for statutory widow's pension following death of husband in industrial accident was civil in nature. Private employment disputes are usually unquestionably disputes over civil rights: *Obermeier* v. *Austria* (1990) 13 EHRR 290. But the position is less clear-cut in relation to the employment of civil servants. The Court generally found in a number of cases that the balance in disputes relating to civil servants' "recruitment, careers and termination" takes such cases outside Article 6.1: *Argento* v. *Italy* (1997) 28 EHRR 719 at para 19 (dispute as to recruitment and career decision to assign to lower staff category on permanent recruitment did not concern a "civil" right); *Huber* v. *France* (1998) 26 EHRR 457 – although this has recently been the subject of sustained criticism; see e.g. Judge De Meyer in *Pierre-Bloch* v. *France* (1997) 26 EHRR 202 at 237 (para 1) and

relation to social insurance;[76] welfare assistance;[77] and liability to
make social security contributions.[78] Pension rights have also been
held to be "civil" in nature in a number of cases.[79] The welfare
(Salesi) and social insurance *(Schuler-Zgraggen)* cases are particularly significant, because they involved pecuniary claims which
depended wholly upon a statutory basis, being non-contributory
and non-employment related benefits. The Court's reasoning is
potentially capable of wide application; in *Schuler-Zgraggen* it held
that as a general rule, Article 6.1 applies in the field of "social insurance" because,

> . . . despite the public law features pointed out by the Government,
> the applicant . . . suffered an interference with her means of subsis-

footnote 95, and Judge Jambrek in *Maillard* v. *France* (1998) 27 EHRR 232. However,
the Court accepted that civil servants' disputes relating purely to remuneration issues
(*Lapalorcia* v. *Italy* (2 September 1997, para 21)) or to pension rights (*Massa* v. *Italy*
(1994) 18 EHRR 266; *Francesco Lombardo* v. *Italy* (1996) 21 EHRR 188; *Sussman* v.
Germany (1998) 25 EHRR 64 at para 42; *McGinley and Egan* v. *UK* (1998) 27 EHRR
1, at para 84) concern civil rights and fall within Article 6.1. Most recently, in *Pellegrin*
v. *France* (judgment of 8 December 1999), the Court has recognised that its own case-
law "contains a margin of uncertainty", and has sought to re-cast the distinction
between civil servants who are within and without the protection of Article 6.1, according to a new "functional criterion" based upon the nature of the employees' duties and
responsibilities: only employees in posts "involving participation in the exercise of
powers conferred by public law" are outside the scope of the Article (paras 64-7). This
radical attempt to escape from the existing case law perhaps surprisingly does not
contain any consideration of the reasons for excluding "public" employees from Article
6.1, nor does it contain any real justification for the functional test as enunciated.

[76] *Schuler –Zgraggen v.Switzerland* (1993) 16 EHRR 405, which concerned a statutory (non-contributory) invalidity pension.

[77] *Salesi* v. *Italy* (1993) 26 EHRR 187.

[78] *Schouten and Meldrum* v. *Netherlands* (1994) 19 EHRR 432. The Court recognised that a dispute as to contributions was different in nature from a dispute as to benefits (in particular, the reasoning as to entitlement to means of subsistence was
inapplicable) but nevertheless, after engaging in a similar balancing process to
Feldbrugge (at paras 52 to 59), held that the obligation to make contributions was
"civil". The Court distinguished, however, this obligation from the obligation to pay
taxes under tax legislation, and from other pecuniary obligations which are "otherwise a
part of the normal civic duties in a democratic society", which the Court tentatively
indicated ("*may* exist") would be considered as belonging exclusively to the realm of
public law and "accordingly" would be classified as non-civil (para 50).

[79] *Francesco Lombardo* v. *Italy* (1996) 21 EHRR 188; *Massa* v. *Italy* (1994) 18
EHRR 266; *Pauger* v. *Austria* (1997) 25 EHRR 105.

tence; she was claiming an individual economic right flowing from specific rules laid down in a federal statute.[80]

(e) Other rights found to be "civil" include not only rights over land[81] (unsurprisingly), but a variety of rights relating to land, such as a "right to build" notwithstanding building regulations and planning procedures which are firmly parts of a public law system.[82] The Court has also held family law rights by their nature to be civil,[83] as well as the right to reputation.[84]

Bradley has commented, in surveying the case-law, that "the Strasbourg Court is well on the way to recognising that there is a developing human right to administrative justice".[85] Certainly, the most significant point is not simply that the Court has still kept open the *possibility* of bringing within the scope of "civil" rights the formal category of "public" or administrative law rights. It is rather that as a matter of practice, it has classified as "private rights and obligations" (and hence as "civil") a wide swathe of entitlements created or located firmly within an administrative law context. In the welfare entitlement cases, in particular, it is difficult to see a real or genuine connection with a "private law" entitlement which can sustain the theory that "civil" rights only cover "private" rights, albeit in a public law context.[86] On the other hand, it is notable that the Strasbourg cases adopting the broader approach are all concerned with a claimed pecuniary benefit; it is a substantial further step to seek to apply them to

---

[80] *Schuler –Zgraggen v.Switzerland,* at para 46; cf. *Salesi* at para 19.

[81] *Sporrong and Lönnroth* v. *Sweden* (1982) 5 EHRR 35.

[82] *Allan Jacobsson* v. *Sweden* (1989) 12 EHRR 56 at para 73; cf. *Håkansson and Sturesson* v. *Sweden* (1990) 13 EHRR 1 at para 60; *Mats Jacobsson* v. *Sweden* (1990) 13 EHRR 79 at para 87; *Skarby* v. *Sweden* (1991) 13 EHRR 90; *Fredin* v. *Sweden* (1991) 13 EHRR 784 at para 63; *Bryan* v. *UK* (1995) 21 EHRR 342 at para 31.

[83] *Rasmussen* v. *Denmark* (1984) 7 EHRR 371 (paternity proceedings); *Airey* v. *Ireland* (1979) 2 EHRR 305 (legal aid in family proceedings); cf. *Keegan* v. *Ireland* (1994) 18 EHRR 342 (application for guardianship and custody by father).

[84] *Fayed* v. *UK* (1994) 18 EHRR 393.

[85] A.W. Bradley, "Administrative Justice: a Developing Human Right" (1995) 1 *European Public Law* 347.

[86] *Salesi* and *Schuler-Zgraggen, supra.* See also the recent decision in *Georgiadis* v. *Greece* (1997) 24 EHRR 406 at paras 34-5 where the Court held that a discretionary right created by the Greek Code of Criminal Procedure to compensation for an acquitted person for periods spent in detention was a "civil" right, notwithstanding that it concerned "public law issues".

non-pecuniary entitlements.[87] The question nevertheless arises: even on the Strasbourg case-law, is there any principled objection (outside possibly *sui generis* fields such as civil servants' conditions, and tax obligations) to the proposition that Article 6.1 presumptively applies to all interests capable of giving rise in national law to an application for judicial review or other similar administrative law recourse? Such a conclusion might, as we shall see, have substantial implications in imposing the rigid Article 6.1 protections upon categories of administrative law rights and obligations which most Contracting States have assumed may be protected by more flexible procedures (or in some cases, no procedures). But we should first note certain real constraints upon such a conclusion which do exist in the Strasbourg case-law.

Rights Held not to be "Civil" Rights

The first and most important limitation derives not from the definition of a "civil" right, but rather from the very definition of a "right" itself.[88] In a number of recent cases, the Court has re-asserted that it is a real precondition for the application of Article 6.1 that the applicant have an "arguable *right*": if the applicant's interest under national law is a mere hope or expectation, Article 6.1 is for that reason alone not applicable. This appears most clearly from two contrasting cases involving compensation claimed by an acquitted person for detention pending trial. In *Masson and Van Zon* v. *Netherlands*,[89] the applicants claimed compensation under a Dutch law which allowed them to recover in the criminal courts, the claim being determined on "equitable principles". The Court held that because the statute merely stated that, even if certain threshold conditions were met, the domestic court "may" (if it took the view that there were sufficient "reasons in equity") award compensation, "the grant to a public authority of such a measure of discretion indicates that no actual right is recognised in law".[90] By

87 See further below at pp. 113–114.
88 See above, pp. 95–96.
89 (1996) 22 EHRR 491; cf. *Gustafson* v. *Sweden* (1997) 25 EHRR 623.
90 (1997) 24 EHRR 406, at para 51. The case was more extreme, because there was a separate statutory entitlement (which the Applicants did not pursue) which provided that expenses "shall" be refunded to a suspect where certain conditions were met. The Court took the view that under *this* provision, a duty is imposed upon the State to reimburse expenses where the conditions were met, and a "right" arises: para 50.

contrast, in *Georgiadis* v. *Greece*[91] the Greek Code for Criminal Procedure was held to create a "right" to compensation under domestic law, subject only to certain conditions (excluding situations where the detained person was "intentionally or by gross negligence" responsible for his detention), and thus was held to be subject to Article 6.1.

The real difference between the two cases is surely no more than the extent to which the discretion to award compensation was structured and confined under national law. In each case, the applicant had an entitlement to apply for compensation, and the authority had a measure of discretion in assessing the claim. In one case, that discretion was a broad and unfettered one; in the other, it was closely confined to establishing that detention was not (in effect) the responsibility of the applicant. Other recent cases confirm this analysis. In *Allan Jacobsson* v. *Sweden*, the Court considered the argument that the wide discretion accorded to the administrative authorities by the Swedish Parliament in the grant of a building permit meant that the applicant could not claim any "right" to build before a permit had been granted. The Court found, however, that subject to meeting various statutory conditions (some relatively wide) he could arguably have claimed a permit as of right. As the Court put it:

> True, the issue of a permit under these circumstances would have involved the exercise of a certain discretion by the authorities, but their discretion would not have been unfettered: *they would have been bound by generally recognised legal and administrative principles.*[92] (emphasis added).

Similarly, in *Zander* v. *Sweden*, the applicants' standing in Swedish law to ask a Licensing Board to impose conditions upon a proposed permit in favour of a neighbouring occupier of land to dump waste was an entitlement which was sufficiently "concrete" to found a (civil) right.[93]

The practical extent of the apparent proposition that an "unfettered" discretion does not give rise to a "right" within Article 6.1 is unclear.

---

[91] (1997) 24 EHRR 606; followed in *Werner* v. *Austria; Szucs* v. *Austria* (1998) 26 EHRR 310 at paras 32-5, where the law conferred an entitlement to compensation for detention for an acquitted or freed person if "the suspicion that he committed the offence has been dispelled".

[92] (1989) 12 EHRR 56 at para 69; followed in *Mats Jacobsson* v. *Sweden* (1990) 13 EHRR 79 at paras 31-2. The same reasoning can be seen in cases involving the withdrawal of an existing entitlement: see *Tre Traktörer Aktiebolag* v. *Sweden* (1989) 13 EHRR 309 (withdrawal of licence did affect a "right" because the withdrawal was not an exercise of pure discretion; it could only be done on "structured" grounds).

[93] (1993) 18 EHRR 175 at para 24.

Almost every discretion, at least in English law, is now confined at least by "recognised legal and administrative principles" (quoting the words which in *Allan Jacobsson* were said to indicate that the discretion was fettered and therefore within the scope of Article 6.1).[94] On this basis, very few administrative powers would escape the reach of Article 6. According any wider ambit to the concept of an "unfettered discretion" would appear to reincarnate the uncomfortable distinction between "rights" and "mere privileges" which existed in English law[95] until "scotched" by *Ridge* v. *Baldwin*[96] and *Re HK*.[97] But, as noted below, it must be recognised that this distinction would in principle provide a way out (however unattractive it might appear) from what the Court evidently sees as the dangerous prospect of subjecting all administrative law rights to the rigours of Article 6.1. For this reason, a further expansion of the category of "civil" rights may increase the temptation restrictively to define what is a "right" at all.

The case-law reveals two other apparent limitations upon the scope of a "civil" right. In *Pierre-Bloch* v. *France* (1997),[98] the Court held that the right to stand for election to the National Assembly in France, and hence all disputes related thereto (including disputes as to limitations on election expenditure and consequent forfeiture of the applicant's seat) was a "political" one and not a "civil" one within the meaning of Article 6.1, notwithstanding the obvious pecuniary interests of the applicant at stake. No justification was given for this distinction, and it is hard not to sympathise with the powerful dissent of Judge De Meyer, who pointed out that the distinction between civil and political rights is "strange in itself if one considers the etymology of the two adjectives, seeing that the Latin words from which the former is derived (*civile, civis, civitas*) and the Greek words from which the latter is derived (*politikon, politis, politeia*) mean the same thing".[99]

---

[94] Perhaps excluding only cases where the decision is "non-justiciable"; see, in that regard, p. 118 below.

[95] See *Nakkdua Ali* v. *Jayaratne* [1951] AC 66; *R* v. *Metropolitan Police Commissioner, ex p Parker* [1953] 1 WLR 1150 and similar cases; cf. de Smith, Woolf and Jowell, *Judicial Review of Administrative Action*, 5th edn. (London, Sweet & Maxwell, 1995) at para 7-029.

[96] [1964] AC 40.   [97] [1967] 2 QB 617, 630, 631.

[98] (1997) 26 EHRR 202 at paras 50-1.

[99] *Ibid.* at paras 1-2 of the dissent. As it stands, the decision would appear to exclude from the scope of Article 6 domestic rights under the Representation of the People Acts;

It is similarly difficult to understand the reasoning of the Commission in the application *Adams and Benn* v. *UK*,[100] that Gerry Adams' right under Article 8A(1) of the EC Treaty[101] to move and reside freely within the Community was not, even if the right was directly effective in domestic law, a civil right within Article 6.1. The Commission suggested that a treaty provision providing in general terms for freedom of movement was of a "public law nature, having regard to the origin and general nature of the provision, which lacks the economic or individual aspects which are characteristic to the private law sphere". It is surely open to question whether the guarantee of free-dom of movement can be said to lack the necessary economic aspect, given both the purpose of the Treaty and its application by the European Court of Justice. The decision could be interpreted as excluding from the definition of a civil right all inchoate or non "personal" rights, but this may be to over-state the significance of the Commission's view, particularly given the Commission's long-standing tradition of interpreting Article 6.1 even more restrictively than the Court.[102]

To sum up the state of the Strasbourg case-law, a principle does appear to be developing that "public law" entitlements (or at least those which are not in the pure and unfettered discretion of the relevant authority) are civil rights for the purpose of Article 6.1 – but only, thus far, as regards pecuniary rights.[103] Indeed, cases such as *Pierre-Bloch* and *Adams* suggest that the Strasbourg organs are still instinctively

---

and, arguably, access to Court in fact situations such as *R* v. *Broadcasting Complaints Commission, ex p Owen* [1985] QB 1153; *R* v. *Rowe, ex p Mainwaring* [1992] 1 WLR 1059 (corrupt election practice).

[100] Application 28979/95 and 30343/96, relying upon *Schouten and Meldrum, supra* n. 78.

[101] See now EC Treaty (as amended by Treaty of Amsterdam), Article 18.

[102] See also decisions of the Court on the admission and expulsion of aliens: App 2991 and 2992/66 *Alam, Kahn and Singh* v. *UK* 10 *Yearbook* 478; *Uppal* v. *UK* (1980) 3 EHRR 391. But see, recently, App 4222/98 *J.E.D.* v. *UK* (admissibility decision of the Court, 2 February 1999), where the Court expressly held open the possibility that the guarantees contained in Article 6 could apply to the judicial review procedures by which the Applicant had challenged the rejection of his asylum request (but held, unnecessary to consider because those procedures satisfied the requirements of Article 6.1).

[103] See, in addition to the cases referred to above, *Editions Periscope* v. *France* (1992) 14 EHRR 597; *Procola* v. *Luxembourg* (1995) 22 EHRR 193; *Werner* v. *Austria, supra*, at para 347 ("For a right to be a 'civil' one, it is *sufficient* that the subject-matter of the

suspicious of any attempt to broaden "civil rights" even to include "public" entitlements having an indirect pecuniary effect – unless the right is separately recognised under the Convention, such as the right to reputation.

Application to English Law

The uncertain state of the Strasbourg case-law makes it difficult to predict the likely attitude of the English courts to the equivalent provision of the Human Rights Act 1998. But the difficulty is also conceptual, because the distinction between "civil" rights and "public" or "administrative law" rights is not one which is familiar to English lawyers. It is quite plain, from the cases reviewed above, that the distinction does not even approximately correspond to the public/private divide as enunciated in *O'Reilly* v. *Mackman,*[104] either in its original incarnation or as more recently softened by successive decisions.[105] There is some precedent for a distinction between "civil" and "public" rights in domestic law: section 38(2) of the Crown Proceedings Act 1947 provides that for the purposes of the Act, "civil proceedings"

> includes proceedings in the High Court or the county court for the recovery of fines or penalties, *but does not include proceedings on the Crown side of the King's Bench Division.*[106]

But that distinction is principally a procedural or remedial one, and is therefore of limited assistance because, as we have seen, the European Court has repeatedly stressed that the procedural allocation of the right

action should be pecuniary and that the action should be founded on an alleged infringement of rights which are likewise pecuniary rights"). In other cases, however, the Court has continued to stress that even though a dispute is "pecuniary" in nature, that may *not* be sufficient to bring it within Article 6: *Schouten and Meldrum, supra,* at para 57; *Pierre-Bloch, supra,* at para 51; *Pellegrin* v. *France* (8 December 1999), para 60.

[104] [1983] 2 AC 237.

[105] See e.g. *Roy* v. *Kensington Chelsea and Westminster Family Practitioner Committee* [1992] 1 AC 624; *British Steel plc* v. *Customs & Excise Commissioners* [1997] 2 All ER 366; *Trustees of Dennis Rye Pension Fund* v. *Sheffield City Council* [1998] 1 WLR 840.

[106] See also the analysis in *M* v. *Home Office* [1994] 1 AC 377, where Lord Woolf analysed separately the availability of injunctive relief against the Crown in "civil" proceedings and in judicial review proceedings where a prerogative order was sought.

to an administrative forum is of little concern compared with the nature of the right itself. For similar reasons, the fact that Order 53 is now located under the umbrella of the "Civil Procedure Rules" is surely of little significance.[107]

It is suggested that a more fundamental reason for the English courts to distrust the distinction is that, even on its own terms, it is open to serious question. Van Dijk[108] has built a powerful case, based upon a landmark article by Newman examining the antecedents of the Convention,[109] showing that the framers of the Convention, like the framers of the equivalent provisions of the International Covenant on Civil and Political Rights and the Universal Declaration of Human Rights, did not intend to make a distinction between "public" and "private" rights. Rather, the word "civil" was simply used, as might be guessed from a straightforward linguistic analysis of the Article, in contradistinction to the word "criminal" in the same sentence.[110]

Van Dijk also points out that the distinction is not a familiar one to Continental systems of law any more than in England. As Judge De Meyer has put it, in his dissenting Opinion in *Pierre-Bloch*, the distinction (like that between civil and political rights),

has all too often served to remove from the scope of the ordinary law situations affecting the exercise of what is called public authority (*puissance publique*) and to reduce the scope of the protection of citizens in

---

[107] See further, Dawn Oliver, *Common Values and the Public-Private Divide* (London, Butterworths, 1999): academics are also questioning the validity of traditional dichotomies between the spheres of public and private law.

[108] "The interpretation of 'civil rights and obligations' by the European Court of Human Rights – one more step to take", at 131 in Franz Matscher and Herbert Petzold (eds.), *Protecting Human Rights: the European Dimension* (Köln, Carl Heymanns Verlag KG, 1990).

[109] Newman, "Natural Justice, Due Process and the New International Covenants on Human Rights: Prospectus" [1967] *PL* 274.

[110] See van Dijk's conclusion (n. 108 *supra*) at 137: "From this legal history one cannot draw any other conclusion than that it was not the intention of the drafters to restrict the scope of Article 14 of the [ICCPR], apart from determinations of a criminal law character, to determinations of rights and obligations of a private law character. On the contrary, one is struck by the fact that proposals whose wording might have entailed the risk of such a restriction, were criticised for that reason and rejected or amended". At pp 137-148 van Dijk demonstrates that the intentions of Article 14 of the Covenant were effectively carried over in to Article 6 of the Convention.

relation to such situations . . . Are "civil" rights . . . not essentially, in the most literal meaning of the term, the rights of the citizen (*civis*)?[111]

Van Dijk therefore advocates that the Court "should take that one further step which would remove the existing uncertainty [*sc.* expressly bringing 'public rights' within Article 6], while the consequences it would have for the national systems of administrative law protection could and should be accepted as implications for the rule of law which States opted for when drafting and/or ratifying the Convention".[112]

There would appear to be no reason of principle why the English courts should not accept that invitation even while the European Court remains reluctant to interpret "civil" rights and obligations as referring to all non-criminal rights and obligations. As noted earlier, the English courts are fully entitled to develop an interpretation of the Convention as found in the HRA which offers a higher level of protection than that accorded by the Strasbourg institutions. The case for doing so, both by reference to the antecedents of the Convention and the conceptual difficulties of the equation of "civil" with "private", is persuasive. Furthermore, the position which the European Court appears to be reaching, namely that "pecuniary" public rights are accorded protection under Article 6.1 but other non-private rights are not, is surely not an attractive one. It is not only artificial (in setting its face against non-direct pecuniary rights, such as the EC right to free movement)[113] but difficult to justify in principle. Why, for example, should rights in the field of immigration not be accorded protection?[114] Or even statutory rights to information under Freedom of Information legislation?

---

[111] (1997) 26 EHRR 202, at para 2 of Judge De Meyer's dissent.

[112] van Dijk (n. 108, *supra*) at 142-3.

[113] *Adams and Benn* v. *UK* (n. 100 *supra*).

[114] See n. 102 *supra*. One example would be discretionary decisions of the Secretary of State to grant or refuse exceptional leave to remain or to grant citizenship (see *R* v. *Secretary of State for the Home Department, ex p Montana*, Turner J, 21 December 1999). Such decisions do not fall into the category of "unfettered discretions" (and hence outside the category of "rights" at all), because they are subject to the constraints of judicial review, and indeed subject to specific constraints by way of legitimate expectations encouraged by the Secretary of State. Sir Robert Walker has identified immigration decisions as a "likely no go area" under the Human Rights Act, in the light of the Strasbourg case-law: "Opinion: The Impact of European Standards on the Right to a Fair Trial in Civil Proceedings in United Kingdom Domestic Law" [1999] *EHRLR* 4, at p.7. But see the recent decision of the European Court in *J.E.D.* v. *UK*, n. 102 *supra*.

It is right that the range of decisions opened up to the protections of Article 6.1 would be considerably extended as a result of the *Golder* principle.[115] The Court there held that Article 6.1 secures the right to have any claim relating to civil rights and obligations brought before a domestic court or tribunal; in other words, that Article 6.1 secures a right of *access* to Court, as well as a right to Article 6.1 protections for proceedings already in progress.[116] This being the case, a wide interpretation of "civil rights and obligations" would have the consequence that any administrative determination of a public or private right or entitlement would become subject to Article 6.1, even if national law contemplated that the decision would be simply taken by an administrative authority and not at any stage by a court or tribunal.

This is plainly the concern of the European Court which has prompted (at least in part) its restrictive decisions on the meaning of "civil" rights and obligations, but is it a concern which should be shared and taken into account by the English courts (or, indeed, persisted in by the European Court)? The root of the concern is the inflexible nature of the protections mandated by Article 6.1: unlike the principles of procedural propriety or natural justice, Article 6.1 cannot be described as a "flexi-principle"[117] whose protections depend on "the circumstances of the case, the nature of the inquiry, the rules under which the tribunal is acting, the subject matter under consideration and so forth".[118] By its terms it requires a hearing in public, before an "independent and impartial tribunal established by law". For "administrative"

---

[115] *Golder* v. *UK* (1975) 1 EHRR 524, especially para 36; see also *Le Compte, van Leuven & De Meyere* v. *Belgium, supra,* at para 44; *Ashingdane* v. UK (1985) 7 EHRR 528 (mental patient).

[116] Interestingly, van Dijk (see n. 108 *supra*) at pp. 138-40 suggests that on this point as well, the Court has disregarded the intentions of the framers of the Convention, albeit this time in the opposite direction. His analysis of the antecedents of the Convention suggests that the framers anticipated (contrary to *Golder*) that Article 6.1 would apply *only to those rights and obligations which, in the tradition of the legal system concerned, came within the competence of a court or tribunal,* and not those determined solely by administrative bodies. As van Dijk recognises, it is far too late in the day (and it may well not in any event be desirable) for a reversal of the decision in *Golder,* but it is surely right as a matter of legal history that the "distortion" introduced by *Golder* helped to produce an equal and opposite distorted reaction in the case-law limiting civil rights to "private rights".

[117] Michael Fordham, *Judicial Review Handbook,* 2nd edn. (London, Wiley Chancery Law Publishing, 1995) at para 60.2.

[118] *Russell* v. *Duke of Norfolk* [1949] 1 All ER 109, per Tucker LJ at 118.

decisions as to entitlement, particularly for decisions which have to be taken for large numbers of people, the Article 6.1 protections may be seen as at best unsatisfactorily judicialised or juridified,[119] or at worst utterly unrealistic.

There are, however, two ways by which an unsatisfactory application of Article 6.1 to inappropriate circumstances might be avoided. The first relies upon the distinction between "rights" and "unfettered discretions" enunciated by the European Court in cases like *Masson and Van Zon*.[120] This distinction, as noted above, is itself at best unsatisfactory. But if it stands, then a category of unstructured and unconfined discretionary decisions which are more likely to be unsuitable for the judicialised Article 6.1 procedure[121] will in any event be taken outside the realm of Article 6.1, for the reasons explained above. This path is likely, however, to be unattractive to English judges: not only is it conceptually unsatisfactory, but it is a blunt instrument with which to seek to mitigate the rigours of Article 6.1.

More promising is the flexibility more recently shown by the European Court in its application of the Article 6.1 procedural protections, and in particular its willingness to consider the fairness of proceedings in the round, taking into account any appeal or review rights. As the Court pointed out as long ago as *Le Compte*, Article 6.1

> does not oblige the Contracting States to submit *"contestations"* over "civil rights and obligations" to a procedure conducted at each of its stages before "tribunals" meeting the Article's various requirements. Demands of flexibility and efficiency, which are fully compatible with the protection of human rights, may justify the prior intervention of administrative or professional bodies and, *a fortiori*, of judicial bodies which do not satisfy the said requirements in every respect . . .[122]

---

[119] See, for example, the treatment of "red light theories" in Carol Harlow and Richard Rawlings, *Law and Administration*, 2nd edn. (London, Butterworths, 1997), ch 1. See also the concerns of Sir Robert Walker (pp. 11-12) as to the effects upon hearings which are private *to suit the Applicant*.

[120] Note 89 *supra*, pp. 20-2.

[121] Although it is ironic that even in *Masson and van Zon* itself, the "unfettered discretion" was to be exercised by a (criminal) court, in a public and judicialised setting.

[122] *Le Compte* (n. 17 *supra*), para 51(a); see also *Kaplan* v. *UK* (1980) 4 EHRR 64 where the Court noted that to provide a full appeal on the merits of every administrative decision affecting rights protected by Article 6 would lead to a result which was inconsistent with the long-standing legal position in most Contracting States (para 161).

Crucially, the European Court has shown an increasing willingness to entertain the argument that an avenue of challenge of an administrative decision by way of judicial review is sufficient to meet Article 6.1. As is well known, particularly in specialised areas of law, the Court may be satisfied by an appeal in the nature of the judicial review jurisdiction: i.e. an appeal which permits challenge for error of law, but only for error of fact in very limited circumstances such as perversity.[123] The sufficiency of review must be assessed against a number of factors, such as the subject matter of the decision appealed against; the nature of the decision-making process at first instance; the content of the dispute; and the desired and actual grounds of appeal.[124] The circumstances in which review will be sufficient to meet Article 6.1 is itself a subject for debate beyond the scope of this paper, and there are some recent indications of a retreat from *Bryan*[125] but it is plain from recent decisions that the Court has moved appreciably towards an

---

[123] *Bryan* v. *UK* (1995) 21 EHRR 342. In this case, the Court held that although the statutory planning procedure did not itself comply with all aspects of Article 6.1 (in particular, the Inspector was held not to constitute an independent tribunal), those defects were cured by the availability of judicial review, in the context of a specialised form of administrative decision-making where there were limited factual disputes. See also *Air Canada* v. *UK* (1995) 20 EHRR 150 (no breach of Article 6.1 where judicial review proceedings largely concerned issue of statutory construction). Compare *Le Compte* (para 51(b)), where the inability of the Court of Cassation to hear an appeal on anything other than a point of law meant that that appeal could not "cure" a first instance hearing which did not comply with Article 6.1.

[124] See *Zumtobel* v. *Austria* (1983) 17 EHRR 116 at paras 31-2; *Ortenberg* v. *Austria* (1995) 19 EHRR 524. In relation to the sufficiency of judicial review in particular, see (in addition to the cases cited above) *Stefan* v. *General Medical Council* (Admissibility Decision, 8 March 1999) (appeal from GMC's decision to suspend doctor to Privy Council on point of law was sufficient to meet Article 6.1); *ABP and others* v. *UK* (Admissibility Decision, 15 January 1998); *X* v. *UK* (Admissibility Decision, 19 January 1998); *Wickramasinghe* v. *UK* (Admissibility Decision, 9 December 1997). Compare also the similar approach of the European Court of Justice, which has held that Community law does not require national courts to substitute their assessment of the facts for that of competent national authorities, provided that this does not render the exercise of community rights "virtually impossible or excessively difficult": *Upjohn Ltd* v. *Licensing Authority Established by the Medicines Act 1968* [1999] 1 CMLR 825.

[125] See *Kingsley* v. *United Kingdom*, ECtHR, 7 November 2000; *The Times*, 9 January 2001. See also *County Properties Ltd* v. *The Scottish Ministers* (outer House, Court of Session, 25 July 2000); *R* v. *Secretary of State of the Environment, Transport and the Regions ex p Alconbury Developments Ltd and others* (Div.Ct., 13 December 2000).

acceptance that judicial review of an administrative decision affecting civil rights may satisfy Article 6.[126]

Furthermore, the domestic courts will be able to assist that acceptance by extending or modifying the principles of judicial review (having regard, not least, to their statutory obligation, as public authorities, to act compatibly with Convention rights) so as to provide, in an appropriate case, for "heightened scrutiny" of administrative decisions to comply with Article 6.1;[127] for an inquiry into whether a "sanction" is proportionate to the fault found; and/or, in appropriate cases, by exercising their little-used powers of factual investigation to ensure, for example, that jurisdictional facts for the exercise of the discretion exist. In other situations, it may be that only the introduction of new rights of appeal giving greater powers to investigate issues of fact or policy will satisfy Article 6.1. But that is already a process which occurs when either EC law or human rights concerns prompt the Government to act.[128]

In conclusion, if Article 6.1 is to be given its full application to administrative and public law rights and decisions, then it is surely vitally neces-

---

[126] But judicial review may well still be inadequate where an initial administrative decision is taken by a non "judicial" body, and the facts cannot be re-opened thereafter: *Terra Woningen* v. *Netherlands* (1996) 24 EHRR 456. Even if judicial review is in principle an adequate remedy, there is a difficult question as to whether a domestic court, hearing a Human Rights Act challenge to the decision of an administrative body on the grounds that it did not satisfy Article 6.1 (which challenge may or may not be brought by way of an application for judicial review), can itself supply the procedural protection lacking below, or whether its role is confined to adjudicating upon whether or not there has been a breach of Article 6.1. It is submitted that compatibility with the Act should in general be assessed in the light of an available appeal or review, and that the Court should be ready to consider (if the matter is brought by way of an application for judicial review) whether on domestic principles the applicant is entitled to relief.

[127] For example, to provide "heightened scrutiny" required by *Smith and Grady* v. *UK* and *Lustig-Prean and Beckett* v. *UK* [1999] IRLR 734. Indeed, the courts may have had that power even before the Human Rights Act came into force: *R* v. *Secretary of State for the Home Department, ex p Simms* [2000] 2 AC 115; Fordham and de la Mare, "Identifiying the Principles of Proportionality" above. See, more generally, Grosz, Beatson and Duffy (n. 125 *supra*) at para 5-02.

[128] E.g. the new appeal procedure from determinations of the Director-General of Telecommunications, introduced by regulation (to implement an EC Directive as well as to satisfy human rights concerns). The grounds of appeal replicate the grounds of judicial review, but also include review for "a material error as to the facts" and where "there was some other material illegality, including unreasonableness or lack of proportionality": see Telecommunications Act 1984, section 46B, as inserted by the Telecommunications (Appeals) Regulations 1999 (SI 1999 No.3180).

sary for a degree of flexibility to be injected into the process to mediate the procedural requirements of Article 6.1 and to avoid the juridification of public decision-making. This flexibility can in many cases be achieved by a reliance on judicial review as providing a right of appeal compatible with Article 6.1. The courts will in many cases have the ability, we suggest, to tailor the scope and intensity of review to the requirements of Article 6, and should thereby be able to retain the flexibility of the principles of procedural fairness, together with the Convention's guarantee of access to open justice from an independent and impartial tribunal.

"RECOGNISED" BY DOMESTIC LAW

The Strasbourg case-law repeatedly states that Article 6.1 extends only to disputes over civil rights and obligations "*recognised* under domestic law", though this includes disputes "in which the actual existence of a 'civil right' may be at stake". Moreover, Article 6.1 "does not in itself guarantee any particular content for the 'rights and obligations' in the substantive law of the Contracting States" and "it is clear that the Convention organs could not create by way of interpretation of Article 6.1 a substantive right which has no legal basis whatsoever in the State concerned".[129] Only in extreme circumstances, perhaps, would the Strasbourg Court review a rule of substantive national law – if, say, a legislature or judge removed all rights to sue for damages for the negligent actions of all public authorities. The Court said as much in *Fayed* v. *UK*:[130]

> . . . it would not be consistent with the rule of law in a democratic society or with the basic principle underlying Article 6.1 — namely that civil claims must be capable of being submitted to a judge for adjudication — if, for example, a State could, without restraint or control by the Convention enforcement bodies, remove from the jurisdiction of the courts a whole range of civil claims or confer immunities from civil liability on large groups or categories of persons.

In normal times, the question whether national law "recognises" a civil right or obligation emerges most starkly in relation to immunities and other exclusionary rules.

---

[129] *Sporrong* v. *Sweden* (1983) 5 EHRR 35.
[130] (1994) 18 EHRR 393.

The Nature of Exclusionary Rules and Immunities

While it is doubtful (or controversial) whether, if at all, Article 6.1 should control the existence and extent of national "substantive" law on civil liability, it is clear that "procedural" bars to obtaining a full hearing on the merits of a case fall within its ambit. The dichotomy is probably not a helpful one; certainly, it is[131]

> not always an easy matter to trace the dividing line between proce-
> dural and substantive limitations of a given entitlement under domes-
> tic law. It may sometimes be no more than a question of legislative
> technique whether a limitation is expressed in terms of the right or its
> remedy.

The following types of rules have been held to fall within scope of Article 6.1. From one perspective, they may plausibly be characterised as rules which define the scope of a substantive right *in limine* (i.e. at the initial stage of the right's definition) but may, from another point of view, be seen as rules which hamper a person's capacity to litigate or complain about infringements of an existing substantive right.

- Rules creating limitation time periods outside which (otherwise arguable) claims will not be entertained.[132]
- Rules completely removing a defendant (against whom, applying principles to which others are subject, an arguable claim would lie) from the jurisdiction of a court.[133]

---

[131] *Fayed* v. *UK*, para 67.

[132] E.g. *Stubbings* v. *UK* (1997) 23 EHRR 213.

[133] E.g. *Waite and Kennedy* v. *Germany* (1999) 6 BHRC 499. The applicants were computer programmers employed first by a British company and later by an Irish company; for many years, their employers placed them "at the disposal" of the European Space Agency (ESA) Operation Centre in Darmstadt, Germany. A dispute arose and the applicants instituted proceedings in the Darmstadt Labour Court against the ESA, argu-ing that they had acquired the status of employees of the ESA. The German courts held that the ESA was conferred with immunity from jurisdiction in domestic courts (by the ESA Convention and German domestic law) and rejected the applicants' argument that a waiver of that immunity had been agreed upon by the body which preceded the ESA. On an application to Strasbourg, the court held that there was no violation of Article 6.1 – the immunity from jurisdiction had a legitimate objective and, in the circum-stances, it was proportionate.

- Rules which create a defence in terms of an immunity from suit in respect of a type of conduct by a defendant.[134]
- Rules which expressly frame an element of a cause of action so as to require a court to weigh up public policy considerations for and against imposing liability.

It is in relation to the last of these categories that difficulties have arisen recently (at least from the perspective of English tort law). Most legal systems have some form of summary hearing procedure in which a judge may consider preliminary points of law raised by a defendant to a civil claim.[135] The application of immunities and other exclusionary rules is particularly apt to be considered at a summary trial as they normally constitute "knock-out" defences without the need for detailed oral testimony, cross-examination and the other features of a full trial on the merits of a claim. What is objectionable about immunities and exclusionary rules is that they have a tendency to prevent claimants receiving full hearings of their cases. The concern is therefore with the "fair hearing" entitlement of Article 6.1, and also the implied right of "access to a court".[136] Contracting States are not totally prohibited from having immunities and exclusionary rules within their legal systems; such rules are acceptable to the extent that they (i) do not

---

[134] E.g. the defence of privilege in defamation actions (considered in *Fayed* v. *UK*); *Tinnelly & Sons Ltd and McElduff* v. *UK* (1999) 27 EHRR 249 (Article 6.1 applied to issue of certificate under Fair Employment (Northern Ireland) Act 1976 which enacts: "(1) This Act shall not apply to an act done for the purpose of safeguarding national security or of protecting public safety or public order. (2) A certificate signed by or on behalf of the Secretary of State and certifying that an act specified in the certificate was done for a purpose mentioned in subsection (1) shall be conclusive evidence that it was done for that purpose"; cf. the different outcome in *Powell and Rayner* v. *UK* (1990) 12 EHRR 355 (Civil Aviation Act 1982, s. 72 which bars rights of action in trespass and nuisance in respect of aircraft noise, held not to be an exclusionary rule, but to prevent any civil right arising in the first place).

[135] In England and Wales, summary justice under the Civil Procedure Rules 1998 includes: the power of the court to strike out a statement of case, or part of one, as disclosing no reasonable grounds for bringing or defending the claim (CPR, r. 3(4)(2) – "striking out" means the court ordering written material to be deleted so that it may no longer be relied upon); and summary judgments under CPR, Part 24 on the ground that the claimant has no real prospect of succeeding on the claim or issue or that defendant has no reasonable prospect of successfully defending the claim or issue. See further Derek O'Brien, "The New Summary Judgment: Raising the Threshold of Admission" (1999) 18 *CJQ* 132.

[136] *Golder* v. *UK* (1975) 1 EHRR 524.

restrict the access of the individual in such a way or to such extent that the very essence of the right of access under Article 6.1 is impaired; (ii) pursue a legitimate objective and (iii) are proportionate.

Strasbourg Reasoning about Exclusionary Rules and Immunities

In *Osman* v. *UK* the Strasbourg Court had to consider issues arising from an attack by a school teacher on one of his former pupils (about whom the teacher had become obsessive) and the pupil's father (who was killed in the attack). The Osman family's negligence claim against the Metropolitan Police had been struck out by the Court of Appeal as disclosing no reasonable cause of action;[137] applying principles developed by the House of Lords in *Hill* v. *Chief Constable of West Yorkshire*[138] it had held that in the circumstances of the case, the police owed no duty of care to the Osman family as it would not be "fair, just and reasonable" to impose one. The Strasbourg Court found there was no violation of Articles 2 or 8 but held that there was a breach of Article 6.1. The requirement of the cause of action in negligence that a claimant must plead and prove (at least in novel situations) that it is "fair, just and reasonable" for the law to impose a duty of care on the defendant, was characterised by the Strasbourg court as an "exclusionary rule". Although the exclusionary rule did pursue a legitimate objective in the present case (the aim of maintaining the effectiveness of the police service, and hence the prevention of disorder or crime), the "blanket immunity on the police for their acts and omissions during the investigation and suppression of crime" was disproportionate.

In September 1999, the European Commission on Human Rights returned to the problems of exclusionary rules in English tort law and the use of the strike out procedure. In *Z and others* v. *UK*, the allegation made on behalf of the child claimants was that social workers had wrongfully failed to intervene, leaving them in conditions of abject squalor for several years. Their claims for damages were struck out by the House of Lords as revealing no cause of action because, *inter alia*, it was not fair, just and reasonable to impose a duty of care.[139] The

---

[137] *Osman* v. *Ferguson* [1993] 4 All ER 344.

[138] [1989] AC 53.

[139] *Z* v. *UK* [2000] 2 FCR 245; *X (minors) and other* v. *Bedfordshire County Council* [1995] AC 633.

Commission found, unanimously, that there had been a violation of Article 3; in relation to the striking out of the negligence claim,[140] the Commission applied the reasoning in *Osman* v. *UK* and found there to be a breach of Article 6.1.

In the litigation leading to *TP and KM's* application to Strasbourg, the claimants were a mother and child. The child was removed from the family home into local authority care on the basis of allegedly careless assumptions of fact: the child had told social workers that she was sexually abused by a man named "X". The mother's boyfriend was named X and social workers assumed he was the abuser; in fact, the child was referring to another man named X. The mother's claim for damages was based on breach of statutory duty and the direct liability of the local authority. The child's claim relied on the vicarious liability of the local and health authorities for their professionals.[141] The House of Lords had struck out all the claims made by the claimants as revealing no cause of action. The House of Lords found that a social worker acting as a professional to advise a local authority in the exercise of its public functions owed a duty of care to the local authority but not to the child concerned. The relationship was not sufficiently proximate to create a duty of care situation. The Commission held that in striking out the child's claim – based on vicarious liability – there was a violation of Article 6.1.[142] In reasoning that is perplexing, the Commission found that there *was* a determination of the "merits" of the vicarious liability claim, but that *if* the claim had been formulated in terms of direct liability, it *would* have been rejected on the basis of the exclusionary rule.[143] The Commission found no violation of Article 6.1 in relation to the mother's claims in negligence and breach of statutory duty: she had no arguable claims in domestic law and therefore no "civil right" to which Article 6.1 was applicable (alternatively,[144] she did have a civil right, but this was satisfactorily

---

[140] Issues to do with the claim of breach of statutory duty were not considered in any detail: see para 109.

[141] Cf. *Z's* case (n. 139, *supra*) which was based on the direct liability of the local and health authorities.

[142] (2000) LGLR 181.

[143] In his partly dissenting opinion, Sir Nicolas Bratza states: "Since the second applicant's claim as formulated was fully considered and determined in accordance with ordinary principles of domestic law, it cannot in my view be said that there was any denial of access to court". Surely this is correct?

[144] See the partly dissenting opinion of Sir Nicolas Bratza.

"determined"). It remains to be seen whether the Court will adopt a similar approach.

The reasoning utilised in this series of Strasbourg cases is, in places, difficult to understand – as Lord Browne-Wilkinson observed in *Barrett* v. *London Borough of Enfield*[145] (decided before the most baffling of the Strasbourg decisions, the Commission's reports in *TP and KM* v. *UK*). The Strasbourg cases are capable of being given either a restrictive or an expansive reading by an English lawyer.

A restrictive reading?

The restrictive reading is that the cases are concerned with the narrow issue of how, in some situations, English courts have approached the question of whether it is "fair, just and reasonable" to recognise a duty of care in negligence. The problem was that in *Osman*, the Court of Appeal "in the *instant* case" had "*proceeded on the basis* that the rule was a watertight defence". In *X* v. *Bedfordshire*, the error was that the House of Lords had "*unequivocally* rejected the children's claims on the basis that actions against the social services for decisions taken in relation to their child protection functions were to be excluded".[146] The disapproval is not of some element of domestic substantive law, but rather of the manner in which English courts in particular cases conducted the inquiry into public policy questions in this context.[147] So long as English courts refrain from treating the question of "fair, just and reasonable" as a blunt instrument, by being prepared to consider countervailing arguments, there can be no objection.[148] If this is done, policy based arguments on tortious liability may be considered as

---

[145]   [1999] 3 WLR 79.

[146]   See *TP*, para 90.

[147]   As the Strasbourg Court has stated elsewhere (*Ashingdane* v. *UK* (1985) 7 EHRR 528): "Without losing sight of the general context of the case, the Court would recall that, in proceedings originating in an individual application, it has to confine its attention, as far as possible, to the concrete case before it . . . Accordingly, the Court's task in assessing the permissibility of the limitation imposed is not to review section 141 [of the Mental Health Act 1959] as such but the circumstances and the manner in which that section was actually applied [to the applicant]".

[148]   This is a principle familiar to English administrative law: decision-takers must not "fetter" their discretions by adopting overly rigid policies and closing their ears to arguments that a policy should not be applied in the particular circumstances.

preliminary issues of law.[149] The Strasbourg reasoning has no application to other substantive elements of the cause of action in negligence:
questions of "proximity", "foreseeability" and, moreover, "voluntary
assumption of responsibility" are unaffected.[150]

The restrictive reading also emphasises that there is no real difference
between English law and the Convention requirements. As Auld LJ has
recently commented:[151]

> ... it was evident even before the recent decision ... in *Osman* v. *UK*, that
> such an assessment [of "fair, just and reasonable"] could normally only
> properly be made after full consideration of the evidence and circum-
> stances at trial. In *E (A Minor)* v. *Dorset CC* [1995] 2 AC 689 ... Sir
> Thomas Bingham MR, indicated at 694E-F, that if all that remains to a
> judge hearing a strike-out application is the question whether the
> claimant has an arguable case that the duty of care for which he or she
> contends is fair, just and reasonable in the circumstances, the case is not
> appropriate for a strike-out.

The importance of *Waite and Kennedy*[152] is to illustrate that even a
categorical, "blanket immunity" from jurisdiction may be justifiable
under Article 6.1.

An expansive reading?

The cases may, however, be read differently and more expansively. They
show a new willingness by the Strasbourg institutions to regard Article
6.1 as applicable to issues of substantive domestic law. In *Osman*, the
Strasbourg court accepted that the question whether it is "fair, just and
reasonable" to impose a duty of care on a defendant *is* a constituent
element of the cause of action,[153] but nevertheless held that a claimant
who failed to establish that criterion was denied a fair hearing. The
practical effect has to be that questions of liability in negligence are
shifted from being determined in terms of whether or not a duty of care
exists, to whether the defendant has breached the standard of care (or,
perhaps, whether there is causation).[154] Here, too, at the breach of duty

---

[149] See *Kinsella* v. *Chief Constable of Nottinghamshire*, *The Times*, 24 August 1999,
discussed below.

[150] See p. 135.   [151] *G* v. *Bromley LBC*, (2000) 2 LGLR 237.

[152] See n. 133, *supra*.   [153] *Osman*, para. 138.

[154] See e.g. *Barrett* v. *Enfield LBC* [1999] 3 WLR 79.

stage, the Strasbourg cases indicate that English law ought to re-conceptualise itself to recognise a distinction between "ordinary" and "gross" negligence.[155] The cases also lower, considerably, the threshold of what counts as an "arguable" claim to a civil right or obligation.[156]

The expansive reading requires us to go well beyond negligence claims; the approach is applicable to any "exclusionary rule" or "immunity" (broadly defined) affecting disputes about any civil right and obligation.[157] The cases also reveal that Article 6.1 encompasses an independent right – to call public authorities "to account", in an adversarial trial, for their errors and omissions.[158] It was insufficient that, in the striking out applications, the English courts *assumed* that the facts pleaded by the claimants were true. Trials, in which witnesses give testimony and are cross-examined and where the judge considers the "merits" are an indispensable element of the rule of law; legal proceedings short of this may not count as "determinations". Other methods of accountability, including ombudsmen and public inquiries, are inadequate substitutes.

The cases also show an absolute intolerance by Strasbourg of any rule of law (whether procedural or substantive) which offends the new regime. Even if a claimant has not pleaded and argued her case in a way which opens it up to being dismissed by application of an exclusionary

---

[155] *Osman*, para. 151 (". . . the applicants' case involved the alleged failure to protect the life of a child and their view that the failure was the result of a catalogue of acts and omissions which amounted to grave negligence as opposed to minor acts of incompetence"); *TP and KM*, para. 91 (". . . the exclusionary rule gave no consideration to the seriousness or otherwise of the damage or the nature or degree of the negligence alleged or the fundamental rights of the applicants [sic] which were involved."); *Z and others*, para 114.

[156] In striking out applications, the threshold of arguability for the claimant is already low: see *Barrett* v. *Enfield LBC* [1999] 3 WLR 79, per Lord Browne-Wilkinson ("In my speech in *The X Case* (at pp. 740-1) . . . I pointed out that unless it was possible to give a *certain* answer to the question whether the plaintiff's claim would succeed, the case was inappropriate for striking out. I further said that in an area of law which was uncertain and developing (such as the circumstances on which a person can be held liable in negligence for the exercise of a statutory duty or power) it is not normally appropriate to strike out."). And see also *Gower* v. *Bromley LBC*, n. 151 *supra*.

[157] The right claimed in *Waite and Kennedy* was a contractual one.

[158] *Z and others*, para.115 (". . . the applicants were entitled to have the local authority account for its acts and omissions in adversarial proceedings"); *TP and KM*, para. 92; *Osman*, para. 153 ("They may or may not have failed to convince the domestic court that the police were negligent in the circumstances. However, they were entitled to have the police account for their actions and omissions in adversarial proceedings").

rule, there will be a breach of Article 6.1 if the claimant *could have* chosen to frame her claim in such a way.[159]

A synthesis

Neither a restrictive nor expansive reading is wholly satisfactory. In an attempt to steer a third way, we offer the following synthesis of the Strasbourg approach.

- Article 6.1 does not in itself guarantee any particular content for the "rights and obligations" in the substantive law of the Contracting States;
- but a person does have a Convention right to have disputes about "civil rights and obligations" determined.
- This right includes the capacity to seek adjudication on whether or not a particular civil right or obligation actually exists in national law. In other words, an arguable claim that a cause of action is or ought to be "derived" from national law[160] is in itself sufficient to ensure the applicability of Article 6.1;
- A "right to a court" and a fair hearing may require a case to proceed to trial where the facts of a claim, and the particular merits of its legal basis, are tested in adversarial proceedings; Article 6.1 creates an entitlement for claimants to have public authorities "account for their acts and omissions"[161] where there is an allegation of particularly grave wrong doing. Where a national court disposes of a claim in summary proceedings confined to the preliminary issue[162] as to the application of an exclusionary rule or immunity, especially if the court is required to assess public policy arguments for and against imposing liability, this may in and of itself breach Article 6.1.
- The application of an exclusionary rule or immunity may violate Article 6.1 unless it can be demonstrated that the "exclusionary rule":

---

[159] See p. 125.

[160] On the concept of arguability, see further p. 93 above. In *TP and KM* (at para 84), factors lending weight to the claim included: that the Legal Aid Board had funded the litigation; that the Court of Appeal has granted permission to appeal to the House of Lords on a point; and that there was no precedent establishing that a claimant cannot make a claim.

[161] *Osman*, para. 153; *TP and KM*, para. 92; *Z*, para 115.

[162] In England and Wales, e.g. the strike out procedure and summary judgments (see n. 135, *supra*); and applications for permission to proceed with a claim for judicial review.

(i) does not restrict the access of the individual in such a way or to such extent that the very essence of the right of access is impaired; (ii) pursues a legitimate objective[163] and (iii) is proportionate. For an exclusionary rule of a national court's own making to be proportionate, it must be open to a national court to have regard to the presence of other public interest considerations which pull in the opposite direction to the application of the rule; this may require a case to be considered on its merits.[164]

• The Contracting State enjoys a certain margin of appreciation, but the final decision as to the observance of the Convention's requirements rests in Strasbourg. In carrying out its assessment, the Strasbourg Court may approach the question hypothetically: there may be a denial of access to a national court contrary to Article 6.1 even where a claimant's claim as formulated was fully considered and determined in accordance with ordinary principles of domestic law if, had the claim been formulated and argued differently, it would have been rejected by the national court on the basis of an exclusionary rule.[165]

The general approach of *Osman* v. *UK* and the other cases under discussion is apt to apply to litigation between private parties in so far as it requires *the court* to conduct itself in a particular way (i.e. avoid applying exclusionary rules in an impermissible way).[166] The requirement

---

[163] These include e.g.: ensuring that international organisations are able to function free from unilateral interference by individual governments (*Waite and Kennedy*, n. 133 *supra*); preserving the efficiency of a vital sector of public service (*TP and KM*, para 91); the avoidance of defensive policing and the diversion of police manpower (*Osman*, para 143).

[164] In *TP and KM* the following factors were held by the Commission not to be of much weight in the calculus (see para 91): the multidisciplinary aspects of child protection work; the risk that liability would open a floodgate of litigation from discontented parents; the argument that liability would render the social services more cautious in the exercise of their powers. The weight to be afforded to the fact that a claimant has a reasonable alternative form of redress is problematic. In *TP and KM*, the Commission held that access to the Local Commission for Administration (the ombudsman) was not adequate since "it does not provide any enforceable right to compensation in respect of the damage suffered, the ombudsman having only recommendatory powers" (para 92). In *Z*, the Criminal Injuries Compensation Scheme was dismissed (para. 115). In *Waite and Kennedy*, however, it was held that the applicants did have reasonable alternative means to protect effectively their rights (para 69).

[165] *TP and KM*; cf. Partly dissenting opinion of Sir Nicolas Bratza and others (p. 27).

[166] E.g. *Osman* v. *UK* was raised in argument, but not pursued, in *Aldrich* v. *Norwich Union Life Insurance Society Co Ltd*, [1999] 2 All ER (Comm) 707.

for a claimant to establish that it is "fair, just and reasonable" to recognise a duty of care is, of course, as much part of the cause of action in negligence against a private body as it is against a public one.[167] Whether, however, in private party litigation there is any right to "call to account" (if indeed that be a separate right) is open to doubt.

Is the Strasbourg approach a proper one?

Several criticisms may be made of the Strasbourg reasoning in general, and its impact on the civil justice system of England and Wales in particular.[168]

First, it pushes the concept of a "right to a court" too far. While it has long been understood to include the right of access "in fact, as well as law" and to provide "practical and effective" rather than "theoretical and illusory" protection,[169] in none of the cases considered above did the claimants have what may appropriately be characterised as "access" problems. In *Waite and Kennedy*,[170] the applicants had been able to argue the question of the European Space Agency's immunity from suit at three levels of German labour courts and petitioned the Constitutional Court;[171] in the child abuse cases, the claimants had hearings in the High Court, Court of Appeal and House of Lords, supported by legal aid; in the *Osman* case, there was a hearing in the High Court and in the Court of Appeal. The Strasbourg approach arguably also attaches insufficient importance to the benefits claimants receive in striking out proceedings in England and Wales where the Court assumes the facts pleaded by the claimant are true. The Strasbourg decisions now make it difficult for courts to determine cases on the basis of legal argument of preliminary issues – something that goes against the grain of the overriding objectives of the new Civil Procedure Rules in England and Wales.[172] There is no

---

[167] E.g. *British Telecommunications Plc* v. *James Thomson & Sons (Engineers) Ltd* [1999] 1 WLR 9; *Perrett* v. *Collins* [1998] 2 Lloyd's Rep. 255.

[168] See also Lord Hoffmann, "Human Rights and the House of Lords" (1999) 62 *MLR* 159, 162-6; Paul Craig and Duncan Fairgrieve, "*Barrett*, Negligence and Discretionary Powers" [1999] *PL* 626.

[169] *Airey* v. *Ireland* (1979-80) 2 EHRR 305.   [170] See n. 133 *supra*.

[171] There was held to be no breach of Article 6.1, but for other reasons.

[172] As Lord Woolf MR acknowledged in *Kent* v. *Griffith*, 3 February 2000, CA ("The possible consequences [of *Osman* v. *UK*] also concern me from a procedural point of view in the light of the new culture of litigation in this jurisdiction as a result of the introduction of the CPR").

evidence to show that, as a matter of routine, summary proceedings fail to give proper weight to claimants' arguments on questions of law or fact. Arguably, the Strasbourg Court ignores the fact that defendants, too, have rights under Article 6.1 to have a fair hearing without unreasonable delay, and summary hearings on preliminary points of law are an important method of achieving this.

Secondly, the Strasbourg decisions expound as one of the rights contained in Article 6.1 that claimants may be "entitled to have the [public] authority account for its acts and omissions" at a trial. The insistence on the need for access to court, distinct from other alternative forms of redress and accountability now provided by ombudsmen and the routine use of public inquiries, seems a generation out of date. The courts are not the only, or the best, way in which aggrieved citizens can question the conduct of officials; litigation is certainly not necessarily the best "fact finding" mechanism.

Thirdly, there is, arguably, a sleight of hand by the Strasbourg institutions. Although the cases still purport expressly to deny that Article 6.1 guarantees any particular content for the "civil rights and obligations" (except perhaps in extreme situations), in effect the recent cases do just that. As we have noted, it has effectively required English law to recognise that a duty of care exists in relation to certain police and social worker operations where previously this was not so; it has shifted the emphasis in tort litigation from the question of whether a duty of care exists, to the different question of whether a breach of a standard of care has occurred, or whether causation is present; there are also hints that the creation of a new concept for English law of "gross negligence" may be necessary.

Fourthly, the concept of an "immunity" or "exclusionary rule" is seemingly so broadly defined as to be uncertain. To fall into the prohibited category, a rule need not "automatically doom to failure . . . a civil action from the outset".[173] As well as the types of rules considered above,[174] where a court rejects a claim on the basis that the matter in dispute is "not justiciable", this may constitute an exclusionary rule within the scope of Article 6.1.[175]

---

[173] *Osman*, para 138.

[174] See text at p. 122.

[175] Consider, e.g. a court refusing permission to apply for judicial review of a refusal or grant an honour (a category of decision held in the GCHQ case to be non-justiciable) or to review the rationality of a government decision to allocate scarce resources among

Fifthly, the "hypothetical" approach adopted by the Commission in *TP and KM*, focusing on the outcome of domestic litigation *if* the claimant had presented her case differently, must surely be wrong for the reasons set out in Sir Nicolas Bratza's partly dissenting opinion.[176]

The arguments are not, of course, all one way. The recent Strasbourg cases build upon understandings that are now well-accepted: Article 6.1, expressly, concerns itself with the "determination" of rights – including whether such rights actually exist; Article 6 protects rights to institute proceedings, not just the conduct of proceedings once begun;[177] and there must be access in fact as well as law;[178] and may require an adversarial trial. It also must be said that the area of English tort law found wanting in the Strasbourg case-law is, indeed, inadequate – a "blunt instrument".[179] The assessment of public policy factors pointing in favour and against the imposition of liability on public authorities has often been based on surmise and anecdote rather than rigorous analysis and evidence.[180] The recent developments also remind the English legal system of the importance of deciding cases "on the basis of actual facts found at trial not on hypothetical facts assumed (possibly wrongly) to be true for the purpose of the strike out".[181]

The expansive (or alarmist) reading of the cases needs to be set off against the reassurance given by Strasbourg,[182] that there is in this context a margin of appreciation accorded to national legal systems. It is to this we now turn.

---

competing claims. On justiciability, see further Le Sueur, "Justifying Judicial Caution: Jurisdiction, Justiciablity and Policy", ch. 8 in Brigid Hadfield (ed.), *Thematic Approach to Judicial Review* (Dublin, Gill & MacMillan, 1995) and Lord Woolf, Jeffrey Jowell and A.P. Le Sueur, *de Smith's Principles of Judicial Review* (London, Sweet & Maxwell, 1999) pp. 168-73.

[176] See n. 143 *supra*. [177] *Golder* v. *UK* (1975) 1 EHRR 524.

[178] *Airey* v. *Ireland* (n. 69 *supra*): this expression has become a *double entendre!*

[179] Sir John Freedland in *Osman*, p. 53.

[180] See *de Smith, Woolf and Jowell's Principles of Judicial Review* (1999), pp. 639-41.

[181] See Lord Browne-Wilkinson in *Barrett* v. *Enfield LBC* [1999] 3 WLR 79, 83 (referring to a mistaken understanding of the role of educational psychologists, corrected by the Court of Appeal in *Phelps* v. *Hillingdon LBC* [1999] 1 WLR 500).

[182] *Osman*, para 147 ("However, this right [the 'right to a court'] is not absolute, but may be subject to limitations; these are permitted by implication since the right of access by its very nature calls for regulation by the State. In this respect, the Contracting States enjoy a certain margin of appreciation, although the final decision as to the observance of the Convention's requirements rests with the Court.")

How Have the English Courts Responded?

It is too soon to assess the full impact of *Osman* in English law; what can be said, however, is that the predominant reaction of English judges has been to seek to minimise the reach of the Strasbourg case-law[183] in relation to several issues. There is much uncertainty. Along with Lord Browne-Wilkinson, "one can only hope that the law applicable under Article 6 is further interpreted".[184]

Does Osman apply to questions of "foreseeability" and "proximity"?

In *Palmer* v. *Tees Health Authority*[185] the Court of Appeal was dealing with a negligence claim by a mother of a child who was sexually abused and murdered by a former patient in the defendant's hospital. The judge at first instance held that while it was not disputed that the injuries to the child and her mother were arguably foreseeable, there was no sufficient proximity between the defendants and the claimant; and also that it was not fair, just and reasonable to impose a duty of care on the defendants. Thus, the claim was struck out as disclosing no cause of action on the grounds that the second and third requirements for the existence of a duty of care laid down in *Caparo Industries plc* v. *Dickman*[186] were not satisfied. On appeal, the claimant sought to rely upon *Osman* v. *UK*, as interpreted by the House of Lords in *Barrett* v. *Enfield LBC*. For the defendants, it was accepted that it was impossible to sustain the second ground of the judge's decision to strike out (i.e., that it was not fair, just and reasonable to impose a duty of care); the Court of Appeal held that nevertheless the first ground (i.e., proximity) could stand. Stuart-Smith LJ held that "it is implicit in the judgment of the Strasbourg Court in *Osman* that it is appropriate to strike out actions on the grounds that in law proximity is not established".[187] Pill LJ agreed, stating that

---

[183] In the period of almost two years between October 1998 when *Osman* was decided by the Strasbourg Court and 2 October 2000 when the Human Rights Act 1998 came fully into force, courts were not under a statutory duty to take account of Strasbourg case-law.

[184] *Barrett* v. *Enfield LBC* [1999] 3 WLR 79, 86.

[185] (2000) 2 LGLR 69. *Palmer* was followed by the CA in *Gallagher* v. *Berrow*, 7 October 1999.

[186] [1990] 2 AC 605.

[187] Transcript. Cf. the comment of Auld LJ in *G* v. *Bromely LBC*, (2000) 2 LGLR 237: "And if, as Lord Browne-Wilkinson considered in *Barrett*, at 199j-200b, the effect

"*Barrett* does not require the transposition of the 'blanket exclusion-ary rule,' condemned in *Osman*, to the assessment of proximity".[188] Is such certainty about the reach of *Osman* warranted? In *Osman* itself, the Strasbourg Court stated:[189]

> On that understanding [[190]] the Court considers that the applicants must be taken to have a right, derived from the law of negligence, to seek an adjudication on the admissibility and merits of an arguable claim *that they were in a relationship of proximity with the police*, that the harm caused was foreseeable and that in the circumstances it was fair, just and reasonable not to apply the exclusionary rule outlined in the Hill case.

There is also surely some merit in the argument (made by counsel for the claimant in *Palmer*) that since the three stages in the *Caparo* approach overlap, and may be described as "facets of the same thing", it is artificial to limit *Osman* considerations only to the question of whether to impose a duty of care is fair, just and reasonable.

Does Osman apply in "voluntary assumption of responsibility" situations?

As an alternative to seeking to establish a duty of care on the basis of the *Caparo* approach, a claimant may argue that there had been a "voluntary assumption of responsibility" by the defendant.[191] Such a duty of care often arises in relation to negligent advice on which the claimant has relied to his detriment. In *Qazi* v. *Waltham Forest LBC*,[192] Richards J

---

of *Osman* is uncertain, say in that it may also apply to the ingredient of proximity, that is a further and equally powerful reason for concluding that it is not a clear and obvious case for a striking out order".

[188] Transcript.   [189] *Osman*, para 139 (emphasis added).

[190] I.e., the factors the Court refers to in para 138, namely: that the Court accepted the government's contention that the rule did not automatically doom to failure such a civil action from the outset but in principle allowed a domestic court to make a consid-ered assessment on the basis of the arguments before it as to whether a particular case is or is not suitable for the application of the rule.

[191] See *Hedley Byrne & Co Ltd* v. *Heller* [1964] AC 465; *Henderson* v. *Merrett Syndicates Ltd* [1995] 2 AC 145.

[192] (2000) 32 HLR 689. This was a test case action for damages in relation to the local authority's scheme for allocating means-tested housing renovation grants under the Local Government Act 1989. Richards J held that it would have been "plainly arguable" that the scheme was unlawful as a matter of public law, but rejected the claimants' action for negligent misstatement and misfeasance in public office.

held that *Osman* and *Barrett* do not apply to strike out applications in this context:

> But the specific question is whether there was a voluntary assumption of responsibility by the defendant such as to give rise to a duty on the *Hedley Byrne* principle. That is a well established category and does not in itself require separate consideration of whether it is fair, just and reasonable to impose a duty of care. Nor is it contended by the defendant that, if there was a voluntary assumption of responsibility, the defendant's statutory functions were such that a duty should be excluded for reasons of public policy or because it would not be fair, just and reasonable to impose it. The approach I have indicated seems to me to accord with what was said by Lord Goff in *Henderson v. Merrett Syndicates Ltd* and by the Court of Appeal in *Welton v. North Cornwall District Council* about the relationship between the *Hedley Byrne* duty and the "fair, just and reasonable" test.
>
> For similar reasons *Osman* v. *UK* does not in my view pose significant problems. In determining whether a factual situation arguably fits within the category into which the claimants seek to fit it, the court is not applying any exclusionary rule. No question arises of balancing private hardship against considerations of public policy, as in determining whether it is fair, just and reasonable to impose a duty of care. Nevertheless in deciding whether a duty of care might be found to exist I have borne in mind the extent of private hardship arguably suffered by the claimants.
>
> Another respect in which the observations in *Barrett* apply with less force in the present case is that, although of course the full facts have not been found, the claim is based on written material which the court has before it and which is not itself the subject of any dispute.

Do all pre-trial determinations of "fair, just and reasonable" fall foul of Osman?

In *Kinsella* v. *Chief Constable of Nottinghamshire*,[193] the claimant made a negligence claim for damage caused to her property while police were searching her house. Tucker J held that the question of immunity can be decided pre-trial if there is sufficient information in the pleadings;

---

[193] *The Times*, 24 August 1999. See also *A and B* v. *Gloucestershire County Council,* 14 March 2000, CA (in an appropriate case, a summary hearing can be a fair hearing for the purposes of Article 6.1).

the decision as to whether the immunity applies is not restricted to the full hearing. On the restrictive reading of the Strasbourg cases, this may be correct.[194] If, however, the cases should be interpreted as creating a right "to call into account in adversarial proceedings", nothing short of a trial may suffice.[195]

[194] See p. 126.
[195] See p. 127.

Positive Obligations Under the Convention

Keir Starmer

INTRODUCTION

In many respects, the European Convention on Human Rights is mainly concerned with setting limits on the ability of state authorities to interfere with individual rights. The scheme of the Convention is therefore to spell out a number of rights and then to set out the circumstances (if any) in which those rights can be restricted. In this sense the Convention defines the negative obligations of state authorities: i.e. obligations to refrain from certain action.

However, the Convention is also concerned with positive obligations: i.e. obligations on state authorities to take positive steps or measures to protect the Convention rights of individuals. These obligations take a number of forms. The most straightforward arise where, by very definition, a Convention right requires the provision of resources. The right to free legal assistance in criminal cases under Article 6(3)(c), the right to education under Article 2 of Protocol 1 and the duty to hold elections under Article 3 of Protocol 1 are obvious examples.

Other positive obligations arise more discreetly. Their foundation lies in the recognition that a purely negative approach to the protection of human rights cannot guarantee their effective protection and that the acts of private individuals can threaten human rights just as much as the acts of state authorities. Their scope and content are more controversial.

Unfortunately, the European Court has expressly declined to develop any "general theory" of positive obligations[1] and any attempt, such as this, to extract the key principles from its jurisprudence and to locate them in a coherent framework is inevitably somewhat precarious. However, as the case-law referred to in this chapter demonstrates, there

---

[1] *Platform Artze fur das Leben* v. *Austria* (1991) 13 EHRR 204.

is no longer any question of whether the European Convention on Human Rights imposes positive obligations on state authorities, only the questions, when and to what extent? And for public authorities anxious to know the extent of the duties and liabilities under the Human Rights Act 1998, these are questions which cannot be left unanswered.

THE THEORETICAL BASIS FOR POSITIVE OBLIGATIONS

Any search for a theoretical basis for the imposition of positive obligations under the European Convention has to grapple with, and try to explain, the fundamental difference in approach between the US Supreme Court and the European Court of Human Rights to positive obligations. The cases of *DeShaney* v. *Winnebago Social Services Department*[2] and *A* v. *UK*[3] provide good examples.

In March 1984, Randy DeShaney beat Joshua, his four-year-old son, so severely that he fell into a life-threatening coma. Emergency brain surgery revealed a series of haemorrhages caused by traumatic injuries to his head inflicted over a long period of time. Joshua did not die, but suffered brain damage so severe that he is expected to spend the rest of his life confined to an institution for those with profound learning difficulties. Randy DeShaney was subsequently tried and convicted of child abuse.

There was a history. The local Department of Social Services (DSS) had first learnt that Joshua might be the victim of violence two years earlier, but when Randy DeShaney denied the allegations made against him, the DSS did not pursue the matter. One year later Joshua, then three years old, was admitted to hospital with multiple injuries. He was temporarily placed in the custody of the hospital, but later returned to his father, who had entered a voluntary agreement with the DSS to attend a counselling course and to enrol Joshua on a preschool programme.

Over the next six months the DSS caseworker made monthly visits to the DeShaney home, during which she observed a number of suspicious injuries on Joshua's head; she also noticed that he had not been enrolled in school. The caseworker dutifully recorded these injuries in

---

[2] (1989) 489 US 189.   [3] (1999) 27 EHRR 611.

her files, along with her suspicions that Joshua was still the victim of violence, but did nothing more.

In November 1983, the hopital emergency services notified the DSS that Joshua had again been treated for injuries consistent with violence. And on the caseworker's next two visits to the DeShaney home, she was told that Joshua was too ill to see her. Still the DSS took no action; leaving Randy DeShaney to inflict the beating that irreversibly changed Joshua's life in March 1984.

Joshua's mother (who lived separately) brought an action on Joshua's behalf against the DSS in the United States District Court, Eastern Wisconsin. Relying on the Due Process Clause of the Fourteenth Amendment, which provides that "[n]o state shall . . . deprive any person of life, liberty, or property, without due process of law", they claimed that the DSS had deprived Joshua of his liberty interest – widely defined to include "unjustified intrusions on personal security"[4] – by failing to provide him with adequate protection against his father's violence.

They lost. The District Court granted summary judgment for the DSS and this was upheld by the Court of Appeals for the Seventh Circuit on the basis that the Due Process Clause of the Fourteenth Amendment does not require state or local government authorities to protect their citizens from "private violence, or other mishaps not attributable to the conduct of its employees".[5] In so holding, the Court specifically rejected the position endorsed in two previous decisions[6] that once the State learns that a particular child is in danger of abuse from third parties and actually undertakes to protect him from that danger, a "special relationship" arises between it and the child which imposes an affirmative constitutional duty to provide adequate protection.

Joshua and his mother appealed to the Supreme Court. They lost again. Delivering the judgment of the majority, Chief Justice Renquist observed that:

> . . . nothing in the language of the Due Process Clause itself requires the State to protect the life, liberty, and property of its citizens against

---

[4] *Ingraham* v. *Wright* (1977) 430 US 651 at 673.

[5] *DeShaney* v. *Winnebago City Social Services* Department (1987) 812 F.2d 298.

[6] *Oare* v. *County of York* (1985) 470 US 1052, and *Jensen* v. *Conrad* (1984) 474 F.2d 185.

invasion by private actors. The Clause is phrased as a limitation on the State's power to act, not as a guarantee of certain minimal levels of safety and security. It forbids the State itself to deprive individuals of life, liberty, or property without "due process of law", but its language cannot fairly be extended to impose an affirmative obligation on the State to ensure that those interests do not come to harm through other means. Nor does history support such an expansive reading of the constitutional text. Like its counterpart in the Fifth Amendment, the Due Process Clause in the Fourteenth Amendment was intended to prevent government "from abusing [its] power, or employing it as an instrument of oppression" . . . Its purpose was to protect the people from the State, not to ensure that the State protected them from each other. The Framers were content to leave the extent of governmental obligation in the latter area to the democratic political processes.

Consistent with these principles, our cases have recognised that the Due Process Clauses generally confer no affirmative right to governmental aid, even where such aid may be necessary to secure life, liberty, or property interests of which the government itself may not deprive the individual.[7]

From this, the Supreme Court reasoned, if state authorities are under no duty to protect their citizens from the acts of other individuals, the DSS could not be liable to Joshua and his mother where it had failed to do so.

In *A* v. *UK*,[8] the European Court of Human Rights took a different stance. There the applicant, a nine year-old child, had been regularly beaten at home by his stepfather with a stick. He was examined by a consultant paediatrician who found the following marks on his body: (a) a fresh red linear bruise on the back of the right thigh, consistent with a blow from a garden cane, probably within the preceding twenty-four hours; (b) a double linear bruise on the back of the left calf, consistent with two separate blows given some time before the first injury; (c) two lines on the back of the left thigh, probably caused by two blows one or two days previously; (d) three linear bruises on the right bottom, consistent with three blows, possibly given at different times and up to one week old; (e) a fading linear bruise, probably several days old. The paediatrician considered that the bruising was consistent with the use

---

[7] *DeShaney* v. *Winnebago Social Services* Department (1989) 489 US 189 at 195-6.
[8] (1999) 27 EHRR 611.

of a garden cane, applied with considerable force on more than one occasion.

A's stepfather was charged and prosecuted for an offence of assault occasioning actual bodily harm, but acquitted by the majority verdict of a jury. He did not deny causing A's injuries, but claimed that caning the child was necessary and reasonable because A was a difficult boy who did not respond to parental or school discipline. In criminal proceedings for assault of a child, the burden of proof is on the prosecution to satisfy the jury, beyond a reasonable doubt, that the assault did not constitute lawful punishment. Such an approach affords the defendant broad protection, but is obviously somewhat less generous to the alleged victim.

When A subsequently petitioned the European Court of Human Rights on the basis that the State had failed to protect him from illtreatment by his stepfather, the government argued that no direct responsibility could attach to the State in respect of the acts of a parent or step-parent within the home. The European Court disagreed. In a unanimous judgment, it held that:

> . . . the obligation on the High Contracting Parties under Article 1 of the Convention to secure to everyone within their jurisdiction the rights and freedoms defined in the Convention, taken together with Article 3, requires States to take measures designed to ensure that individuals within their jurisdiction are not subjected to torture or inhuman or degrading treatment or punishment, including such ill-treatment adminsistered by private individuals. Children and other vulnerable individuals, in particular, are entitled to state protection in the form of effective deterrence against such serious breaches of personal integrity.[9]

Since the criminal offence of assault permitted lawful punishment amounting, in A's case, to inhuman and degrading treatment, the protection it provided was not effective and the State was liable.

Of course, legitimate distinctions can be drawn between the cases of *DeShaney* and *A* v. *UK*: not least that in *DeShaney*, Joshua's father was successfully prosecuted for child abuse; and in *A* v. *UK* no allegation was being made that the local social services had failed to protect A in any way – the focus of the case was effectiveness of the criminal law as a mechanism for protecting him. However, these distinctions cannot

---

[9] Paragraph 22.

mask the fact that the approach of the US Supreme Court – the Constitution cannot fairly be extended to impose a duty of affirmative action on the State – and the European Court of Human Rights – states are required to take positive measures to protect private individuals – reflect a fundamentally different concept of human rights protection.

For the US Supreme Court the position is relatively straightforward. The purpose of the Bill of Rights provisions in the Constitution is to protect individuals from the State and hence only negative obligations can be derived from them. Positive obligations are for the democratically-elected legislature. And herein lies the difference. It is not that the US Supreme Court disapproves of positive obligations, nor that the European Convention on Human Rights is necessarily a better instrument than the US Constitution for the protection of human rights. It is simply that the US Supreme Court takes the view that the legislature, not the judges, should make decisions with resource implications.

As noted above, in reviewing the history of the Due Process Clause in the Fourteenth Amendment in *DeShaney*, the Supreme Court observed that "The Framers were content to leave the extent of governmental obligation in the latter area to the democratic political processes". And, in concluding, Chief Justice Rehnquist said:

> The people of Wisconsin may well prefer a system of liability which would place upon the State and its officials the responsibility for failure to act in situations such as the present one. They may create such a system, if they do not have it already, by changing the tort law of the State in accordance with the law-making process. But they should not have it thrust upon them by this Court's expansion of the Due Process Clause of the Fourteenth Amendment.[10]

In other words, to the extent that they are legitimised by the democratic process, positive obligations can find reflection in the law, but they cannot simply be read into the human rights provisions of the Constitution.

The European Convention on Human Rights was drafted in different times and incorporates different values. Unlike the US Constitution, the purpose of the Convention is not primarily to safeguard individual freedom from over-mighty government. It is to safeguard human dignity. It was born out of the experiences of the Second

---

[10] Page 203.

World War; in particular, the ruthless oppression and annihilation of minorities and dissidents by the Nazis, assisted by the collaboration of millions of ordinary people.

Along with the Universal Declaration of Human Rights, the adoption of the European Convention on Human Rights represented the beginning of a new era in the protection of human rights. The idea that the majority could necessarily be trusted to protect the rights of minorities, or that private individuals did not need state protection from the acts of other private individuals, was morally discredited. The emphasis in the Convention is therefore on the "effective" protection of human rights, not the entrenchment of "theoretical" or "illusory" rights.

Take, for example, the approach of the European Court to the protection of Article 11 rights in the case of *Plattform Ärzte für das Leben* v. *Austria;*[11] chosen here because the Article 11 right to peaceful assembly is manifestly not an absolute right under the Convention and, it might therefore be assumed, not one that necessarily attracts any special kind of protection. The applicants in that case, a group of anti-abortion protestors, complained to the European Court that they had been unable to exercise their right of peaceful assembly because every time they organised a rally or march, they were attacked by counter-demonstrators. The Austrian Government responded by claiming that, since it had not interfered with the applicants' rights, it could not be responsible for any breach of Article 11 of the Convention. This was robustly rejected by the European Court on the basis that:

> . . . a demonstration may annoy or give offence to persons opposed to the ideas or claims that it is seeking to promote. The participants must however be able to hold the demonstration without having to fear that they will be subjected to physical violence by their opponents; such a fear would be liable to deter associations or other groups supporting common ideas or interests from openly expressing their opinions on highly controversial issues affecting the community. In a democracy the right to counter-demonstrate cannot extend to inhibiting the exercise of the right to demonstrate.

Genuine, effective freedom of peaceful assembly cannot, therefore, be reduced to a mere duty on the part of the state not to interfere; a purely negative conception would not be compatible with the object and purpose of Article 11. Like Article 8, Article 11 sometimes requires

[11] A/139 (1988) 13 EHRR 204.

> positive measures to be taken, even in the sphere of relations between individuals, if need be.[12]

What was needed was effective policing to enable the applicants to exercise their right to peaceful assembly free from the attacks of counter-demonstrators.[13]

This notion of effectiveness runs like a thread through Convention jurisprudence. It was the basis for the European Court's judgments in the seminal cases of *Airey* v. *Ireland*,[14] *X and Y* v. *Netherlands*,[15] *Soering* v. *UK*[16] and, more recently, *Aydin* v. *Turkey*.[17] It was also the springboard for the European Court's development of an extended notion of state liability under the Convention and its wide definition of a "victim"; and, it is suggested, provides the theoretical basis for the imposition of positive obligations on state authorities under the Convention, the scope of which will now be addressed.

THE SCOPE OF POSITIVE OBLIGATIONS UNDER THE CONVENTION

The European Court has emphasised that the way in which state authorities go about protecting individuals from the actions of other individuals is largely a matter for their discretion because "regard must be had to the fair balance that has to be struck between the competing interests of the individual and of the community as a whole".[18] As a result cases often appear to turn on the character of the Convention right engaged and the seriousness of the breach in issue. However, the suggestion advanced in this chapter is that close analysis reveals that a number of general principles can be discerned from the Court's case-law. In particular, five broad positive duties can be identified, namely:

(1) A duty to put in place a legal framework which provides effective protection for Convention rights.
(2) A duty to prevent breaches of Convention rights.

---

[12] Paragraph 32.

[13] On the facts, however, the Court held that the policing provided by the Austrian authorities was sufficient to discharge this duty.

[14] (1979) 2 EHRR 305.   [15] (1985) 8 EHRR 235.

[16] (1989) 11 EHRR 439.   [17] (1997) 25 EHRR 251.

[18] *Powell and Rayner* v. *UK* A/172 (1990) 12 EHRR 355.

(3) A duty to provide information and advice relevant to a breach of
Convention rights.
(4) A duty to respond to breaches of Convention rights.
(5) A duty to provide resources to individuals to prevent breaches of
their Convention rights.

Each of these will be examined in turn.

THE DUTY TO PUT IN PLACE A LEGAL FRAMEWORK
WHICH PROVIDES EFFECTIVE PROTECTION FOR
CONVENTION RIGHTS

The duty to put in place a legal framework which provides effective
protection for Convention rights in many respects represents the minimum obligation of Contracting States under the Convention. The
Convention does not require its terms to be incorporated directly into
domestic law, but it does require a framework of effective remedies.

Broadly speaking the Court and Commission have been content to
leave it to the domestic authorities to decide how best to set up the
required legal framework. So, for example, in a number of cases against
the UK, the Commission has accepted that the availability of civil
remedies for defamation or malicious prosecution can be sufficient to
protect privacy rights under Article 8.[19] However, there are some
circumstances where breach of a Convention right is so serious that the
Court has insisted that criminal law sanctions must be put in place.

In *X and Y* v. *Netherlands*,[20] the perpetrator of a sexual assault on the
second applicant had not been prosecuted because under Dutch law
the fact that the victim was a sixteen year-old woman with a mental
disorder prevented her from initiating a criminal "complaint". The
government argued that since it was possible to bring civil proceedings
for compensation, its obligations under Article 8 had been fulfilled.
The Court disagreed. In its view:

> . . . the protection afforded by the civil law in the case of wrongdoing of
> the kind inflicted on Miss Y is insufficient. This is a case where funda-
> mental values and essential aspects of private life are at stake. Effective

[19] See *Stewart-Brady* v. *UK* (1997) 24 EHRR CD 38 and *Winer* v. *UK* (1986) 48
DR 154.
[20] A/91 (1985) 8 EHRR 235.

deterrence is indispensable in this area and it can be achieved only by criminal-law provisions; indeed, it is by such provisions that the matter is normally regulated.[21]

Since Dutch law was defective in this respect, state responsibility was engaged.

In *Stubbings* v. *UK*,[22] the applicants attempted to extend the reach of the decision in *X and Y* v. *Netherlands* by arguing that the widespread problem of child sexual abuse, which was only beginning to be properly understood, demanded new measures for the protection of minors. Their complaint was that the House of Lords' interpretation of the Limitation Act 1980 in *Stubbings* v. *Webb*[23] restricting the scope for extending the limitation period in civil proceedings based on child sexual abuse, effectively deprived them of a remedy against their abusers contrary to Article 8 of the Convention.

The European Court began its analysis by reiterating that "[s]exual abuse is unquestionably an abhorrent type of wrongdoing, with debilitating effects on its victims. Children and other vulnerable individuals are entitled to State protection, in the form of effective deterrence, from such grave types of interference with essential aspects of their private lives". However, in its view:

> In the instant case . . . such protection was afforded. The abuse of which the applicants complained is regarded most seriously by the English criminal law and subject to severe maximum penalties. Provided sufficient evidence could be secured, a criminal prosecution could have been brought. . . .
>
> In principle, civil remedies are also available provided they are brought within the statutory time-limit . . . Article 8 does not necessarily require that States fulfil their positive obligation to secure respect for private life by the provision of unlimited civil remedies in circumstances where criminal law sanctions are in operation.[24]

Where the law provides no remedy at all for Convention breaches the position will be different.

In *Young, James and Webster* v. *UK*,[25] the government argued that it was not responsible for the applicant's dismissal by British Rail for non-

---

[21] Paragraph 27.
[22] Appl. 22083/93 and 22095/93 (1996) 23 EHRR 213.
[23] [1993] AC 498. [24] Paragraph 64. [25] A/44 (1980) 4 EHRR 38.

membership of a trade union. Rather than analyse the extent to which the State was responsible for running British Rail, the Court approached the case on the basis that since Article 1 of the Convention imposed a duty on the State to "secure" Convention rights to everyone within its jurisdiction:

> . . . if a violation of one of those rights and freedoms is the result of non-observance of that obligation in the enactment of domestic legislation, the responsibility of the State for that violation is engaged.

Notwithstanding the fact that the immediate cause of the applicants' dismissal was an agreement between British Rail and the railway unions, the Court took the view that:

> . . . it was the domestic law in force at the relevant time that made lawful the treatment of which the applicants complained. The responsibility of the Respondent State for any resultant breach of the Convention is thus engaged . . .[26]

In effect, therefore, the Court extended state responsibility into the sphere of relations between private individuals because it was responsible for legislation which allowed others to breach the applicants' Convention rights.

The principle articulated in *Young, James and Webster* v. *UK*[27] was applied in *Stedman* v. *UK*[28] which involved an allegation that the applicant had been dismissed because of her religious beliefs contrary to Article 9 of the Convention. Adopting the reasoning of the Court in *Young, James and Webster* v. *UK*,[29] the Commission held that it was irrelevant that the dismissal was the act of a purely private company if the dismissal was lawful in domestic law. On the facts, however, it found that the applicant had not been dismissed because of her religious beliefs.

---

[26] Paragraph 49.   [27] A/44 (1980) 4 EHRR 38.
[28] Appl. 29107/95 (1997) 23 EHRR 168 CD.
[29] A/44 (1980) 4 EHRR 38.

THE DUTY TO PREVENT BREACHES OF
CONVENTION RIGHTS

It appears that, in some circumstances, providing a legal framework which provides effective protection for human rights will not be enough, and more specific steps are needed. The Court has never defined the circumstances in which such steps are needed, but its case-law seems to suggest that the duty to prevent breaches of Convention rights arises in (at least) three situations:

(1) Where fundamental rights such as those in Articles 2 and 3 are at stake.
(2) Where intimate interests such as those protected in Article 8 are at stake.
(3) Where Convention rights cannot be effectively protected by the legal framework in place.

Each of these requires examination.

Positive obligations where fundamental rights are at stake

The fundamental nature of the rights protected by Article 2 (the right to life) and Article 3 (the prohibition on torture and inhuman treatment/punishment) demand special protection. After the event remedies for breach are not sufficient: reasonable preventative measures are called for.

The positive duty to protect the right to life under Article 2 requires that reasonable steps be taken by the state (and its officials) to protect life. This includes a duty to put in place "effective criminal law provisions to deter the commission of offences against the person backed up by law-enforcement machinery for the prevention, suppression and sanctioning of breaches of such provisions".[30] It may also include, in certain well-defined circumstances, a positive obligation on the authorities to take preventative operational measures to protect individuals whose lives are at risk from the criminal acts of another individual.[31]

---

[30] *Osman* v. *UK*, 28 October 1998 (2000) 29 EHRR 245 at para 115.
[31] *Ibid.*

In *Osman* v. *UK*,[32] the Court held that such obligations arise where it can be established that:

> ... the authorities knew or ought to have known at the time of the existence of a real and immediate risk to the life of an identified individual or individuals from the criminal acts of a third party and that they failed to take measures within the scope of their powers which, judged reasonably, might have been expected to avoid that risk.[33]

In that case, an argument that the police failed to take adequate steps to prevent a teacher, who was infatuated with the second applicant, attacking him and killing his father failed on the facts.

In *Soering* v. *UK*,[34] the Court held that the absolute prohibition on torture and inhuman treatment/punishment would render the UK Government responsible for a breach of Article 3 if it extradited the applicant to another State in circumstances where there were substantial grounds for believing that he would be in danger of being subject to such treatment/punishment. The fact that the State was not itself responsible for the treatment/punishment in question was irrelevant. In the earlier case of *Altun* v. *Germany*[35] the Commission recognised that this principle applied even where "the danger does not emanate from public authorities for whom the receiving State is responsible".

It also appears that state authorities have positive duties to protect life even where death or serious injury is not *intentional*. In *X* v. *UK*,[36] the applicant association complained that the vaccination programme organised by the government caused severe damage to some babies and had sometimes even resulted in death. In its decision on admissibility the Commission stated that:

> The concept that "everyone's life shall be protected by law" enjoins the State not only to refrain from taking life *intentionally* but, further, to take appropriate steps to safeguard life.[37]

It went on to find that, on the facts, it could not be said that the State had failed to take adequate and appropriate measures to protect life.[38]

---

[32] *Osman* v. *UK.*   [33] *Ibid.* para 116.   [34] A/161 (1989) 11 EHRR 439.
[35] (1983) 36 DR 209.   [36] 14 DR 31.   [37] Paragraph 2.
[38] See also *Tavares* v. *France* Appl 16539/90 (1991) unreported and *H* v. *France* (1989) 12 EHRR 74 concerning allegations of medical negligence resulting in death.

Whether a right to medical treatment can be read into the Convention by this route is not clear. In *Tanko* v. *Finland*[39] the Commission expressly refused to exclude the possibility that "a lack of proper medical care in a case where someone is suffering from serious illness could in certain circumstances amount to treatment contrary to Article 3". And the question of whether Article 2 imposes a duty on state authorities to provide free medical care for those whose lives are at risk was left open by the Commission in *X* v. *Ireland*.[40]

Positive obligations where intimate interests are at stake

Many of the cases on positive obligations have involved Article 8, which protects a number of intimate interests under the umbrella of "private and family life". These have mainly turned on the question of whether or not the state has put in place a legal framework which effectively protects Convention rights. So, for example, the Court's decision in *Marckx* v. *Belgium*[41] that the non-existence in Belgian law of measures to safeguard the integration of all children, including illegitimate children, into their families, effectively called for legislative reform.

In *Airey* v. *Ireland*[42] what was in issue was not the existence of a satisfactory legal framework for the protection of Convention rights, but the applicant's access to it. The applicant there complained that her rights under Article 8 had been breached because she was unable to divorce her alcoholic and violent husband because she could not afford legal representation and no legal aid was available to her. Having recognised that protection of family life included the right to separate, the Court held that:

> Effective respect for private or family life obliges Ireland to make this means of protection effectively accessible, when appropriate, to anyone who may wish to have recourse thereto.

In other words, some positive steps were needed to enable the applicant to realise her legal right to separate from her husband.

The principle of effectiveness also underpinned the Court's decision in *Lopez Ostra* v. *Spain*.[43] On the basis that ". . . severe environmental

---

[39] Appl 23634/94 (1994) unreported.
[40] (1976) 7 DR 78.
[41] A/31 (1979) 2 EHRR 330.
[42] A/32 (1979) 2 EHRR 305.
[43] A/303-C (1994) 20 EHRR 277.

pollution may affect individuals' well-being and prevent them from enjoying their homes in such a way as to affect their private and family life adversely, without, however, seriously endangering their health",[44] the Court held that a positive obligation was imposed on the authorities to take appropriate measures to protect the applicants' right to live their lives free from the adverse effects of severe pollution.[45] By opposing the applicants' legal action to close the waste-treatment plant, the Spanish authorities had failed in that duty and prolonged the applicants' exposure to pollution.

A different result followed in *Osman* v. *UK*[46] where, in addition to their argument under Article 2, the applicants also advanced an argument under Article 8. The nub of their complaint was that the police had failed to bring to an end the campaign of harassment, vandalism and victimisation, which the second applicant's teacher had waged against their property. The Court accepted that an obligation on the police to take preventative measures could arise under Article 8, but found that, on the facts, the police had done all they could reasonably have been expected to do.

Positive obligations where Convention rights cannot be effectively protected by the legal framework in place

The circumstances in which a positive obligation is imposed on state authorities to take some action on the basis that Convention rights cannot be effectively protected by the legal framework in place are inevitably varied. The basis for the Court's decision in *Plattform Ärzte für das Leben* v. *Austria*[47] was a recognition that effective protection for the right of peaceful assembly required immediate police action on the streets. Legal proceedings after the event were no substitute for the practical exercise of the right in issue. And remedies such as preventative injunctions were of limited use without police enforcement.

---

[44] Paragraph 51.   [45] Paragraph 55.   [46] (2000) 29 EHRR 245.
[47] A/139 (1988) 13 EHRR 204.

THE DUTY TO PROVIDE INFORMATION AND ADVICE
RELEVANT TO A BREACH OF CONVENTION RIGHTS

In a number of recent cases, the Court has recognised that in many situations, individuals can only protect their Convention rights if they have access to relevant information. In *Guerra* v. *Italy*,[48] the Court took the principles it had established in *Lopez Ostra* v. *Spain*[49] a step further and established a positive obligation to provide information to those affected by environmental pollution. The facts in that case were similar: the applicants lived near a chemical factory which was classified as "high risk". However, their complaint was framed more broadly. They claimed that the authorities had failed to properly respect their right to family life and home by failing to provide them with information about the risks of living near the factory and how to proceed in the event of an accident.

Although the Commission had proceeded on the basis that the applicants had a right to the information they sought under Article 10, the Court rejected this. In its view, Article 10 "basically prohibits a government from restricting a person from receiving information that others wish or may be willing to impart to him".[50] However, the Court found a breach of Article 8 on the basis that once the authorities became aware of essential information about the dangers inherent in the running of the factory, they delayed for several years before passing that information to the applicants and therefore prevented them from assessing the risks they and their families ran by continuing to live in the vicinity of the factory.

In *LCB* v. *UK*[51] the applicant, the daughter of a man who had been present during nuclear testing at Christmas Island in the late 1950s when he was serving in the RAF, complained that the authorities had failed to advise her parents to monitor her health prior to her diagnosis with leukaemia. The Court approached the case on the basis that;

> . . . the State could only have been required of its own motion to take these steps in relation to the applicant if it had appeared likely at that time that any such exposure of her father to radiation might have engendered a real risk to her health.[52]

---

[48] (1998) 26 EHRR 357.   [49] A/303-C (1994) 20 EHRR 277.
[50] Paragraph 53; see also *Leander* v. *Sweden* A/116 (1987) 9 EHRR 433.
[51] (1998) 27 EHRR 212.   [52] Paragraph 38.

On its analysis of the facts known at the time, it concluded that the authorities could not reasonably have been expected to have established any link between the exposure of the applicant's father to radiation and the likelihood that his children might develop leukaemia.

The position was different in *McGinley and Egan* v. *UK*[53] where the applicants had themselves been exposed to radiation in the same tests and claimed, under Article 8, that they should have been provided with information sufficient to enable them to assess the possible consequences of the tests for their health. The Court held that Article 8 was applicable because:

> . . . given the fact that exposure to high levels of radiation is known to have hidden, but serious and long-lasting, effects on health, it is not unnatural that the applicants' uncertainty as to whether or not they had been put at risk in this way caused them substantial anxiety and distress . . .
>
> . . . since the [radiation level records] contained information which might have assisted the applicants in assessing radiation levels in the areas in which they were stationed during the tests, and might indeed have served to reassure them in this respect, they had an interest under Article 8 in obtaining access to them.[54]

In those circumstances the Court took the view that a positive obligation under Article 8 arose. As a matter of principle:

> Where a Government engages in hazardous activities, such as those in issue in the present case, which might have hidden adverse consequences on the health of those involved in such activities, respect for private and family life under Article 8 requires that an effective and accessible procedure be established which enables persons to seek all relevant and appropriate information."[55]

On the facts, however, the Court found no breach of this positive obligation because the applicants could have sought access to the relevant documents in proceedings before the Pension Appeal Tribunal but had failed to do so.

Establishing the scope of the duty to provide information is, however, difficult. In *Gaskin* v. *UK*[56] the applicant, who had been

---

[53] (1998) 27 EHRR 1.   [54] Paragraph 99.   [55] Paragraph 101.
[56] (1989) 12 EHRR 36.

taken into care when his mother died, wished to obtain details of the foster homes in which he had been brought up, but was refused access to some of the local authority's records on the ground that the information in question was private and confidential. Having decided that this was a case in which effective respect for the applicant's private and family life imposed a positive obligation, the Court was divided as to its scope. A minority considered that the local authority had gone as far as it reasonably could by writing to each contributor to the case file, asking for permission to release the relevant part of the record. The majority, on the other hand, acknowledged that a system which made access dependent on the contributors' consent was not objectionable in principle, but ruled that the interests of those in the applicant's position could only be secured if there was an independent authority to decide on the issue of access when a contributor was not available or refused consent improperly.

THE DUTY TO RESPOND TO BREACHES OF CONVENTION RIGHTS

Where fundamental rights are in issue, such as those under Articles 2 and 3, the Court has imposed an obligation on states to respond diligently to any breaches. The payment of compensation is insufficient, an efficient investigation must be carried out, backed up with criminal prosecutions where appropriate.

This duty is particularly strict where it is suggested that police officers or other public officials may be responsible for the breach. Its scope was examined by the Court in *Aydin* v. *Turkey*[57] where the applicant complained that during her detention by the security forces in Turkey she was raped and subjected to other forms of ill treatment amounting to torture under Article 3 of the Convention. The Court held that:

> Given the fundamental importance of the prohibition of torture and the especially vulnerable position of torture victims, Article 13 imposes, without prejudice to any other remedy available under the domestic system, an obligation on states to carry out a thorough and effective investigation of incidents of torture.

---

[57] (1997) 25 EHRR 251.

Accordingly it formulated the following principle:

> . . . where an individual has an arguable claim that he or she has been
> tortured by agents of the state, the notion of an "effective remedy"
> entails, in addition to the payment of compensation where appropriate,
> a thorough and effective investigation capable of leading to the identifi-
> cation and punishment of those responsible and including effective
> access for the complainant to the investigatory procedure.[58]

Having regard to this principle, the Court found a breach of the
Convention because the Turkish authorities had carried out an incom-
plete enquiry to determine the veracity of the applicant's complaint.

THE DUTY TO PROVIDE RESOURCES TO INDIVIDUALS
WHOSE CONVENTION RIGHTS ARE AT STAKE

As noted above, some Articles of the Convention by their very nature
impose a duty on the State to provide resources such as free legal assistance etc. In *Airey* v. *Ireland*[59] this principle was extended on the basis
that the right there in issue – family life – could not be effectively
protected without the provision of resources, legal aid in divorce
proceedings, by the State. And the principle is one of general application.

On several occasions applicants have argued that the right to family
life under Article 8 of the Convention imposes a positive obligation on
state authorities to provide them with financial assistance to enable one
of two parents to stay at home and take care of their children. So far,
the Commission has rejected such arguments. In *Andersson and
Kullman* v. *Sweden*,[60] the Commission rejected a complaint that the
decision of the Swedish social services to terminate family allowance
payments and replace them with free creche places to enable the second
applicant to work breached Article 8. And in *A.P.* v. *Austria*[61] it rejected
a complaint that failure to make long-term parental leave payments to
enable a father to stay at home and look after his children breached
Article 8.

There may be circumstances in which a local authority comes under
a positive obligation under the Convention to provide housing to those

---

[58] *Ibid.*   [59] A/32 (1979) 2 EHRR 305.   [60] 46 DR 251.
[61] (1995) 20 EHRR CD 63.

within its catchment area. However, they are only likely to arise in exceptional cases. In *Burton* v. *UK*,[62] the Commission rejected an argument that in failing to provide an individual suffering from cancer with a place where she could live out her days in a caravan according to her Romany gypsy background, a local authority had failed in its obligations under Article 8.

THE RELATIONSHIP BETWEEN POSITIVE AND NEGATIVE OBLIGATIONS

The boundaries between a state's positive and negative obligations do not lend themselves to precise definition. In many situations the applicable principles are the same. As the Court observed in *Powell and Rayner* v. *UK*:[63]

> In both contexts regard must be had to the fair balance that has to be struck between the competing interests of the individual and of the community as a whole; and in both contexts the State enjoys a certain margin of appreciation in determining the steps to be taken to ensure compliance with the Convention. Furthermore, even in relation to the positive obligations flowing from the first paragraph of Article 8, in striking the required balance the aims mentioned in the second paragraph may be of a certain relevance.[64]

That case and *Lopez Ostra* v. *Spain*[65] provide striking examples of the interrelationship between the two types of obligations.

In *Powell and Rayner* v. *UK*[66] the applicants, who lived near Heathrow Airport, complained that the excessive noise from the airport breached their rights under Article 8 to respect for their private life and home. As a preliminary issue, the government argued that the complaint disclosed no direct "interference by a public authority" because Heathrow Airport and the aircraft using it were not and never had been owned, controlled or operated by the government or any agency of the government. The Court disagreed. In its view:

---

[62] (1996) 22 EHRR CD 134.
[64] Paragraph 41.
[66] A/172 (1990) 12 EHRR 355.

[63] A/172 (1990) 12 EHRR 355.
[65] A/303-C (1994) 20 EHRR 277.

Whether the present case be analysed in terms of a positive duty on the State to take reasonable and appropriate measures to secure the applicants' rights under paragraph (1) of Article 8 or in terms of an "interference by a public authority" to be justified in accordance with paragraph (2), the applicable principles are broadly similar.[67]

State responsibility was therefore engaged, although, on the facts, it found no breach of the Convention.

A similar approach was taken in *Lopez Ostra* v. *Spain*,[68] where the Court found that state responsibility was engaged where the local authority had failed to take adequate steps to curtail pollution emitted from a privately run waste-treatment plant on the two-fold basis that:

- Although the local authority had not been directly responsible for the plant, it had given permission for it to be built and subsidised its construction.[69]
- And, in any event, under Article 8, the local authority was under a positive obligation to take such measures as were necessary for the protection of the applicants' private and family life.[70]

As noted above, on the facts the Court found that the measures taken by the local authority were inadequate.

CONCLUSION

In many respects positive obligations are the hallmark of the European Convention on Human Rights, and mark it out from other human rights instruments; particularly those drafted before the Second World War. They are clearly not confined to any particular kind of Convention right, although, equally clearly, the extent of any positive obligation arising will vary according to the nature of the issue at stake (a stricter obligation being attached to serious or intimate issues). However, what is important, so far as the Human Rights Act 1998 is concerned, is an appreciation that for the European Court of Human Rights, positive obligations are an integral aspect of Convention rights – part of their very definition – and, as such, they should be given effect in domestic law.

---

[67] Paragraph 41.   [68] A/303-C (1994) 20 EHRR 277.
[69] Paragraph 52.   [70] Paragraph 55.

The "Horizontal Effect" of the Human Rights Act: Moving Beyond the Public–Private Distinction

Murray Hunt

INTRODUCTION

During the two year phoney war between the passage of the Human Rights Act in November 1998 and its entry into force in October 2000, one of the questions which has been the subject of most analysis and speculation has been the so-called question of the Act's "horizontal effect": to what extent will the Act and the Convention rights it brings directly into our law, affect the law which governs relations between private parties, and in particular the common law. In an earlier article on this subject,[1] I argued that the supposed choice between a wholly "vertical" and a directly "horizontal" approach to the reach of fundamental rights legislation was a false one, and that in fact there is a spectrum of possible positions between those two extremes. In other words, how far such a constitutional instrument affects the law governing wholly private relations is a matter of degree.

The article also argued that, following enactment of the Human Rights Act, precisely where on that spectrum the UK will stand when the Act comes into force will no longer be a matter of unconstrained choice. After considering the text and scheme of the Act, its legislative history, and the long established practice of both our domestic courts and the European Court of Human Rights (ECHR), as well as comparative Commonwealth material, the article concluded that the Human Rights Act achieves a significant degree of "horizontal effect", going significantly beyond the "indirect effect" of the equivalent instruments in countries such as Canada and Germany, but stopping short of the full or direct "horizontality" of Ireland, where certain constitutional rights are directly enforceable against other individuals. This meant that,

[1] "The 'Horizontal Effect' of the Human Rights Act" [1998] PL 423.

although the Act would not immediately create any new causes of action against private parties where none previously existed, it would inevitably lead to the development of the common law by the incremental expansion of existing causes of action, or of defences to such causes of action.

Like any debate concerning the public-private distinction, whether fundamental rights instruments have any "horizontal effect" is a deeply ideological one which textual arguments alone are never going to resolve, even in a debate between lawyers. When the Human Rights Act was passed by Parliament containing a provision expressly making courts public authorities and therefore subject to a clear duty to act compatibly with Convention rights,[2] there was every prospect of a highly charged debate erupting between proponents of the limited government school of constitutionalism advocating a narrow, "vertical" interpretation of the Act and the Convention, and advocates of a more social-democratic version of constitutionalism arguing for a more expansive "horizontal" interpretation which can accommodate the positive dimension of Convention rights.

In fact, far from there being a debate raging between "verticalists" and "horizontalists", there has now emerged a remarkable degree of consensus[3] about the extent to which the Human Rights Act makes the Convention relevant to the law governing private relations. The only real area of disagreement, it will be suggested, is over the extent to which the common law governing private relations is affected by the Act, and in particular whether it imposes an *obligation* on courts to develop the common law in such a way as to give effect to Convention rights, and, if so, the extent of that obligation.

This chapter tries to take that debate forward by doing the following. First, it reviews the range of opinions that have emerged on this question in the burgeoning literature on the Act, in an attempt to identify the real area of disagreement that remains. Second, it reflects further on the lessons to be learned from the comparative material, in the light of competing claims in the literature about the support it lends. Third, it argues that what Stephen Sedley in his 1998 Hamlyn Lectures has called "the geometric metaphor" of verticality/horizontality is an inappropriate

---

[2] Sections 6(3)(a) and 6(1) respectively of the Human Rights Act 1998.

[3] In *Michael Douglas and others* v. *Hello! Ltd.* (decision of the Court of Appeal, 21 December 2000), Sedley LJ at para.129 observed that "there is widespread support among commentators on the Act" for the proposition that the step from confidentiality to privacy is "precisely the kind of incremental change for which the Act is designed".

way to conceptualise the questions and will lead to misunderstandings which may frustrate one of the central purposes of the Human Rights Act, which is to make Convention rights practically effective. Fourth, it seeks to suggest an approach which courts should take to this question which is practical, understandable and consistent with the scheme of the Act.

THE RANGE OF OPINIONS

Curiously, the only commentator so far who appears to have taken the extreme view that the Act makes Convention rights directly enforceable against private parties (that is, gives them full horizontal effect) is William Wade.[4] In his 1998 Judicial Studies Board lecture,[5] he argued that the effect of making courts "public authorities" who are obliged to act compatibly with the Convention is that private individuals and bodies are subjected to the Convention rights, which can be enforced directly against them through the courts. Wade has continued to be an advocate of this position, arguing that it is compelled by both the letter of the Act and its spirit.[6]

For reasons which will be explained below, in my view this claim that the Act achieves full or direct horizontal effect for Convention rights is unsustainable: it is plainly inconsistent with the scheme of the Act; it is directly contrary to the explanations of its effect which were given by the ministers promoting it during its passage; and it does not pay sufficient heed to the nature of Convention rights themselves. Wade's view, however, is a useful reference point in the debate about the reach of the Human Rights Act: it occupies the most extreme position at the "full horizontality" end of the spectrum.

At the other end of the spectrum, by comparison, not a single commentator so far has sought to defend the extreme verticalist position, that the Convention rights are entirely irrelevant to the law which governs private relations and the Act therefore has no effect on private law rights and obligations. In one sense this is hardly surprising, given

---

[4] "Curiously", because, as the paradigm "red light" theorist, Wade has been considered by many administrative lawyers to be a staunch defender of the private sphere against the incursion of more "public" values imposed by an overmighty state: see Harlow and Rawlings, *Law and Administration*, 2nd edn. Butterworths 1999).

[5] (1998) EHRLR 522.

[6] H.W.R. Wade, "Horizons of Horizontality" (2000) 116 *LQR* 217.

that the language of the Act, its legislative history and the case-law of the Convention make such an extreme position entirely untenable.[7] But it is highly significant, because it immediately reveals that (Wade apart) the real debate is taking place on a relatively narrow part of the spectrum somewhere in between the two extremes.

The narrowest views so far expressed have been those of Richard Buxton[8] and Sydney Kentridge.[9] Buxton has argued that there are "substantial limitations" on the effect that the Human Rights Act and the ECHR will have on private law.[10] He recognises, as he must, that even before the Human Rights Act indirect use has been made of the ECHR's provisions and values in the interpretation of domestic law, including private law.[11] He also acknowledges that the principle of effectiveness and the fact that courts themselves, as public authorities, have responsibilities imposed on them by the ECHR, "have significance when considering the ability of individuals to resist claims made against them which if upheld would entail a breach of the requirements of the ECHR".[12] To this extent, therefore, he falls short of being an outright verticalist. However, in his view there are "substantial limitations" on the effect of the Act on private law because the rights created by the ECHR are limited to rights against states or against public bodies for which the state is responsible,[13] and human rights values "remain, stubbornly, values whose content lives in public law".[14] On this view, the effects of the Act are safely confined to the realm of public law by asserting the traditional distinction between public and private as if it were uncontroversial that such a clear distinction exists.

Sydney Kentridge, in his comments to a conference on constitutional reform in Cambridge in January 1998, argued that the inclusion of courts in the definition of "public authority" in the Human Rights Act "means only that the courts in their own sphere must give effect to

---

[7] Richard Buxton, however, at times comes very close to this extreme position in his article, "The Human Rights Act and Private Law" (2000) 116 *LQR* 48, in which he invokes the traditional view that there is a rigid distinction between public and private to assert that the Human Rights Act and the ECHR both properly belong "in the sphere of public law".

[8] *Ibid.*

[9] S. Kentridge, "The Incorporation of the European Convention on Human Rights" in *Constitutional Reform in the United Kingdom: Practice and Principles* (1998 Hart Publishing) 69 at 70.

[10] (2000) 116 LQR 48 at 65.

[11] *Ibid.* at 49.   [12] *Ibid.* at 52.   [13] *Ibid.* at 55.   [14] *Ibid.* at 59.

such fundamental rights as the right to a fair trial, and to more particular rights such as a right to an interpreter. The courts must also in their own sphere observe general prohibitions, such as the prohibition of discrimination".[15] It did not mean that the Convention applied as between individual litigants, such as the plaintiff and defendant in a defamation case. In such cases the Convention would influence the common law, but only indirectly, on the German *drittwirkung* model.

Less narrow than Kentridge's view, but stopping significantly short of the position that the Convention applies to all law, is that of Ian Leigh, who has drawn up a typology of horizontal effect, identifying no fewer than six forms of "horizontal effect" which could be said to arise under the Human Rights Act, five of which he accepts exist.[16] Two of these are the types that Kentridge also acknowledges: "remedial horizontality", whereby judges exercising discretionary powers in private litigation must do so in conformity with Convention rights; and "indirect horizontality", which is the indirect influence the Convention exerts over the general development of the common law as it applies between private parties.

In addition to these, Leigh acknowledges what he labels "direct statutory horizontality", which refers to the fact that even statutes which apply to private relations are still subject to the interpretive obligation in section 3(1) to give effect to Convention rights so far as it is possible to do so. "Public liability horizontality" refers to the fact that under the Act the definition of "public authority" may be wider than the category of bodies or persons for which the State may be liable in Strasbourg. And "intermediate horizontality" refers to the situation where a Convention right may be claimed against a public authority in respect of its failure to take action against a third party whose actions harm the plaintiff.

Leigh therefore acknowledges that the Act has a considerable degree of horizontal effect, but he cannot accept that the Act has what he calls "full or direct horizontal effect" in the sense that courts, as public authorities, are required to create appropriate rights and remedies by developing the common law.[17] He sees this as the most contentious

---

[15] Cf. the early arguments made in New Zealand about the significance of the judicial branch being bound by the New Zealand Bill of Rights Act 1990, considered below.

[16] I. Leigh, "Horizontal Rights, the Human Rights Act and Privacy: Lessons from the Commonwealth" (1999) 48 *ICLQ* 57.

[17] See also G. Phillipson, "The Human Rights Act, 'Horizontal Effect' and the Common Law: a Bang or a Whimper?" (1999) 62 *MLR* 824, who argues that no general

type of horizontal effect and in his view it is unsupported by the drafting of the Act, the scheme of the Convention, or constitutional principle elucidated by courts in other jurisdictions which have faced identical problems.[18]

Anthony Lester and David Pannick, on the other hand, explicitly accept that the consequence of courts being public authorities is that they are under a duty to develop the common law in order to achieve compatibility:

> "Because the courts are public authorities, they have a duty to ensure that Convention rights are protected even in litigation between private parties. The obligation of the court under s. 6 will apply where the Convention has effect on the legal relationship between private parties because the state (acting through its courts) is obliged, under the Convention, to protect individuals against breaches of their rights."[19]

This brief survey of the literature reveals a surprisingly large amount of consensus about the extent to which the law governing "private" disputes is affected by the Act. All commentators appear to be agreed that the Convention is relevant to the development of the common law governing private relations, and the only area of real disagreement is whether, and if so to what extent courts are *obliged* to develop the common law to protect Convention rights. It appears that the debate is not so much about whether the law governing private relations should be compatible with Convention rights (that debate has largely been settled by the form of the legislation); it seems to be more concerned

---

duty to ensure the compatibility of all private common law with Convention rights can be deduced from the Act. Instead, he argues that the most satisfactory interpretation of the Court's duty under s. 6(1) is that "the rights will figure only as principles to which the courts must have regard", *ibid.* at 848.

[18] Leigh, n. 16 *supra*, at 87. Although I am attributed with having reached a similar conclusion, *ibid.*, at n. 126, Leigh's analysis does not distinguish between an entirely new cause of action and an incremental development in the scope of an existing cause of action, a distinction which is crucial to maintaining a meaningful difference between illegitimate horizontality under the Human Rights Act and permissible development of the common law pursuant to the obligation on courts to act compatibly.

[19] Lester and Pannick (eds.), *Human Rights Law and Practice* (Butterworths, 1999) para. 2.6.3, n. 3 (pp. 31-2). This also appears to be the view taken by Lord Hope in *R* v. *DPP, ex p Kebilene* [1999] 4 All ER 801 at 838h-j, who said "It is now plain that the incorporation of the ECHR into our domestic law will subject the entire legal system to a fundamental process of review and, where necessary, reform by the judiciary".

with the extent to which development of the common law will tread on Parliament's toes. In which case the issue has become less a philosophical one about public and private, and more an issue of relative institutional competence between the courts and Parliament.[20]

COMMONWEALTH COMPARISONS

One of the main arguments relied on to support Ian Leigh's conclusion, that courts are not required to revise the common law to protect Convention rights, is that this is the lesson to be learned from the experience of those Commonwealth countries that have recently undergone similar constitutional reform, and in particular Canada, South Africa and New Zealand. Since in my view the experience of those countries lends strong support to the view that UK courts under the Human Rights Act are *required* to make the common law governing private relations compatible with the Convention, it is necessary briefly to consider these comparisons.

Canada and South Africa can be dealt with relatively shortly. In both Canada under the Charter of Rights and Freedoms and South Africa under the 1993 Interim Constitution, the courts expressly refused to hold that the common law governing private disputes is subject to, and must therefore be compatible with, the constitutional Bill of Rights. In both countries the highest court preferred instead to say that the common law was affected only "indirectly", in the sense that its development should be "informed" by the values underlying the constitutional document.[21] This is certainly a good deal weaker than an obligation to make the common law compatible, but the main value of the comparison, in my view, is not to demonstrate the approach which UK courts should take when confronted with the same abstract question, but to demonstrate the crucial difference between the position here and that both in Canada and in South Africa under the Interim Constitution.

Whereas in the UK courts are expressly made "public authorities" and therefore obliged to act compatibly with the Act, neither the

---

[20] Though inescapably this remains a normative question, raising difficult issues of legitimacy, and is not merely a value-free, factual question about which decision-maker is "best-placed" to make a decision.

[21] See, in Canada, *Dolphin Delivery* [1986] 2 SCR 573 and *Manning* v. *Hill* (1995) 126 DLR (4th) 129; and, in South Africa, *Du Plessis* v. *de Klerk* 1996 (3) SA 850.

Canadian Charter nor the South African Interim Constitution included courts or the judicial branch in the "application section" defining who is bound by those instruments. In both the Canadian and the South African case-law, this omission was central in the reasoning by which the highest courts arrived at the conclusion that the common law is not subject to the constitutionally protected rights in those countries. While this remains the case in Canada, the final Constitution of the Republic of South Africa, adopted in 1996, was deliberately altered so as to ensure that the position reached under the Interim Constitution was not repeated; in short, the Constitution was amended to give effect to Kriegler J's dissent in *Du Plessis*. The final Constitution provides explicitly in its "application clause" (clause 8) that the Bill of Rights "applies to all law", and it expressly includes the judiciary in the list of organs of the State that are bound.[22] The experience of both Canada and South Africa therefore lend strong support to the argument that inclusion of courts in the definition of public authorities in the Human Rights Act requires courts to go beyond the weak "indirect effect" approach to developing the common law in Canada and under the South African Interim Constitution, and requires them instead to ensure[23] that the common law is compatible with Convention rights.

The experience of New Zealand is even more instructive for the UK as it grapples with the significance of courts being public authorities for the purposes of the Human Rights Act. Unlike the Canadian Charter and South Africa's Interim Constitution, the New Zealand Bill of Rights Act 1990 more closely resembles the Human Rights Act in that its application clause, section 3, expressly includes the judicial as well as the legislative and executive branches of government in the definition of the bodies to which the Act applies.[24] The significance of this was

---

[22] In fact it goes even further than this, expressly providing in cl. 8(2) that a provision of the Bill of Rights may bind "natural and juristic persons if, and to the extent that, it is applicable, taking into account the nature of the right and of any duty imposed by the right"; and in cl. 8(3) that "In applying the provisions of the Bill of Rights to natural and juristic persons . . ., a court (a) in order to give effect to a right in the Bill, must apply, or where necessary, develop, the common law to the extent that legislation does not give effect to that right; and (b) may develop the rules of the common law to limit the right, provided that the limitation is in accordance with [the general limitation clause]".

[23] Subject to a constraint implicit in the scheme of the Act, explained below.

[24] Section 3(a) New Zealand Bill of Rights Act 1990: "The Bill of Rights applies

the subject of some uncertainty in New Zealand courts in the early days of the Bill of Rights' operation. In *Television New Zealand Ltd.* v. *Newsmonitor Services Ltd.*, for example, which was a private claim for an infringement of copyright in which the plaintiff sought an injunction to restrain the defendant news monitoring company from publishing news and current affairs material produced by the plaintiff, the significance of the judicial branch being bound by the Bill of Rights was canvassed before Blanchard J in the High Court.[25] Although he did not have to decide the point, because in his view the freedom of expression guarantee relied on did not require any change in the interpretation of the Copyright Act, he recorded his tentative thoughts on the matter as follows:[26]

> I note that there is no comparable reference to the judicial branch of government in the Canadian Charter of Rights and Freedoms. It may therefore be that our Parliament intended to go further in this respect than the Canadian Charter, though, equally, [counsel for the plaintiff] may have been correct in saying that the reference to the judicial branch in s. 3 was included because later in the statute there are sections dealing with exclusively judicial decision-making: minimum standards of criminal procedure, retroactive penalties and double jeopardy and the right to observance of the principles of natural justice . . . .. On a wider interpretation it may possibly be that s. 3 requires the Courts to conduct themselves in accordance with the Bill of Rights in terms of their processes and procedures, but that this direction does not extend to the substance of their judgments and the orders which flow out of those judgments. If it was intended that the Bill of Rights is directly to apply in relation to every question of statutory interpretation and every other substantive judicial decision Parliament might have been expected to so enact in plain terms.

It is clear from this passage that Blanchard J was sceptical of the view that the effect of section 3 of the Bill of Rights Act binding the judiciary was to require that the substance of their judgments and orders must be compatible with the Bill of Rights; at the most, in his view, it meant that courts are bound to respect the Bill of Rights when

only to acts done – (a) by the legislative, executive, or judicial branches of the government of New Zealand".

[25] [1994] 2 NZLR 91. [26] *Ibid.* at 96.

conducting their own processes and procedures. In doubting the defendant's submission that section 3 required the court to interpret statutes consistently with the Bill of Rights even in private litigation, his underlying concern was that the logic of this argument led inexorably to the common law governing private relations being subjected to the Bill of Rights:

> I pointed out to counsel that his argument would indistinguishably embrace non-statutory decision-making, e.g. the granting of an injunction to restrain the dissemination of confidential information which was not protected by a statute. Counsel shrank from my invitation so to extend his argument.

If Blanchard J's obiter views in the *Television New Zealand* case represented the current state of New Zealand law, then that country's experience would indeed provide support for Leigh's view that the mere fact that courts are public authorities does not mean that the common law is to be interpreted and applied by them so as to be compatible with the Convention. In fact, however, counsel's timidity in the *TV New Zealand* case proved unwarranted, as in a series of subsequent decisions the New Zealand courts appear to have accepted that the effect of section 3(a) is to require courts to give effect to the Bill of Rights when applying the common law. In *Solicitor-General v. Radio New Zealand*, for example, which involved an application to commit the defendant broadcaster for contempt of court for contacting jurors in a murder trial and broadcasting their comments, the High Court recorded that it was common ground between the parties that "the New Zealand Bill of Rights Act 1990 applies to these proceedings as applying to acts done by the judicial branch of the Government under s. 3(a)", and that the case involved the right to freedom of expression.[27]

This was taken further in *Duff* v. *Communicado Ltd.*, also contempt of court proceedings in respect of comments in the media which had the potential to affect a pending civil trial. Citing the *Radio New Zealand* case, the High Court expressly considered whether the common law approach to contempt of court needed any modification because of the New Zealand Bill of Rights Act.[28] The court considered it to be bound to carry out this exercise because "contempt of court,

---

[27] [1994] 1 NZLR 48 at 58.   [28] [1996] 2 NZLR 89.

like any other part of the common law, is subject to the Bill of Rights by virtue of s. 3(a) thereof".[29]

As in so many other jurisdictions, however, it is in the law of defamation that the clearest statement has been given of the degree to which the common law is affected by the Bill of Rights Act.[30] In *Lange* v. *Atkinson*, which was an action for defamation by a former Prime Minister of New Zealand in which the main issue was whether special defences to defamation claims are required to protect political expression, Elias J in the High Court expressly considered the difference between the weak Canadian approach, according to which the Charter values "inform" the development of the common law, and a stronger obligation to ensure that the common law is applied consistently with the Bill of Rights.[31] She expressly preferred the latter because of the presence in New Zealand of section 3. She said,

> It is convenient to deal at the outset . . . with the submission made on behalf of the plaintiff as to the impact of the [New Zealand Bill of Rights] Act upon the common law. [Counsel for the plaintiff] argues that, while the New Zealand Bill of Rights Act may be taken into account in the development of common law, the common law is not subject to the New Zealand Bill of Rights under s. 3. In this he relies upon *Hill v Church of Scientology of Toronto*. In my view the New Zealand Bill of Rights Act protections are to be given effect by the court in applying the common law. . . . The application of the Act to the common law seems to me to follow from the language of s. 3 which refers to acts of the judicial branch of the Government of New Zealand, a provision not to be found in the Canadian Charter. . . . The New Zealand Bill of Rights Act 1990 is important contemporary legislation which is directly relevant to the policies served by the common law of defamation. It is idle to suggest that the common law need not conform to the judgments in such legislation.[32]

---

[29] *Ibid.* at 99 (emphasis added).

[30] See also *Television New Zealand Ltd.* v. *Quinn* [1996] 3 NZLR 24, a case, like *Rantzen* v. *Mirror Group Newspapers* [1994] QB 670, concerning the practice of directing juries on damages in defamation actions, in which McGechan J. said, at 58, "As a general and opening position, I endorse alignments between jury directions and dictates of the Bill of Rights. It is an inevitability. It is the Court's duty to support freedoms in the Bill of Rights, not to frustrate them".

[31] [1997] 2 NZLR 22 at 32.

[32] Although the point was not expressly considered by the Court of Appeal in its

It would therefore seem now to be well established that in New Zealand the Bill of Rights applies to the common law, including the common law governing disputes between private parties, and that it does so because the acts of the judicial branch are expressly made subject to the Bill of Rights by section 3. It is greatly to be hoped that the benefit of the New Zealand experience will save us in the UK from the wrong turn that was almost made by Blanchard J in the early *Television New Zealand* case. The presence in the House of Lords of Lord Cooke, who fully appreciates the significance of courts being public authorities, should help to ensure this. In his view, "the Convention rights . . . will prevail over the common law, in that the courts will have the responsibility of adjusting the common law as far as may be necessary to give effect to such of them as are capable of application".[33]

THE INAPPROPRIATENESS OF THE GEOMETRIC METAPHOR

Much, though not all of the literature proceeds on the assumption that the geometric language of "vertical" or "horizontal" effect is an entirely appropriate metaphor for the meaningful discussion of the extent to which the Human Rights Act applies to "private" relations. By postulating a spectrum of possible positions between the truly vertical and the fully horizontal position, my earlier article was implicitly questioning the appropriateness of the geometric metaphor, but did not directly confront the question. The purpose of this part of the chapter is to address that question directly and to argue that the language of horizontality mischaracterises the debate and is likely to lead in the

---

decision on appeal, [1998] 3 NZLR 424, it appears that they approved of Elias J.'s approach. Her view about the effect of s. 3 is recited in the Court of Appeal's summary of her decision, *ibid.* at 431, and the Court of Appeal upheld her decision "broadly for the same reasons" (*ibid.* at 428).

[33] "The British Embracement of Human Rights" (1999) *EHRLR* 243 at 257. See also his speech in the House of Lords in *Reynolds* v. *Times Newspapers* [1999] 4 All ER 609, explicitly referring to the role of the European Convention in the development of the common law and to the fact that as public authorities it will be unlawful for courts to act incompatibly with Convention rights. Lord Nicholls in the same case also states that when the Human Rights Act takes effect the common law will have to be developed and applied in a manner consistent with the Convention; and Lord Steyn regards the Human Rights Act as reinforcing the constitutional or "higher order" foundation of freedom of expression.

long run to the frustration of one of the central purposes of the Human Rights Act: to make fundamental human rights pervade our law in order to give them genuine, practical effectiveness.

The most powerful case for abandoning the language of horizontality has been made by Stephen Sedley in his second Hamlyn Lecture, "Public Power and Private Power".[34] In that lecture, Sedley directly challenges the use of the horizontality metaphor because it is premised on an assumed dichotomy between law's public and its private spheres. The metaphor presupposes that there is a fundamental distinction between the public and the private spheres of law's operation, and by framing the debate in this way it "assumes the very thing that needs to be debated".[35] What needs to be debated is not whether or how far rights which are inherently "vertical" in nature should be "extended" into the "private" sphere, but what it means in practical terms for all the institutions of the State, including courts, to be bound to act compatibly with Convention rights.

This is a crucial insight. The vocabulary of "horizontality" commits participants in the discourse to a prior assumption about the separateness of the public and the private spheres which is highly controversial. It concedes the starting point in the debate to those who believe there to be a firm distinction between the public and the private spheres, and who would privilege the private over the public by preserving it immune from the values of public law, including fundamental rights norms. As I argued in my earlier article, there is no such firm distinction, because the very presence of law introduces a public element: private relations are in part constituted by both statute and common law, and the State lurks behind both. For those like Stephen Sedley, who reject the notion that there is a firm distinction between public and private, it follows that the horizontality metaphor cannot serve. It skews the debate from the outset by asking the question to be determined in terms which presuppose a certain answer.[36]

The oddness of the assumption that the common law governing private relations is not subject to Convention rights comes into focus

---

[34] S. Sedley, *Freedom, Law and Justice* (Sweet & Maxwell, 1999).

[35] *Ibid.* at 23.

[36] As Stephen Sedley also explains, rejection of the assumed distinction between law's public and private spheres also requires rejection of the language of "Drittwirkung" or "third party effects", since this "again suggests an artificial extension of the natural ambit of rights": *ibid.* at 23 n. 11.

when one considers the effect of section 3 of the Human Rights Act. The obligation imposed by that section to interpret primary and subordinate legislation, so far as it is possible to do so, in a way which is compatible with Convention rights is in its terms an obligation of general application. It applies as much to the interpretation of statutes which regulate private relations, of which there are many, as it applies to statutes of a more "public" nature. This is uncontroversial. Absolutely no one argues that, where there is a Convention right in play, legislation can be interpreted in a way which is incompatible with that right simply because the question of interpretation arises in litigation between private parties.

Not only does the Human Rights Act itself not attempt to distinguish between different types of legislation, it would be unique if it did: it seems to be universally assumed in legal systems with legal protections for fundamental rights that legislation is *always* amenable to scrutiny for compatibility with those rights, even where the question arises in otherwise purely private proceedings. This is presumably because a legislative intervention is always considered to involve some action by the "State" which satisfies the assumed requirement of a "public" dimension. Even in Canada, for example, where the common law governing private relations is immune from direct Charter scrutiny, it was accepted early on in the life of the Charter that even legislation which governs private relations is subject to the Charter.[37] In this country, the decision of the House of Lords in *Fitzpatrick* v. *Sterling Housing Association Ltd.*, holding that a same-sex partner can qualify as a member of the tenant's family within the meaning of the relevant provision of the Rent Act 1977, entitling him to succeed to an assured tenancy, is a timely reminder of the way in which the judicial interpretation of statutory phrases in legislation governing private relations can have a profound effect on private relations.[38]

---

[37] See e.g. *Re Blainey and Ontario Hockey Association* (1986) 54 O.R. (2d) 513, in which a statutory exemption in provincial human rights legislation concerning discrimination was held to be incompatible with the Charter in a case involving private parties. See generally on "direct statutory horizontality" Leigh, n. 16 *supra* at 75-77.

[38] [1999] 4 All ER 705. Although the "living instrument" approach to interpretation on which the decision is based was not adopted in order to achieve compatibility with the Convention (the decision in fact goes further than the Strasbourg case-law which has yet to recognise the family life of same-sex partners), it is a useful foretaste of the interpretive techniques that will be required by the s. 3(1) obligation.

The fact that the section 3 interpretive obligation clearly applies in proceedings between purely private parties is an important factor in rejecting the appropriateness of the "horizontality" metaphor. It makes something of a mockery of many of the arguments against the Human Rights Act applying to the common law governing private relations, because many of them are in the nature of in-principle objections to human rights having any application in the private sphere at all. Many of Ian Leigh's arguments against the Human Rights Act governing the common law, for example, are based on considerations of certainty and stability:

> if applied in the private domestic sphere, the result would be destabilis-
> ing, with every personal tort open to reinterpretation in the light of
> plausible Article 8 arguments on both sides. Such an undesirable exer-
> cise in uncertainty risks seriously damaging the balancing of private
> interests in the common law.[39]

These are arguments which are of general application in their resistance to the applicability of fundamental rights norms in the "private sphere", and they would apply equally to the applicability of the section 3 inter-pretive obligation to statutes which regulate private disputes. That too will lead to the reinterpretation of law governing private relations in the light of plausible Convention arguments on both sides, leading inevitably to some uncertainty and destabilising of old assumptions, but that is precisely what Parliament has sanctioned. Whether private activity is regulated by statute or common law is often entirely fortu-itous, and it would be a wholly arbitrary distinction if only part of the legal framework within which private relations are conducted were subjected to scrutiny for compatibility with the Convention.

HOW SHOULD THE COMMON LAW BE RENDERED COMPATIBLE?

If the debate about the effect of the Human Rights Act on private law is less about distinguishing public from private than has traditionally

---

[39] Leigh, n. 16 *supra* at 73. For similarly cautious arguments, seeking to privilege the common law over statute law in terms of the effect of the HRA, see Phillipson, n. 17 *supra* at 840: "if the Convention were *always* to override inconsistent common law rules, this could seriously unbalance the common law, which has attempted to reconcile a more comprehensive set of individual interests than has the Convention".

been thought, and if the "horizontality" metaphor is therefore to be abandoned, how are courts to make sense of their confusing role as public authorities, statutorily obliged to act compatibly with the Convention, and therefore to develop the common law where necessary, but at the same time required by the scheme of the Act not to invent entirely new causes of action against private persons, and warned by the Lord Chancellor not to step over the line into forbidden judicial "legislation"?

One of the sure signs of the sheer conceptual difficulty of this question is the prevalence of metaphors. Convention rights have variously been described as the "prism" through which all domestic law must in future be viewed; the "magnetic north" whose gravitational force will rearrange the contours of our law. The most attractive are undoubtedly those which treat our current law as a sort of background cloth, through the fabric of which the Convention rights will spread like a dye,[40] or into which they will be interwoven.[41] This metaphor has the particular attraction that it can graphically capture the reality that the scheme of the model which has been adopted means that there will be some patches which remain impervious to the dye, or some holes in the fabric which cannot be patched by the most skilled judicial weaver.

Stephen Sedley's rejection of the premise underlying the horizontality metaphor leads him to prefer to talk of the "cascade effect" of the Human Rights Act rather than its "horizontal effect". While agreeing on the importance of abandoning the geometric metaphor, its proposed substitute does not do justice to the effect of the Act. Cascading implies differentiated levels, with human rights spilling over from one level to another. The implication is that the primary effect of the Act is on statute law, but that the rights it introduces flow over into the common law. Characterising the effect of the Act in this way risks forfeiting the essential insight that statute and the common law are *both* manifestations of the State in private relations, and are *equally* constitutive of them.[42] Rights which "cascade" or "spill over" into the common law might be thought to be of less force by the time they reach that level.[43] In short, "cascade effect" does not really do justice to the force

---

[40] Sedley, n. 34 *supra* at 19.   [41] Cooke, n. 33 *supra.*

[42] Moreover, the common law continues to regulate vast areas of private activity which are relatively untouched by statutory intervention.

[43] Cf. the now common characterisation of the effect of principles of European public law on our domestic public law as a "spillover effect".

of the Convention's claim under the Human Rights Act to require reshaping of the common law.

This is an important point to keep in mind. The effect of section 6 is that the courts are under an *obligation* to act compatibly with the Convention. They must therefore ensure the common law's compatibility with Convention rights, in so far as it is possible for them to do so. It is not simply a matter of *discretion*: can courts develop the common law in this way if they feel like it? It is a matter of judicial *obligation*. It must be distinguished from the much weaker "indirect effect" doctrine of the Canadian and German approaches. Section 6(3)(a) means that we are not dealing here with mere common law development in line with the underlying values of the common law. We are dealing with something much more concrete: an obligation to ensure that the common law is not incompatible with an individual's Convention rights, subject only to the constraint implicit in the scheme of the Act that Parliament and not the courts should be responsible for changing the law when that amounts to creating a new cause of action against private persons.

Although metaphors can be illuminating and powerful, they can also become an obstacle to understanding or, worse, a substitute for thought. What is required at this juncture is a more practical, metaphor-free articulation of exactly what is required of courts as a consequence of their being public authorities obliged to act compatibly with Convention rights. In plain language, what is required is that courts must ask themselves, even in private litigation, whether there is a Convention right in play. If there is, they must ask themselves whether the substance of the common law they propose to apply, and the order they propose to make, is compatible with that Convention right. That means subjecting the common law to the same process of scrutiny, including for justification where it interferes with Convention rights, as executive actions and legislation.

If application of the common law in the court's order would not be compatible with the Convention right at stake, the court must ask itself whether the common law can be developed so as to avoid the incompatibility. This is only likely to be controversial if it involves filling a gap which exists in the common law scheme of remedies. In trying to decide whether the necessary development in the common law is open to it, the court should remember that it is under an obligation to act compatibly, and should therefore be creative in its incremental development of the common law, but is subject to the ultimate constraint that it must not create entirely new causes of action where nothing analogous previously existed. If (and this is perhaps the most important point) the court decides that the development of the common law that would be required to achieve compatibility would take it beyond its legitimate role of incrementally developing the common law, it should make clear in its judgment that in its view the state of the law is incompatible with the Convention, and requires legislative amendment to remove the incompatibility.

The attraction of this straightforward approach is that it makes the courts' approach to common law compatibility symmetrical with that to statutory compatibility, and therefore fits the scheme of the Human Rights Act, which is to give the courts a central role in ensuring that our law conforms to the Convention, while preserving at the same time a role for Parliament in deciding precisely how such conformity is to be achieved. It achieves a position whereby the Act imposes a judicial obligation to ensure that the law of the UK, including the common law, is compatible with the Convention, except where this would, in the case of statute law, exceed the bounds of the interpretive obligation in section 3 (in which case a declaration of incompatibility should be given) or, in the case of the common law, exceed the legitimate bounds of common law development, in which case the court should indicate clearly to Parliament its view that the common law is incompatible and requires legislative amendment. On this approach to both types of law, courts cannot avoid the compatibility question: they must carry out the inquiry, and either achieve compatibility themselves, or make clear that there is an incompatibility that they are powerless to redress.

The Place of the Human Rights Act in a Democratic Society

Rabinder Singh

This paper will look at three topics:

- the political and philosophical background to the relationship between fundamental human rights and democracy;
- the principles developed in the case law of the European Court of Human Rights on that relationship; and
- the features of the Human Rights Act 1998 which make it a democratic Bill of Rights.

THE POLITICAL AND PHILOSOPHICAL BACKGROUND TO THE RELATIONSHIP BETWEEN FUNDAMENTAL HUMAN RIGHTS AND DEMOCRACY

Although the philosophical origins of human rights go back to ancient times, the modern idea of human rights burst onto the political stage in the eighteenth century. At that time there was in the minds of its proponents a congruence between popular government (or at least a limited form of it, usually confined to white men who had some property) and fundamental rights. When Paine talked of the "rights of man" he was writing in the main about the right of the people to self-government.[1] When the Second Continental Congress adopted the American Declaration of Independence, its famous second paragraph[2] was as

---

[1] T. Paine, *The Rights of Man* (original 1791-2) (Harmondsworth, Penguin, 1984).

[2] The second paragraph reads: "We hold these truths to be self-evident; that all men are created equal; that they are endowed by their Creator with certain unalienable rights; that among these are life, liberty and the pursuit of happiness; that to secure these rights governments are instituted among men, deriving their just powers from the consent of the governed . . ." See further P. Maier, *American Scripture: How America Declared its Independence from Britain* (London, Pimlico, 1999).

much about the legitimate basis of government – the consent of the governed – as it was about the fundamental rights which it announced to be self-evidently the endowments of all "men". The revolutionaries in the United States and France fairly early on decided to impose legal limits on the powers of the new, republican governments they were creating. In 1789 the National Assembly issued the Declaration of the Rights of Man and the Citizen, which in some form has remained a part of the French republican constitutions until today. The US Constitution of 1787 did not originally contain a list of fundamental human rights, although the individual states did usually include such a declaration in their constitutions, most famously Virginia and Massachusetts, which both played a crucial role in the revolution, through such figures as Jefferson, Madison and the "Adams family", Samuel and John. But the Constitution quickly acquired a Bill of Rights in 1791, in the form of the first ten Amendments. Those amendments, together with the important amendments passed after the Civil War, in particular the Fourteenth Amendment, which guarantees due process and the equal protection of the laws against the state governments, became the modern American Bill of Rights. The American system is one that combines commitment to democracy with a profound belief in fundamental rights. As the US Supreme Court judge, Justice Jackson, put it in *West Virginia State Board of Education* v. *Barnette*[3]:

> The very purpose of a Bill of Rights was to withdraw certain subjects from the vicissitudes of political controversy, to place them beyond the reach of majorities and officials and to establish them as legal principles to be applied by the courts. One's right to life, liberty, and property, to free speech, a free press, freedom of worship and assembly, and other fundamental rights may not be submitted to vote; they depend on the outcome of no elections.

The revolutionary tradition which was started in the eighteenth century carried on in the nineteenth and twentieth centuries, as former colonies of the European powers became independent. They usually created a constitution which was based on the Westminster form of parliamentary government, but with an American style Bill of Rights attached to it: the best example is perhaps India, which became a

---

[3] 319 US 624 (1943) at 638.

republic in 1950 (a plaque commemorating Dr Ambedkar, the architect of that constitution, can be found in the garden of Gray's Inn, of which he was a member). And in more recent times, as the former Communist countries of the Eastern bloc have become democracies, they have not rushed to adopt a Westminster style of constitution but rather have joined the family of those democratic nations which recognise that it is essential to have a Bill of Rights for a proper democracy to function (a theme to which I return later).

In contrast, Britain, which had had its revolution earlier than the rest of the world, has for the last two centuries travelled a different path. Its revolution had in a sense occurred a century too soon. The Glorious Revolution of 1688 was concerned with a different problem – wresting power from the Crown and vesting it in the legislature. So in Britain we talk about parliamentary sovereignty rather than the sovereignty of the people. In contrast, the American War of Independence was fought about the limits of Parliamentary power: the Americans did not accept Parliament's assertion in the Declaratory Act 1766 that it had power to make laws for the colonies "in all cases whatsoever".[4]

This was not because Britain has not been a free country for the last two centuries. To the contrary, liberalism "with a small l" has been a powerful creed and for much of the time between 1830 and 1915 the Liberal Party "with a big L" was in power. The economic philosophy of the age was *laissez faire* at home and free trade abroad and much of what governments did was about removing legal barriers to individual achievement, such as religious qualifications for admission to the ancient universities and paper duties, a "tax on public knowledge" the removal of which led to a big increase in the circulation of newspapers.[5] On the political front, although democracy was not fully achieved until after the First World War, the main campaign for reform for a century was for the extension of the franchise, to working class men and to women. Even the People's Charter of 1838, which set out the demands of the Chartists, was not a Bill of Rights: its six points all related to the democratisation of Parliament – all but one of the six points (that there should be annual Parliaments) have been achieved.

The attainment of universal suffrage was a big achievement and its importance should not be underestimated. But the dominant strand in

---

[4] P. Maier, *supra* n.2, p.77.
[5] See R. Jenkins, *Gladstone* (London, Macmillan, 1995) p.225.

British liberalism was utilitarianism. This fitted in well with the general *zeitgeist*: in the economic sphere, it was suited to the creation of free markets, in which the individual would decide what ought to be produced through consumer demand and, in the political sphere, it made sense of the extension of the franchise, which was the equivalent of the free market in that it allowed everyone to have a say and the majority would prevail. When the Labour Party took over from the Liberals as the main party opposed to the forces of conservatism after the First World War, the utilitarians had a new home. Fabian socialism was not particularly concerned about the rights of the individual: it was concerned about improving the general welfare of society and to use parliamentary power once captured through the democratic franchise to effect that improvement. So the dominant creed, although it was progressive, was at best neutral and at worst hostile to the notion of human rights. As Tony Wright MP – the intellectual voice of new Labour - puts it:

> If British socialism was about using the state to achieve social and economic objectives, then the British constitution seemed to put the state at the disposal of majority parties. The left was instrumental in defining a twentieth-century theory and practice of the constitution that sustained this view, and in defending it against those who hankered after something else. . . . Dicey may not have liked socialism . . . but socialists have nevertheless liked Dicey's constitution. Its doctrine of sovereignty, once rooted in an enfranchised people, enabled a parliamentary majority to get its way.[6]

And yet the tension between the majority and the rights of individuals or minorities never went away. The most famous expression of the concern for protection from the tyranny of the majority came in John Stuart Mill's famous essay *On Liberty*.[7] Now, more than two centuries after Paine was convicted in his absence for seditious libel in publishing the second part of *The Rights of Man* we have come to realise that a modern democracy does after all need a Bill of Rights. And in so doing we have re-joined the mainstream of democratic societies.

How is the concept of fundamental human rights to be reconciled with democracy? At first sight it seems obvious that the two are

---

[6] T. Wright, *Citizens and Subjects* (London, Routledge, 1994) pp.59-60.
[7] J. S. Mill, *On Liberty* (original 1859) in J. S. Mill *Utilitarianism* (London, Collins, 1979).

irreconcilable. Democracy seems to fit well with utilitarianism. If one believes that there is no particular view of life which is better than others and the correct course to take is what the majority want, it can be said that this will maximise the greatest happiness of the greatest number. On that view, it does not matter that the opinions of others, however deeply held as a matter of conscience they may be, are crushed on the way.

However, experience has taught us that this is a shortsighted view of democracy. For one thing, if the people are to make informed decisions as they exercise their vote, they must have freedom to receive and impart ideas. So immediately a fundamental right to freedom of expression becomes an integral component in the machinery of democracy. Furthermore, history has also taught us that the views of the eccentric and the heretic sometimes end up becoming the orthodoxy of the majority: Galileo and Darwin provide obvious examples. So the right to freedom of thought and freedom of expression has to be given time to flourish. When experiments are being conducted, no one knows at the outset how things are going to turn out. This gives us the insight that democracy, if it is a good thing, is something we should want to continue. In other words, democracy is entitled to protect itself. Oliver Wendell Holmes famously put it this way in *Abrams* v. *United States*:[8]

> Persecution for the expression of opinions seems to me perfectly logical. If you have no doubt of your premises or your power and want a certain result with all your heart you naturally express your wishes in law and sweep away all opposition. . . . But when men have realized that time has upset many fighting faiths, they may come to believe even more than they believe the very foundations of their own conduct that the ultimate good desired is better reached in free trade in ideas – that the best test of truth is the power of the thought to get itself accepted in the competition of the market . . . Every year if not every day we have to wager our salvation upon some prophecy based upon imperfect knowledge. While that experiment is part of our system I think that we should be eternally vigilant against attempts to check the expression of opinions that we loathe and believe to be fraught with death, unless they so imminently threaten immediate interference with the lawful and pressing purposes of the law that an immediate check is required to save the country.

[8] 250 US 616 (1919) at 630. Holmes J (with whom Brandeis J concurred) dissented but his views have become the orthodoxy in American First Amendment jurisprudence.

But this still leaves a problem. We know from human rights jurisprudence that what it requires is more than just the protection of freedom of expression. How, for example, is the decision that gay people have the right to serve in the armed forces to be reconciled with an apparent decision by the majority that they do not want homosexuals in those forces? In my view, the link is provided by the concept of equality. Democracy is a wonderful thing because it treats everyone as an equal. No matter what your social background or education, when it comes to the ballot box you have one vote – like everyone else. There is no *a priori* reason why this should be so. We could have a rule that the more money a person earns or the more tax they pay (which is not necessarily the same thing) the more votes they should have. But no one would seriously suggest such changes to the franchise today.

This suggests that underlying democracy are more basic notions. Those notions are that legitimate government rests on the consent of the governed and that everyone is equal – we all count but no one counts any more than anyone else. This is reflected in Article 1 of the Universal Declaration of Human Rights, which announces that all human beings are born free *and equal* in dignity and rights. The right to vote in Article 21(3) of the Declaration also refers to the right to universal and equal suffrage. Democracy should therefore be seen as a community of free and equal participants.[9] If the majority from time to time could simply use their power to attack the minority it would be to treat them as not equal or free at all but subjects whose survival depends on the good will of the majority. That cannot be right.

On the other hand, the majority have to be able to get things done. After all, the purpose of government is to govern. This is where the concept of "necessity" comes in. To recognise that a person has a fundamental right is not to say that it must always prevail. Other interests are also important but the fundamental human rights should be curtailed only where there is a need to do so and even then only to the extent that it is necessary to do so. Putting it the other way, why should someone's private life be interfered with unnecessarily? Everyone of the majority who say that they do not want gays in the armed forces would say that their own (heterosexual) private lives are their business and no one else's. So why should others be sacrificed on the altar of popular

[9] See Immanuel Kant, *Political Writings* (ed. H. Reiss) (Cambridge, Cambridge University Press, 1991) p.73; Ronald Dworkin, *A Bill of Rights for Britain* (London, Chatto & Windus, 1990) p.35.

demand simply because they do not have the numerical strength to protect themselves? We know from common sense that, if the tables were turned and we were at risk of interference with our privacy by others – whether those of a different religion, a different race or a different political grouping – we would not think it right that their will could prevail simply because they had strength of numbers on their side. We should be willing to give others the same concern and respect. This common sense insight is what Kant meant when he referred to the principle of universalisability or, even more obscurely, the categorical imperative: we should treat others as we would have them treat us.

The concept of equality also underlies many of the substantive rights which are found in charters of rights such as the European Convention on Human Rights. For example, freedom of expression and freedom of religion are both based on the fundamental notion that it is not the business of the State to choose between different doctrines or ideologies and impose them on individuals. As Justice Jackson once said:

> If there is any fixed star in our constitutional constellation, it is that no official, high or petty, can prescribe what shall be orthodox in politics, nationalism, religion or other matters of opinion to force citizens to confess by word or act their faith therein.[10]

The concept of equality could and should play a greater part in human rights jurisprudence after incorporation than it has necessarily done in the case-law of the European Court of Human Rights. For example, in *Wingrove* v. *United Kingdom*[11], the Court held, by a majority, that the refusal of a classification certificate for the video "Visions of Ecstasy" on the ground that it was blasphemous was permissible under Article 10(2) of the ECHR, having regard to the wide margin of appreciation afforded to Contracting States in the field of morals. However, Judge Loehmus perceptively pointed out in dissent that, although it may be possible to justify such a ban in a democratic society, the justification itself should not be discriminatory[12]: the English law of blasphemy is discriminatory, because it protects Christianity but not other religions.

---

[10] *West Virginia State Board of Education* v. *Barnette* 319 US 624 (1943) at 642. The Supreme Court held in that case that children who were Jehovah's Witnesses could not be compelled to salute the US flag at school. Contrast the decision of the European Court of Human Rights in *Valsamis* v. *Greece* (1997) 24 EHRR 294.

[11] (1997) 24 EHRR 1.   [12] *Ibid.* p.38, para 4.

It remains to be seen whether such discrimination will survive the incorporation of the Convention rights into domestic law.

THE PRINCIPLES IN THE CASE-LAW OF THE EUROPEAN COURT OF HUMAN RIGHTS ON THE RELATIONSHIP BETWEEN DEMOCRACY AND HUMAN RIGHTS

The European Court of Human Rights has long recognised that the rights in the European Convention on Human Rights (ECHR) are essential features of a democratic society. It has placed particular stress on the role of freedom of expression, including freedom of the press, in a democracy. In *Lingens* v. *Austria*[13] the Court said:

> Freedom of the press . . . affords the public one of the best means of discovering and forming an opinion of the ideas and attitudes of political leaders. More generally, freedom of political debate is at the very core of the concept of a democratic society which prevails throughout the Convention.

The Court has also stressed the important link between freedom of expression and the right in Article 3 of Protocol 1 to take part in free elections. In *Bowman* v. *United Kingdom*[14] it said:

> Free elections and freedom of expression, particularly freedom of political debate, together form the bedrock of any democratic system. . . . For this reason it is particularly important in the period preceding an election that opinions and information of all kinds are permitted to circulate freely.

But the Court tends to use the phrase "a democratic society" in a wider sense than just the political system we would call a democracy. It regards the substantive rights in the ECHR as being inherent in the concept of a democratic society. For example, in *Kokkinakis* v. *Greece*[15] the Court said:

> As enshrined in Article 9, freedom of thought, conscience and religion is one of the foundations of a "democratic society" *within the*

---

[13] (1986) 8 EHRR 407, para 42.
[14] (1998) 26 EHRR 1, para 42.
[15] (1994) 17 EHRR 397, para 31 (emphasis added).

meaning of the Convention. . . . The pluralism indissociable from a democratic society, which has been dearly won over the centuries, depends on it.

Even rights such as the right to a fair hearing in Article 6 of the ECHR, which might be thought to be rights associated with the legal system rather than the political system, are regarded by the European Court of Human Rights as defining the concept of a democratic society envisaged by the ECHR. For example, in *Delcourt* v. *Belgium*[16] the Court said:

> In a democratic society within the meaning of the Convention, the right to a fair administration of justice holds such a prominent place that a restrictive interpretation of Article 6(1) would not correspond to the aim and the purpose of that provision.

When it comes to restrictions on the rights in the ECHR, the concept of a democratic society again plays a vital role. There are three kinds of rights in the ECHR:

(1) absolute and unqualified rights;
(2) rights where an interference is permitted where it is "necessary in a democratic society"; and
(3) rights where interference is permitted where some other interest outweighs the right in question.

In category (1) no balancing is required or permitted. Indeed, some of these rights are so important in the Convention system that they cannot be derogated from even in time of war or national emergency.[17] The rights which fall into this category are the right to life in Article 2, the right to be free from torture and inhuman or degrading treatment in article 3, the right to be free from slavery in Article 4(1) and the freedom from retrospective criminal penalties in Article 7. It might be said that, in a democracy, even these rights ought in principle to be capable of being overridden when necessary in a national emergency. However, the view taken by the framers of the ECHR was that they should be non-derogable as well as absolute and all the countries which have accepted the obligations in the ECHR are democracies that did so willingly.

---

[16] (1979-80) 1 EHRR 355, para 26.
[17] Article 15 of the ECHR.

The second category contains the rights which are expressly qualified in the text of the ECHR: the right to respect for private and family life, the home and correspondence in Article 8; the right to freedom to manifest one's religion in Article 9 (though note that the right to freedom of conscience in the same article is unqualified, so making a distinction between what is internal to one's heart and mind and what is manifested externally, because the latter may have an impact on others); the right to freedom of expression in Article 10 and the right to freedom of peaceful assembly and association in Article 11. As is well-known, these rights may be interfered with but only if the interference is "prescribed by law"/"in accordance with the law"; where the interference has a legitimate aim; where there is a pressing social need and where the interference meets the test of proportionality. In *Sunday Times* v. *United Kingdom*[18] the Court said that what is necessary is more than what is "desirable" or "reasonable", although it need not be indispensable. Clearly the more important the right in the scheme of the ECHR, the more convincing the reasons required to justify a restriction on them.

Even in the context of freedom of expression, however, the European Court of Human Rights in fact takes a flexible approach. The right to freedom of expression is given greatest protection in the case of political speech: this is consistent with the view that freedom of expression is essential for the healthy functioning of a democratic society. Other kinds of speech, such as commercial advertising, are less likely to contribute to the democratic process and are given less protection.[19] In any event, those who are regulated by restrictions on commercial speech, such as tobacco companies, can be expected to have the opportunity to lobby politicians and exercise their influence through the democratic process. Commercial speech is, therefore, an area in which the Court tends to take the view that restrictions are best left to the margin of appreciation afforded to Contracting States.[20] More controversially, the Court has not been particularly astute to protect artistic speech, as in *Mueller* v. *Switzerland*[21] (which concerned an exhibition

[18] (1979-80) 2 EHRR 245, para 59.
[19] See e.g. *Casado Coca* v. *Spain* (1994) 18 EHRR 1, which concerned regulation of professional advertising.
[20] See e.g. *Markt Intern and Beermann* v. *Germany* (1990) 12 EHRR 161, para 32, which concerned statements made for the purposes of competition.
[21] (1991) 13 EHRR 212.

of pictures which were said to be obscene) and *Wingrove* v. *United Kingdom*[22] (which, as mentioned above, concerned the ban on the video "Visions of Ecstasy"). It may well be that the courts of this country, when they come to consider similar cases after incorporation, will take a more rigorous approach to the protection of artistic speech. After all, it is difficult to distinguish between art and politics: so much of what people believe comes from habits of mind created over many years through cultural influences. And it is precisely in the context of artistic speech that there is the greatest danger that the lone voice of dissent will be silenced simply because the majority do not like what is said, rather than because it is necessary to meet some pressing social need.

Also in the second category are rights which are not qualified in express terms but which the European Court of Human Rights has held are subject to implied limitations. One of these is the right to a fair hearing in Article 6(1) of the ECHR: for example in *Osman* v. *United Kingdom*[23] the Court engaged in an assessment of proportionality in deciding whether an apparently general immunity conferred on the police from actions for negligence was compatible with the right to a fair hearing of such claims. Another, more controversial, example is the presumption of innocence in article 6(2). On the face of it that provision is entirely unqualified. Yet the Court has held that it is subject to reasonable limitations which maintain the rights of the defence: see *Salabiaku* v. *France*.[24] The case-law on this is relatively under-developed in Strasbourg and the exact scope of the "reasonable limitations" will need to be worked out after incorporation, but the concept of implied qualifications does reflect the common sense view that there will be exceptions to the normal rule that the prosecution should bear the burden of proof on every issue. There are well-known exceptions in English law, for example where a defendant claims the advantage of an exception or an excuse conferred by the statute which creates an offence.[25]

The third category of rights is those which may be qualified but where the test of necessity is not applied. The best example of this is the right to property (or peaceful enjoyment of possessions, as it is put in

[22] (1996) 24 EHRR 1.
[23] (2000) 29 EHRR 245.
[24] (1991) 13 EHRR 379. See further *R* v. *Director of Public Prosecutions, ex p Kebilene* [1999] 3 WLR 972, especially the opinion of Lord Hope of Craighead.
[25] See e.g. *R* v. *Hunt (Richard)* [1987] AC 352.

Article 1 of Protocol 1). This article does not require either the deprivation of property or control of its use to be "necessary in a democratic society". It uses the more flexible phrases "in the public interest" and "in accordance with the general interest". The European Court of Human Rights has made it clear that the question of whether there is a public purpose for which property should be taken or regulated is one for the national authorities and that the Court will interfere only if that judgment is manifestly devoid of reasonable foundation.[26] Likewise, although the test of proportionality is not entirely absent from the case-law on Article 1, the Court has stressed that it will give a wide margin of appreciation to national authorities in this context.

Moreover, it is worth noting two further features of the case-law on the right to property. The first is that the Court has stressed not only the margin of appreciation, in the more general sense that delineates the respective responsibilities of national authorities and the supranational court, but also the special place enjoyed by the legislature in this context.[27] The second point to note is that the Court has also stressed that the Convention does not impose any particular political philosophy on Contracting States. The Court is clearly aware of the controversial nature of the right to property and that decisions about the control of its use are the stuff of democratic debate. It is in that context that most questions arising under Article 1 of Protocol 1 should be resolved.

Although the concept of margin of appreciation is not one which should be imported into national law after incorporation,[28] this is one context in which the alternative concept of "due deference" to the democratically accountable parts of the state should play a prominent role. Otherwise there is a real risk that the courts will be drawn into areas where they are relatively unqualified to tread, as happened in the United States in the early part of the twentieth century, when the Supreme Court struck down state welfare laws such as those which sought to regulate the number of hours that children could work: *Lochner* v. *New York*.[29] As Oliver Wendell Holmes said in dissent in

---

[26] See e.g. *James* v. *United Kingdom* (1986) 8 EHRR 123.

[27] *Ibid.*

[28] See e.g. R. Singh, M. Hunt and M. Demetriou, "Is there a role for the 'margin of appreciation' in national law after the Human Rights Act?" [1999] *EHRLR* 15; and *R* v. *Director of Public Prosecutions, ex p Kebilene* [1999] 3 WLR 972 at 993-4 (Lord Hope of Craighead on the "discretionary area of judgment").

[29] 198 US 45 (1905).

that case, the economic theories of Herbert Spencer are not part of the US Constitution. It would be better if our courts took the same position on which the US Supreme Court settled from the late 1930s: that it would jealously guard certain rights such as freedom of speech and the rights of "discrete and insular minorities"[30] but that questions of economic regulation would be left to the democratic organs of the State, provided they had a rational basis.

It is important to note that the phrase "in a democratic society" has substantive content and is not mere verbiage. The European Court of Human Rights has stressed that the concept of a democratic society which is reflected in the ECHR is not one in which the majority as it is from time to time simply has its way. Rather it is characterised by pluralism, tolerance and broad-mindedness: the classic exposition of this was in *Handyside* v. *United Kingdom*.[31] It is worth dwelling on what a pluralist society is. It is one in which there are fluctuating groups which overlap and which may come together from time to time to form a majority. For example, a person may be wealthy or poor, unemployed or in work, male or female, a trade union member or not, of a particular religion or of no religion, gay or straight, black or white. Most of the time the democratic process should allow people to decide for themselves how they want their political representatives to coalesce around these various interests. The main political parties are coalitions, sometimes uneasy ones, of all these groups and others. Most of the time, at least in theory, it should be possible for today's minorities to become tomorrow's majority by joining forces with others around a common programme. But sometimes there is a systemic failure. There may be no conventional political party that has much interest in representing the interests of a particular group or it may take their support for granted. They may not have the vote at all. It is in such circumstances that the ordinary give and take of the democratic process is unlikely to protect the rights of a vulnerable and unpopular minority.

To make the point less abstract, look at the groups of people who have been "clients" of the European Court of Human Rights from this country. The United Kingdom accepted the right of individual petition under the ECHR in 1966. Most people rightly believe that they have

---

[30] See the famous dicta of Stone J in *United States* v. *Carolene Products Co.* 304 US 144 (1938) at 152-3, n.4.

[31] (1979-80) 1 EHRR 737, para 49.

since that time – and before – been living in a free country. They have not needed to trouble themselves with the ECHR or what it said. But consider the people who have had to take the long and hard road to Strasbourg to vindicate their rights.

The first main group comprised immigrants or potential immigrants. In the notorious *East African Asians* case[32] the European Commission of Human Rights found that the Commonwealth Immigrants Act 1968, passed in a hurry by a Labour Government to stop British passport holders in East Africa from coming to the United Kingdom as they faced persecution in their home countries, was motivated by racism. It held that in such circumstances racial discrimination could amount to degrading treatment contrary to Article 3 of the ECHR. The case was the subject of a "friendly settlement" and did not proceed to the Court. Other famous cases about immigration have included *Abdulaziz, Cabales and Balkandali* v. *United Kingdom*[33] (on the splitting up of families in a way which was discriminatory against women) and *Chahal* v. *United Kingdom*[34] (which concerned, among other things, the absence of effective judicial scrutiny of deportation orders made on the grounds of national security).

The second main group of people who have had to go to Strasbourg were gay men and lesbians: the two famous cases are *Dudgeon* v. *United Kingdom*[35] and the recent one of *Lustig-Prean* v. *United Kingdom*,[36] to which I will return in more detail. Another sexual minority have been transsexuals: four of the five major cases in the Court involving transsexuals have been brought against the United Kingdom: *Rees*,[37] *Cossey*,[38] *X, Y and Z*[39] and *Sheffield and Horsham*.[40] Each time the Court of Human Rights has suggested that in time it might come to view the position of English law, that a person's gender is fixed for all time at birth, as conflicting with the right to respect for private life. The Court has held that Article 8 of the ECHR does not the require the English legal system to recognise a change effected by gender re-assignment surgery but the votes in favour of these judgments have been going down with every case: in *Sheffield and Horsham*, the majority was only eleven judges to nine. Since the decisions have rested on the

---

[32] (1981) 3 EHRR 76. The Commission considered the case in 1973.
[33] (1987) 7 EHRR 471.   [34] (1996) 23 EHRR 413.
[35] (1981) 4 EHRR 149.   [36] (2000) 29 EHRR 548.
[37] (1987) 9 EHRR 56.   [38] (1991) 13 EHRR 622.
[39] (1998) 24 EHRR 143.   [40] (1999) 27 EHRR 163.

Strasbourg concept of the margin of appreciation, and since the rule of English law is a judge-made one (first laid down in *Corbett* v. *Corbett*)[41] rather than a statutory one, there is every chance that, after incorporation, the courts will reconsider it. Other groups of people that have had to go to Strasbourg include mental patients,[42] travellers[43] and prisoners, particularly in cases involving executive decisions in the field of sentencing.[44]

All of these groups had to go to Strasbourg because they had nowhere else to go for legal remedies. English law had failed them. A good example of the European Court approach to the issues in this paper, and how it differs from the traditional English law approach, is provided by the gays in the military case.

In *Lustig-Prean* v. *United Kingdom*[45] the applicants had been compulsorily discharged from the armed forces, after enquiries about their private lives, on the ground that they were homosexual. The absolute policy of the armed forces was to ban homosexuals. The applicants sought judicial review of the ban in the domestic courts. The Divisional Court (Simon Brown LJ and Curtis J) refused the application because the ban was not irrational or *Wednesbury* unreasonable.[46] Simon Brown LJ did express the view that the ban was not likely to survive scrutiny in the European Court of Human Rights. The applicants' appeal to the Court of Appeal was dismissed on essentially the same grounds, although all the members of that court, like Simon Brown LJ, had sympathy for the a1pplicants but felt it inappropriate to speculate on how the European Court might view the ban.

The applicants' petition for leave to appeal to the House of Lords was dismissed. Having exhausted their domestic remedies the applicants then took their case to Strasbourg. The judgment of the Court is a landmark one, not only for its result (that the applicants' rights had been violated) but because the Court's analysis provides a textbook example of human rights reasoning. The Court accepted that the ban on homosexuals in the armed forces, although it constituted an interference with the right to respect for private life in Article 8, was "in accordance with the law" and had a legitimate aim (to ensure the

---

[41] [1971] P 83.   [42] E.g. *X* v. *United Kingdom* (1981) 4 EHRR 188.

[43] E.g. *Buckley* v. *United Kingdom* (1997) 23 EHRR 101.

[44] E.g. *Hussain* v. *United Kingdom* (1996) 22 EHRR 1.

[45] (2000) 29 EHRR 548.   [46] [1996] QB 517.

operational effectiveness of the armed forces). The crucial question was whether the interference was "necessary in a democratic society."

The Court reminded itself that the characteristics of a democratic society are pluralism, tolerance and broad-mindedness.[47] It also noted that, in the intimate context with which it was dealing, the requirements of proportionality required "particularly weighty and convincing reasons" to be demonstrated in justification of the ban.[48] The Court then assessed the reasons advanced by the Government and found them to be less than impressive. In substance what they amounted to was the assertion that the dislike and unwillingness of others to serve with homosexuals would undermine their morale and so the operational effectiveness of the armed forces. The Court said that the perceived problems "were founded solely upon the negative attitudes of heterosexual personnel towards those of homosexual orientation".[49] The Court rejected such reasoning. As the Court said:

> To the extent that they represent a predisposed bias on the part of a heterosexual majority against a homosexual minority, these negative attitudes cannot, of themselves, be considered by the Court to amount to sufficient justification for the interferences with the applicants' rights . . . any more than similar negative attitudes towards those of a different race, origin or colour.[50]

For good measure, in the related case of *Smith* v. *United Kingdom*[51] the Court also held that the applicants' right to an effective remedy for breach of their Convention rights – in Article 13 – had been violated. The Court considered that the principle on which the English courts could interfere with the policy banning homosexuals from the armed forces (irrationality) was, even when applied in a heightened manner in human rights cases, inadequate to provide the protection required by Article 13. The Court said:

> In such circumstances, the Court considers it clear that, even assuming that the essential complaints of the applicants before this Court were before and considered by the domestic courts, the threshold at which the High Court and the Court of Appeal could find the Ministry of Defence policy irrational was placed so high that it effectively excluded any consideration by the domestic courts of the question of whether the

---

[47] Paragraph 80.   [48] Paragraph 87.   [49] Paragraph 89.
[50] Paragraph 90.   [51] (2000) 29 EHRR 493.

interference with the applicants' rights answered a pressing social need or was proportionate to the national security and public order aims pursued, principles which lie at the heart of the Court's analysis of complaints under Article 8 of the Convention.[52]

There could be no better reason for incorporation of the ECHR than this ruling that, despite the advances made by English law in the last decade, it is still doctrinally incapable of engaging in the kind of reasoning which human rights jurisprudence requires.

THE HUMAN RIGHTS ACT:
A DEMOCRATIC BILL OF RIGHTS

The first thing to note about the Human Rights Act is that it did not come suddenly, fully formed from the head of some Olympian god. It did not even happen primarily or even largely because the Government wanted it to. The Human Rights Act came about because a progressive coalition had come together over a sustained period to press for a number of constitutional reforms of which it was only one. Although the structural problems in the constitution of the United Kingdom had long been present, they were only really noticed once the Conservative Party had managed to win four elections in a row between 1979 and 1992. The traditional swing of the pendulum, which had tended to ensure that both main parties could expect to be in office every five or ten years could no longer be relied on. This highlighted the main defects of the constitution. One party could win a majority (often a large majority) of seats in the House of Commons on approximately 43 per cent of the vote. This in turn gave that party access to unlimited power since Parliament may do anything it likes. In reality the sovereignty of Parliament means the sovereignty of the executive. Parliament is dominated by the government through the whip system and by the promise or expectation of ministerial office. The Conservative Government did not have to share power on a regional basis, even though Scotland and Wales consistently voted for Labour. When local government became a nuisance, it could simply be abolished, as happened to the Greater London Council and the other metropolitan councils in 1986. The House of Lords (which had a large Conservative

---

[52] Paragraph 138.

majority) could not stop legislation for long even if it wanted to (on the poll tax it did not even try, as hereditary peers turned out in force to push it through). And, of course, there was no Bill of Rights which could be enforced by the courts, although they did their best to curb the excesses of the government through judicial review, but that (as *Smith* shows) was insufficient to protect human rights.

It was against that background that non-governmental organisations like Charter 88, Liberty, JUSTICE and the Constitution Unit began to create a new climate of opinion on the centre left. In particular the influence of Charter 88, and the *New Statesman* to which it was linked through the editorship of Stuart Weir, cannot be over-estimated. It was no accident that it was at a Charter 88 conference in 1993 that the late John Smith committed the Labour Party to incorporation of the ECHR. His shadow Home Secretary then was one Tony Blair, who has carried through the party's promise in government. As the Prime Minister put it in his preface to the White Paper which accompanied the Human Rights Bill when it was introduced in the House of Lords in October 1997:

> We are committed to a comprehensive programme of constitutional reform. We believe it is right to increase individual rights, to decentralise power, to open up government and to reform Parliament.[53]

To see the significance of the Human Rights Act as part of this comprehensive programme of reform, it may be instructive to start with Scotland, which can be seen now to have become a modern country, like many others in the liberal democratic world. First it has its own Parliament, which is elected on an additional member system, which ensures proportional representation overall while retaining constituency MSPs. This has had the result that the Labour Party, which won the vast majority of seats from Scotland at Westminster on 42 per cent of the vote had to form a coalition government in Edinburgh on the same share of the vote. Secondly, the powers of the Scottish Parliament and Executive are limited by the Convention rights, which are entrenched:[54] in that sense the Human Rights Act is already deemed to have effect in Scotland.[55] Thirdly, the courts are given the power of judicial review to strike down acts of the Scottish Parliament which are

[53] *Rights Brought Home: the Human Rights Bill,* Cm 3782.
[54] Section 29(1) and (4)(d) of the Scotland Act 1998.
[55] Section 129(2) of the Scotland Act 1998.

incompatible with the Convention rights. The question many may be left asking is: if these arrangements are good enough for Scotland, why are they not good enough for the rest of the United Kingdom?

From Scotland it is worth visiting Northern Ireland, where the Good Friday peace agreement included a commitment to human rights which went beyond incorporation of the ECHR. The Northern Ireland Act 1998 too makes the Human Rights Act an entrenched Act, so that the Northern Ireland Assembly may not infringe the Convention rights and may not modify or repeal the Human Rights Act.

Both Scotland and Northern Ireland give an insight into the relationship between democracy and the Human Rights Act in the new United Kingdom which has been created before our eyes in the last three years. It cannot be a democracy based simply on numbers. If numbers were all that mattered, the electorate of England could, if it wished, simply ignore the interests of Scotland – as many people there think it did during the long Conservative Government between 1979 and 1997. Yet devolution has forever ended that concept of democracy. The Northern Ireland Act is based on an even subtler notion of democracy, which recognises that there are two minorities in Ulster: the Unionists are a permanent minority within the United Kingdom and could be expelled from the United Kingdom if that is what Great Britain wanted. But they are a permanent majority within Ulster. This is why the Good Friday agreement seeks to accommodate their interests as well as those of the Nationalist minority. The notion of power-sharing in the Executive and cross-community voting on crucial issues in the Assembly is based on a much more sophisticated kind of democracy than one in which sheer strength of numbers would prevail. And the reason, of course, is a good one: the experience of simple majority rule, where the human rights of a minority are consistently infringed without any realistic prospect of redress through the ballot box leads to violence, which in the end threatens democracy itself.

In an important essay Jeremy Waldron has pointed out that a concern for fundamental human rights need not entail a Bill of Rights which is enforceable by unelected judges.[56] He recalls that, in the US Constitution as originally adopted, James Madison thought it better to protect rights through structural arrangements: the famous "checks and

---

[56] J. Waldron, "Rights and Majorities: Rousseau Revisited" in *Liberal Rights: Collected Papers 1981-1991* (Cambridge, Cambridge University Press, 1993).

balances". But, of course, a particular country may choose to have more than one approach to the protection of rights. One can have checks and balances and as a last resort one can have a Bill of Rights as well. This was the view to which Madison came after 1787 and, with the zeal of a convert, he then drafted the American Bill of Rights, which was ratified in 1791. And there can be variants on the Bill of Rights model. Contrary to popular belief, a Bill of Rights does not have to entail the power of judicial review or the power to strike down legislation.[57]

In the restructuring of the United Kingdom which is currently taking place checks and balances are introduced through devolution, proportional representation in Scotland, Wales and Northern Ireland and for the European Parliament elections, and through possible further reform of the House of Lords and of the electoral system for the House of Commons. But the Human Rights Act introduces a new element: a Bill of Rights. This is not, however, to be enforced only by the courts.

Section 19 of the Human Rights Act, which was brought into force almost two years before most of the Act was due to be brought into force, ordinarily requires ministers to give a statement of compatibility when they introduce a Bill into Parliament. Some have suggested that this is mere "window dressing". I hope they are not proved right. It was certainly intended to be a serious obligation to hold the executive to account in Parliament. If it works it should have two consequences. First, the Government will have had to go through a human rights reasoning process before it introduces legislation: for example, it will have had to assess the proportionality of any measure which appears to infringe a Convention right. Secondly, Members of Parliament will be able to scrutinise legislation and probe the executive if they are not satisfied about compatibility. Whichever way they answer the question, at least they have to ask the question. Of course, one can be cynical and say that MPs will not take the trouble to scrutinise legislation carefully. But there is reason to be more hopeful. Non-governmental organisations like JUSTICE and Liberty will produce the valuable briefing papers for which they are renowned, which will in turn prompt MPs and members of the House of Lords to ask the right questions. The Joint Parliamentary Committee on human rights should be more than

---

[57] P. Craig, 'Constitutionalism, Regulation and Review' in R. Hazell (ed.), *Constitutional Futures* (1999) ch. 5, pp. 67-8.

a rubber-stamping body. And there will be the House of Lords. Even if, as seems likely, its powers are not increased after its reform, it can continue to perform its historic function: to scrutinise legislation with care and to send a Bill back to the House of Commons. It can delay legislation under the Parliament Acts 1911 and 1949: this could be a valuable power if it is not satisfied that a Bill is compatible with the Convention rights.

So the Human Rights Act consciously builds into our constitutional arrangements a democratic scrutiny of the compatibility of legislation with human rights. This reflects what Jeremy Waldron would call a "Rousseauan" model of democracy: one where the legislature asks not only what would be in the interests of the majority but what would be in the general interest (including a consideration of the fundamental rights of minorities):

> we should revise the way we think about rights to accommodate the prospect that voters and representatives in a democratic system will approach their responsibilities in a Rousseauan spirit. If we accept that as a possibility, we should recognize that rights may already be weighed in majoritarian decision-making. If so, the standard opposition between the democratic process and rights as external constitutional constraints would have to be discarded.[58]

But there is no need for the concept of rights as external constraints to be discarded altogether. Of course, Waldron is right to point out that we must admit the possibility that a majority may act in a Rousseauan way because we need it to adopt a Bill of Rights in the first place. But that proves only that a majority at a given point in history takes that view. That same majority could take the view that, as a last resort, a judicially enforceable Bill of Rights should be adopted. If future governments comply there will be no need to resort to it. If they do not, because - as Madison put it - men may not always behave as angels, the Bill of Rights will be there.

Even then it is not a necessary feature of a Bill of Rights that the courts should be able to strike down primary legislation. After incorporation our courts will have to read and give effect to all legislation, whether primary or secondary and whether enacted in the past or in the future, in a way which is compatible with Convention rights, so far as it

---

[58] J. Waldron, *supra* n. 56, p. 420.

is possible to do so.[59] It remains to be seen how imaginative an approach to interpretation this may require: the various members of the House of Lords in *Kebilene*[60] suggested that it might be more or less radical. But everyone accepts that, in principle, there may be legislation which cannot be interpreted in a way which is compatible with Convention rights. When that occurs, the Human Rights Act gives the higher courts the power to make a declaration of that incompatibility. They can declare but they cannot make a coercive order.

But in substance the courts would do what the European Court of Human Rights does when it finds that a breach of an applicant's rights has occurred as a result of an Act of Parliament. The Court does not strike down the legislation. It does not declare it void within the national legal system. It expects the respondent state to remedy the breach by amending the legislation accordingly. This process is, if anything, improved by the scheme of the Human Rights Act. This is because a minister has the power to make a remedial order under section 10 of the Human Rights Act to amend an Act of Parliament to bring it into line with a judgment of the European Court of Human Rights and not only to comply with a declaration of incompatibility made by a court in the United Kingdom.

As is well-known the only legal effect of a declaration of incompatibility will be to permit (but not oblige) a minister to amend the offending Act by a "remedial order" under section 10 and Schedule 2. This will only be used where there are "compelling" reasons to do so.[61] If the declaration of incompatibility is not accepted by the government of the day, and assuming that there is no parliamentary pressure to change the law in the meantime, the applicant will still be able to take the case to Strasbourg. If the European Court of Human Rights takes the same view as the domestic court, which it may not do given the doctrine of the margin of appreciation applied by that Court, precedent suggests that the Government of the United Kingdom would comply at that stage with the Court's judgment.

So the scheme of the Human Rights Act is to establish a relationship of balance between Parliament, the courts of this country and the European Court of Human Rights. But in practice it may well introduce a further, very important player into this relationship: the people. A

---

[59] Section 3 of the Human Rights Act.

[60] *R v. Director of Public Prosecutions, ex p. Kebilene* [1999] 3 WLR 972.

[61] Section 10(2) of the Human Rights Act.

declaration of incompatibility is likely to be made only in relation to the most controversial and sensitive types of legislation: abortion or terrorism may well be the subject-matter. Once a declaration is made, there is likely to be public debate about it. If the government of the day decides not to implement the declaration normal politics can be expected to play their part. Opposition parties and non-governmental organisations will campaign on one side of the issue or the other. There may well be a general election in which the issue registers with the electorate precisely because it has been the subject of a formal declaration by the highest court in the land. In this way, and in others, the Human Rights Act may bind all of us together in support of human rights.[62]

Some commentators have suggested, with apparent relief, that the scheme of the Human Rights Act preserves Parliamentary sovereignty.[63] So it does in a formal sense, although it is hard to see how, after the major reforms of recent years, the constitution can plausibly be said now to rest on the doctrine of Parliamentary sovereignty. But in any event, for me there is no virtue in parliamentary sovereignty as such. Parliamentary democracy is another matter. In a modern constitution there should be no one person or body which enjoys absolute power. This is particularly true when one recalls that Parliament is very largely controlled by the executive. That is simply the modern reincarnation of the old divine right of kings.

As I have suggested, the Human Rights Act, especially when placed in the context of the other reforms which are modernising the United Kingdom, is part of a new constitutionalism in this country, where power is dispersed among regions and shared among institutions. The Human Rights Act is an experiment. It represents a vision that human rights will best be protected when everyone in society is bound into a common enterprise rather than engaged in conflict.[64] It is a democratic Bill of Rights.

---

[62] This is an example of what Francesca Klug has called the "third wave" of human rights: see F. Klug, *Values in a Godless Age* (Harmondsworth, Penguin, 2000), Chs. 5–6.

[63] See e.g. K Ewing, "The Human Rights Act and Parliamentary Democracy" [1999] *MLR* 79.

[64] See further M. Hunt, "The Human Rights Act and Legal Culture: the Judiciary and the Legal Profession" (1999) 26 *Journal of Law and Society* 86 at p. 89, where Murray Hunt says that: "[the Human Rights Act] is designed to institutionalize a creative tension between the judiciary on the one hand and Parliament and the executive on the other".